I0902372

IMAGES
of America

LAKES AND PONDS OF THE GRANITE STATE

IMAGES
of America

Lakes and Ponds of the Granite State

Bruce D. Heald, Ph.D.

ARCADIA
PUBLISHING

Copyright © 2000 by Bruce D. Heald, Ph.D.
ISBN 978-0-7385-0498-8

Published by Arcadia Publishing
Charleston, South Carolina

Printed in the United States of America

Library of Congress Catalog Card Number: 00108829

For all general information contact Arcadia Publishing at:
Telephone 843-853-2070
Fax 843-853-0044
E-mail sales@arcadiapublishing.com
For customer service and orders:
Toll-Free 1-888-313-2665

Visit us on the Internet at www.arcadiapublishing.com

Contents

ACKNOWLEDGMENTS

I would like to thank the following people and organizations: Eric E. Aldrich, the program information officer for the New Hampshire Fish and Game Department; the Appalachian Mountain Club; G.W. Armstrong, DR & N Company; the Boston, Concord, and Montreal Railroad, Boston & Maine Railroad Passenger Service; Chisholm's *White Mountains; Granite State Monthly*; Robert and Mary Julyan; Thomas Starr King, the Lakes Region Association; Robert Lawton, Wendy L'Heureux, the New Hampshire Fish and Game Department; the New Hampshire Department of Resources and Economic Development; *New Hampshire: The American Guide Series*; the New Hampshire Department of Environmental Services; Osgood's *White Mountains*; Robert Sargent, the State Bureau of Labor; Charles J. Swasey, the *Weirs Times Inc.*; and Donald A. Wilson.

INTRODUCTION

Diversity is the one word that best describes the physical characteristics of New Hampshire. Within its borders, the Granite State has majestic mountains, alpine plant and animal communities, forested valleys, fast-flowing streams, large lakes, small ponds, species-rich wetlands, an abundance of fish, a large coastal estuary, and sandy ocean beaches—all acquainting visitors with a richness of sport seldom found in a single state. Of these many gifts, the lakes and ponds are the rarest of gems.

New Hampshire abounds with an almost infinite variety of lakes and ponds, inexhaustible in resources and unlimited in beauty. Each of these sheets of water acts as a magnetic force, attracting thousands of visitors in every season of the year.

Perhaps the first place that comes to mind is Lake Winnipesaukee, the largest in the state, covering an area of 72 square miles, with a mainland shoreline of 186 miles. It is only one of a multitude of beautiful lakes and ponds that glitter in the granite landscape. Others are Sunapee, the dark-eyed "granite-throned queen"; Echo Lake and Profile Lake, hidden amid the mountains of northern New Hampshire; Newfound and Squam, with their milder charms; and Dublin and Spofford, in the smiling southwestern country. Each lake has its own peculiar characteristics and its own host of ardent lovers. Surely such a scenic feast has never been set before the eye of man within such comparatively circumscribed limits of space.

The beauty of a lake or pond cannot be judged from a single point but must be sought in the water's intricate borders, its islands, and on its ever-changing surface. In this way, the observer can find the delicious bits that artists love for studies, the jagged rocks, the shaded beaches, the coy and curving nooks, the limpid water prattling upon amethystine sand.

This lake country of New England is fortunate in having an abundance of fish life: 98 species are found in its rivers, lakes, and ponds. By far the most important, from the standpoint of sportsmen, are the brook trout, common in mountain streams throughout the state, and the black bass, equally common in larger ponds and lakes. Also found, though not so common, are the rainbow and brown trout.

Among game fish, the lake trout is the most eagerly sought and the most plentiful in all the larger lakes. The golden, or aureoles, trout of Lake Sunapee is almost peculiar to the state, but in recent years has been introduced into various other parts of the country. In addition to these popular game fish, the lakes teem with pickerel, yellow and white perch, and the ugly but edible horned pout. Summer shad, smelts, eels, and dace are found in New Hampshire waters, as is the ubiquitous sucker—the delight of small boys who fish these waters.

In these pages are some 200 rare photographic views and maps of the watery gems in New England's crown. Many of these unpublished pictures have been generously loaned by the New Hampshire Fish and Game Department to be shared with all who enjoy the out-of-doors and the sport it offers. While not all of the lakes and ponds appear in this volume, those that do should serve to whet the appetite for the many less renowned but scarcely less lovely ones that are set to be searched out in the Granite State.

—Bruce D. Heald, Ph.D.

New Hampshire's Lakes and Ponds

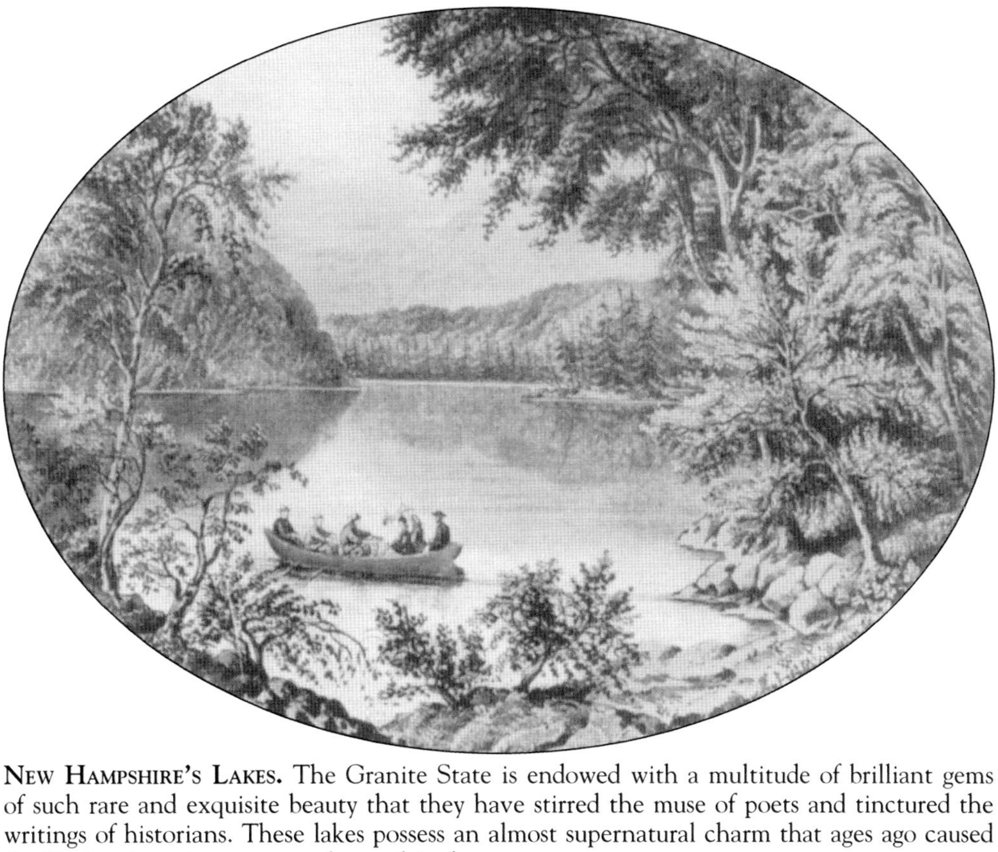

New Hampshire's Lakes. The Granite State is endowed with a multitude of brilliant gems of such rare and exquisite beauty that they have stirred the muse of poets and tinctured the writings of historians. These lakes possess an almost supernatural charm that ages ago caused the Native Americans to mutely worship them.

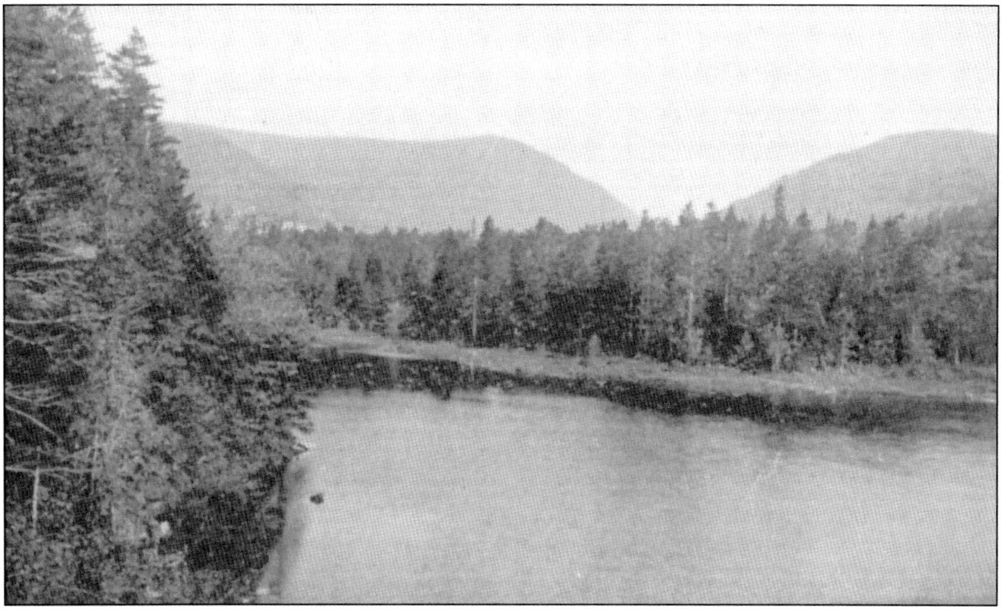

AMMONOOSUC LAKE (4 ACRES), THE CRAWFORD NOTCH AREA. This spruce-shadowed lake, on the plateau north of the gateway to the Crawford Notch, is a small dark body of water enclosed by land within the New Hampshire National Forest. To many it is considered the inner sanctum of the notch. In *The White Mountains* (1890), Julius H. Ward writes, "Half an hour alone on this bit of water, with a wild forest around its entire shore, is of my choicest memories of the Crawford Notch." Brook trout fishing is very good in this lake.

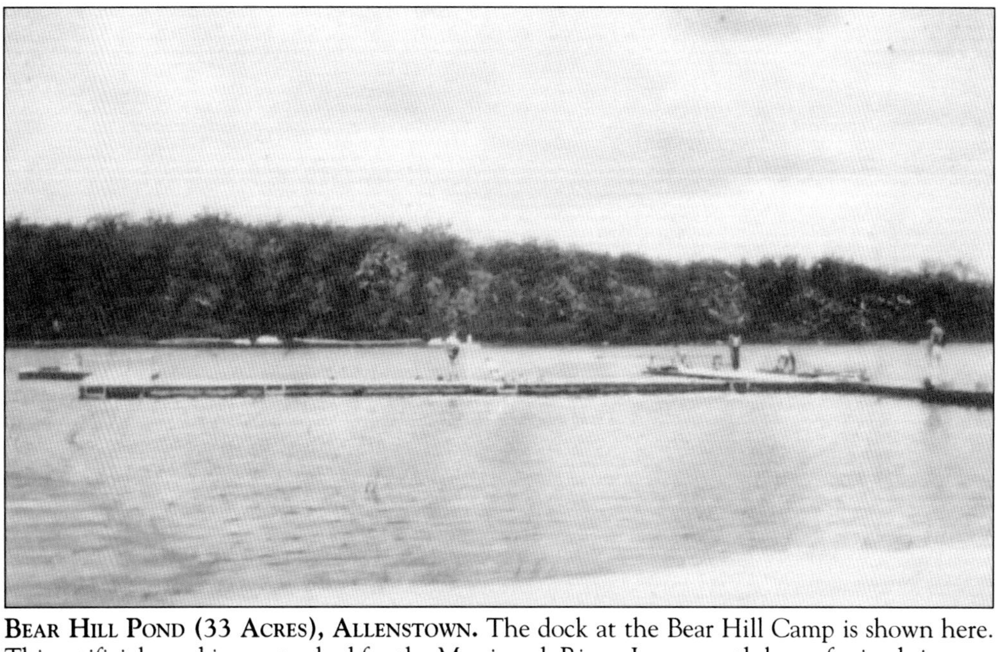

BEAR HILL POND (33 ACRES), ALLENSTOWN. The dock at the Bear Hill Camp is shown here. This artificial pond is a watershed for the Merrimack River. Largemouth bass of mixed sizes are stocked here, along with golden shiners and crayfish.

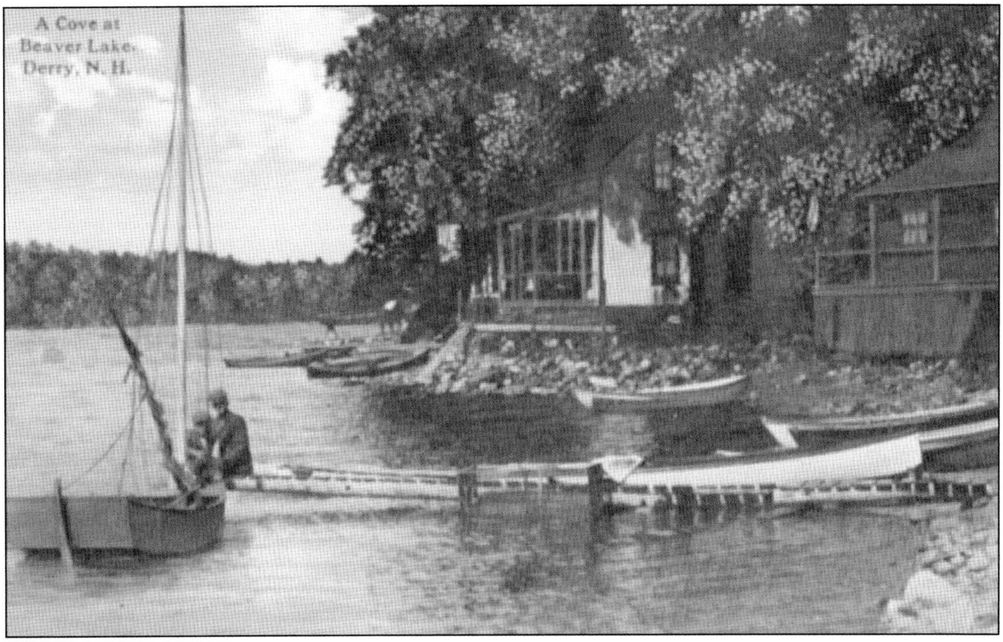

BEAVER LAKE (133 ACRES), DERRY. Near the divide of the Pemigewasset and Ammonoosuc Valleys is Beaver Lake. Teeming with trout, this beautiful tarn has forest-girt shores dotted with small summer cottages.

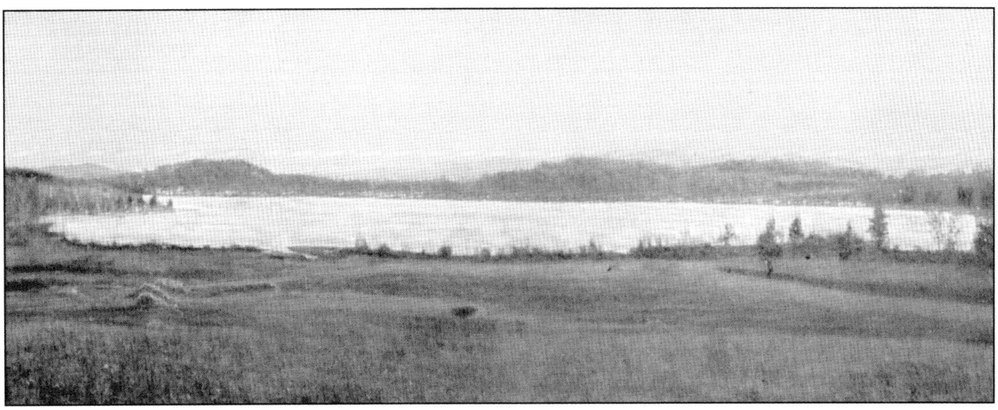

BLAISDELL'S LAKE (158 ACRES), SUTTON. This lovely natural lake acts as a watershed for the Merrimack River. Scattered along its shore are a few select summer residences, but much of its shoreline is still quite wooded and peaceful. This lake is stocked with smallmouth bass, pickerel, and horned pout.

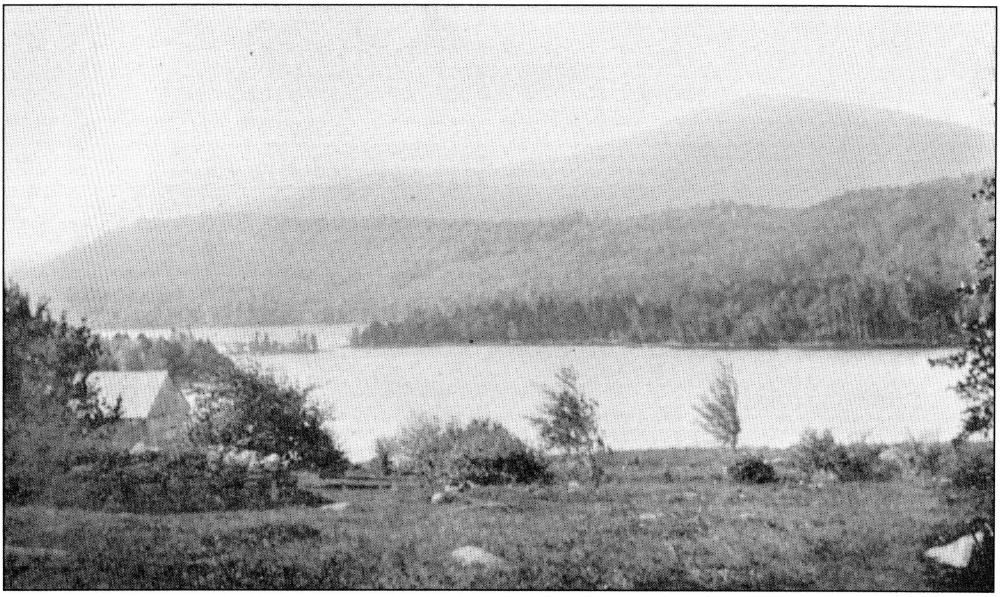

Bradley Pond (169 Acres), Andover. This natural pond was raised by damming. As with many beautiful ponds, a small summer colony has been built along its shore. Mixed sizes of smallmouth bass are stocked here, as well as horned pout, rainbow trout, fingerling trout pickerel, and yellow and white perch.

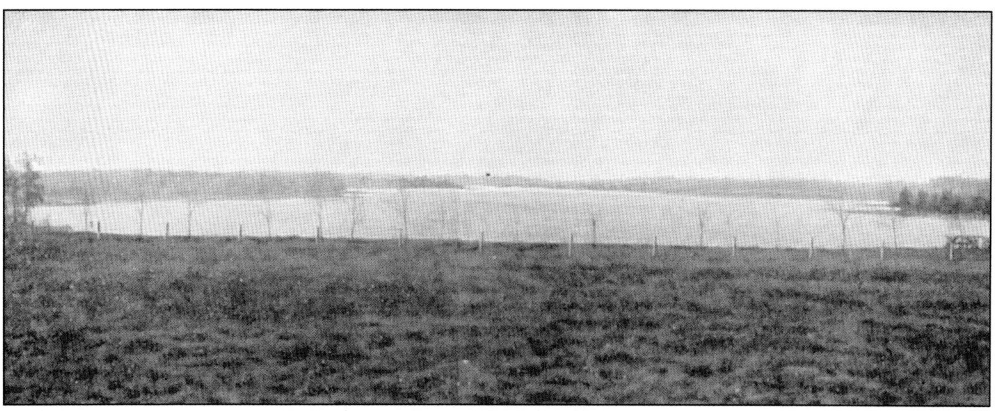

Canobie Lake (373 Acres), Windham and Salem, 1900. Before the incorporation of Salem, this lake was known as Haverhill Pond. It was later called Policy Pond for an Indian chief whose surname was Polis. The name was later changed when the railroad station was built in 1885.

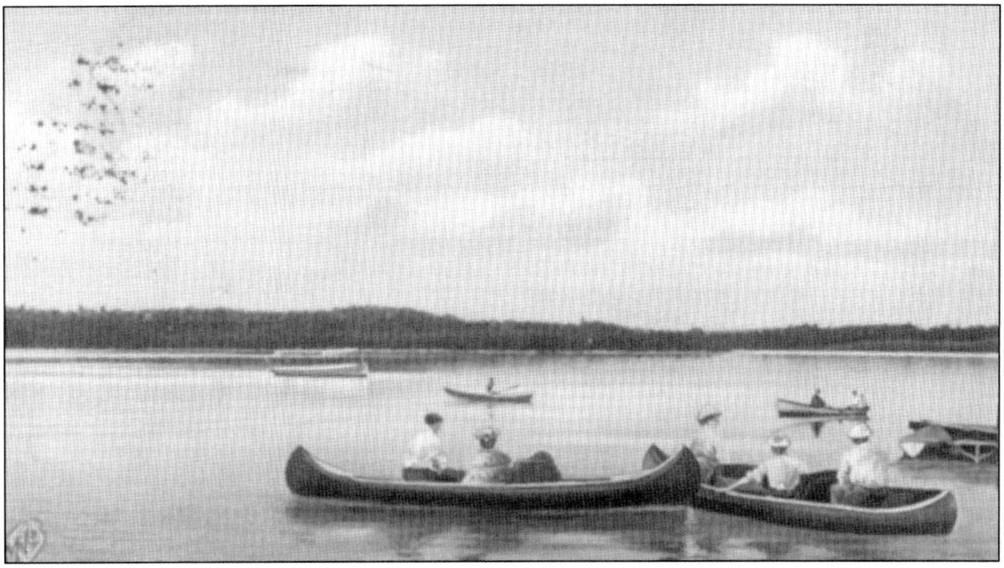

Canobie Lake, 1905. On the northern shore of Canobie Lake is a large and popular recreation park with all types of amusement facilities (above). Boating, fishing, and bathing were very popular for summer tourists who came to this lake (below). The lake is well stocked with fish, including smallmouth and largemouth bass, pickerel, horned pout, and black crappie.

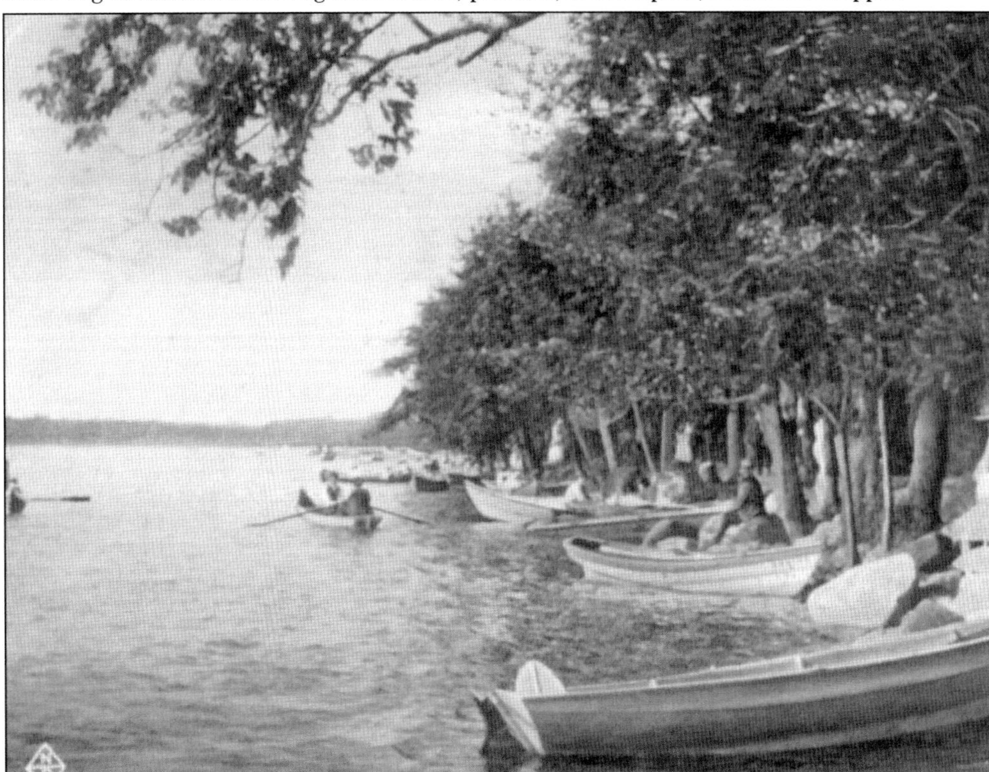

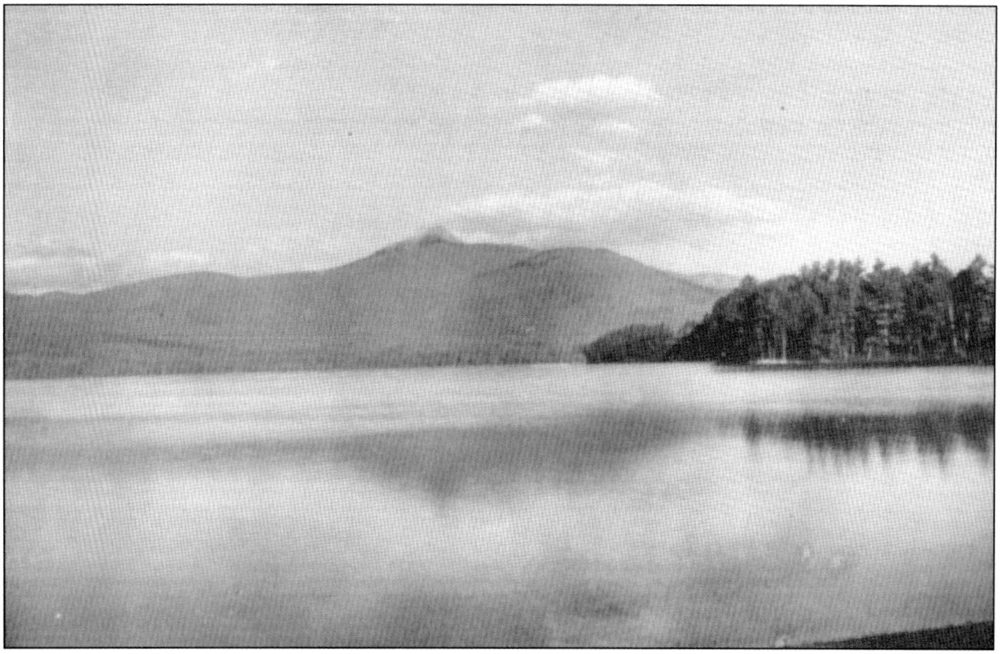

Chocorua Lake (223 Acres), Tamworth. This lake is one of New Hampshire's most delightful bodies of water. Enclosed by tall and densely growing pines, it has an air of perfect peace. At its southern end is a parking place from which there is a superb view of Mount Chocorua mirrored on the silver surface of the lake. Swimming, canoeing, and picnicking along the shore are popular for the visitors. Anglers may cast their lines here for smallmouth bass, chain pickerel, horned pout, yellow perch, and rainbow trout.

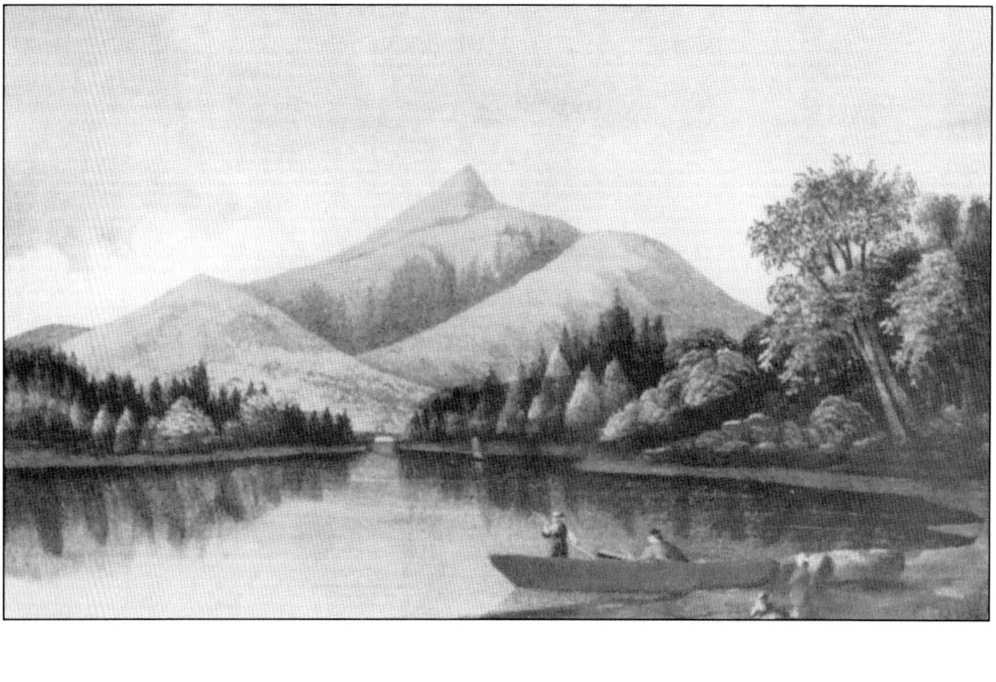

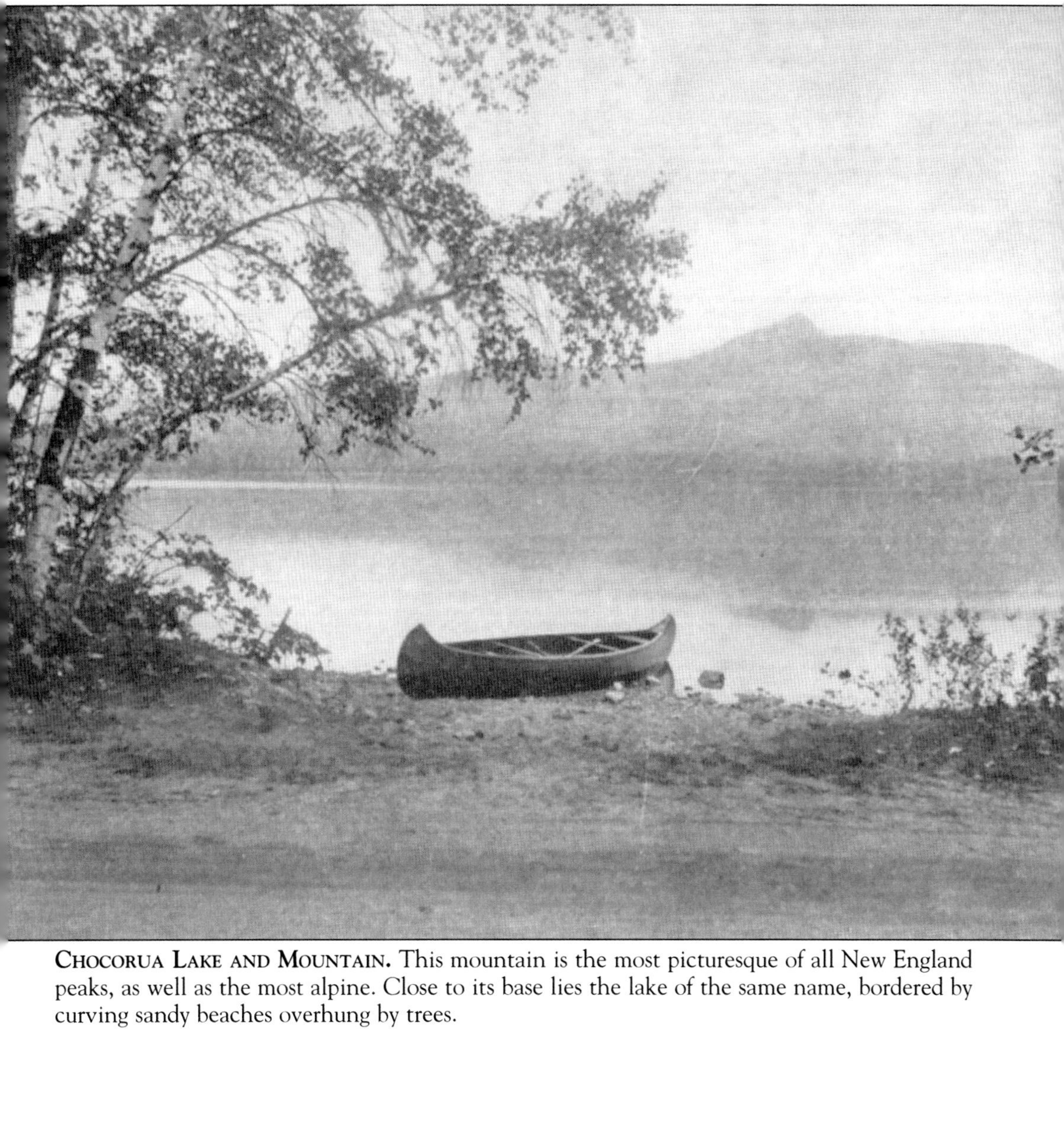

Chocorua Lake and Mountain. This mountain is the most picturesque of all New England peaks, as well as the most alpine. Close to its base lies the lake of the same name, bordered by curving sandy beaches overhung by trees.

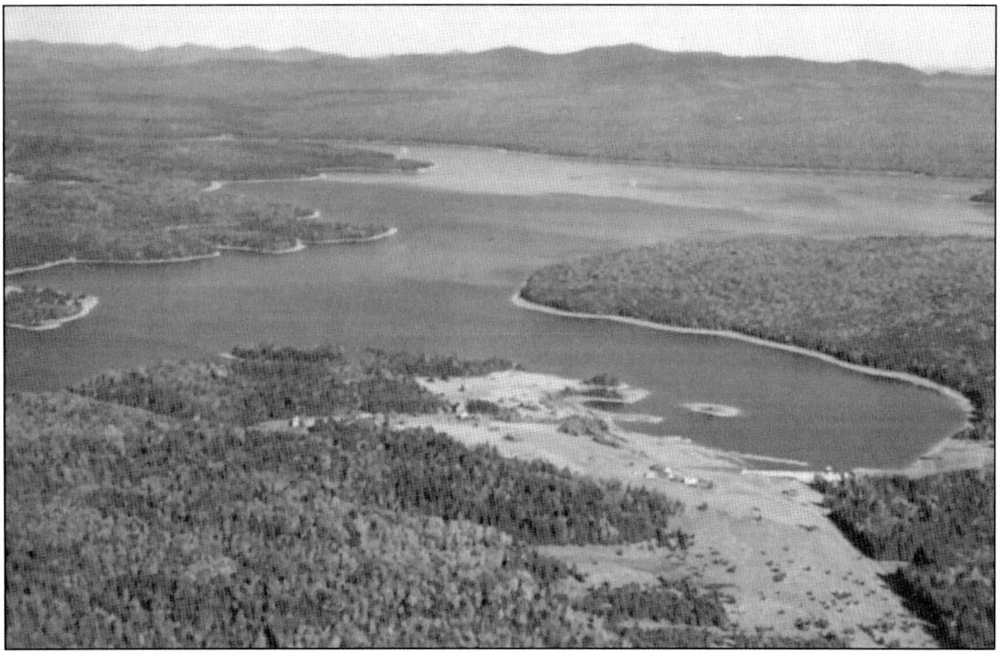

The Connecticut Lakes, Pittsburg. The First Connecticut Lake, the largest of the four, is approximately 4 miles long, with an area of 3 square miles. Having an irregular shoreline, it is one of the most beautiful bodies of water in the state. Its northern and eastern shores are unbroken forests. On the western shore are a few farms with good pastureland extending down to the lake.

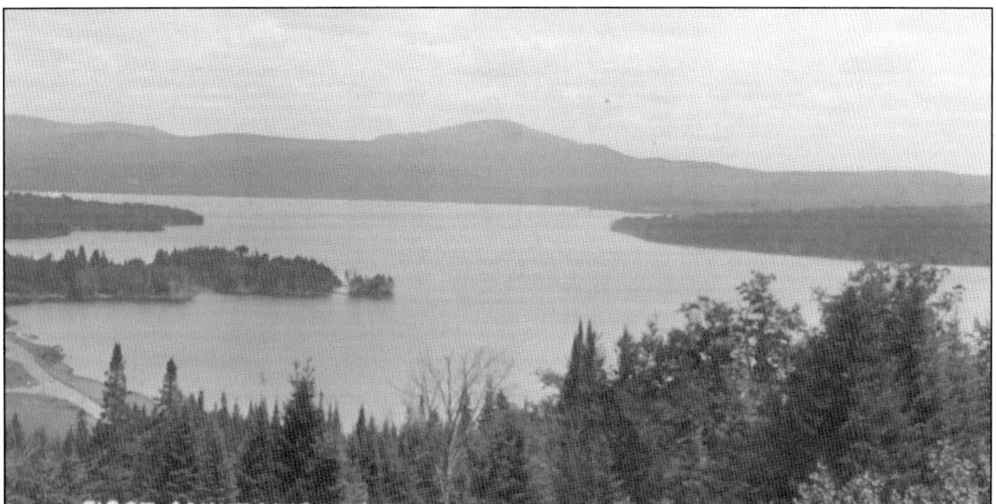

The First Connecticut Lake (2,807 Acres), Pittsburg. At the lower end of this lake is a large cement dam, constructed to hold back not only the water of this lake, but also that of the other Connecticut Lakes farther north. The drainage area of the lake is 83 square miles. Some 20 smaller bodies of water are located in the immediate vicinity. All of them are well stocked with trout, landlocked salmon, chinook salmon, and lake rainbow trout. The country abounds in deer and other game, making it one of the most popular resorts for sportsmen in the state. Near the highway are numerous camps for fishermen and hunters.

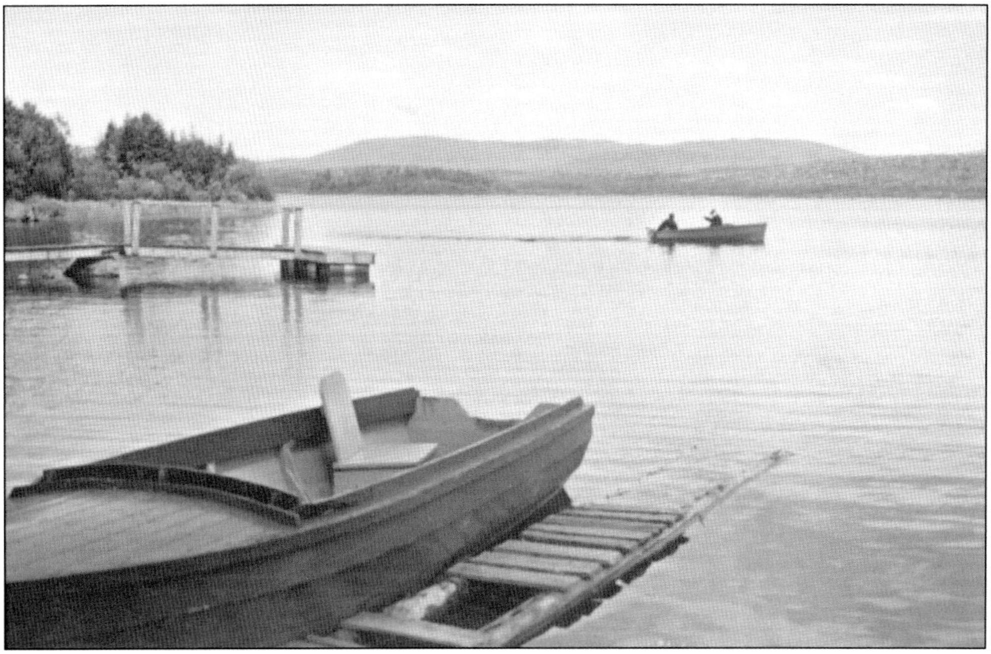

THE SECOND CONNECTICUT LAKE (1,286 ACRES), PITTSBURG. This lake is located due north of the First Connecticut Lake and has a dam at its southern end. Formerly known as Lake Carmel, for a mountain at its northeast end, the lake is 2.75 miles long with an area of 1.75 square miles. The graceful contour of its shore and the receding forested hills create a picture of unsullied serenity.

THE THIRD CONNECTICUT LAKE (289 ACRES), PITTSBURG. This lake is about a mile long with a three-quarter-square-mile area. This lake, known by the Canadians as Lake St. Sophia, is surrounded by hills, with those on the north shore extending into the Canadian territory. Its isolation gives it a wild beauty, and its waters are well stocked with brook trout.

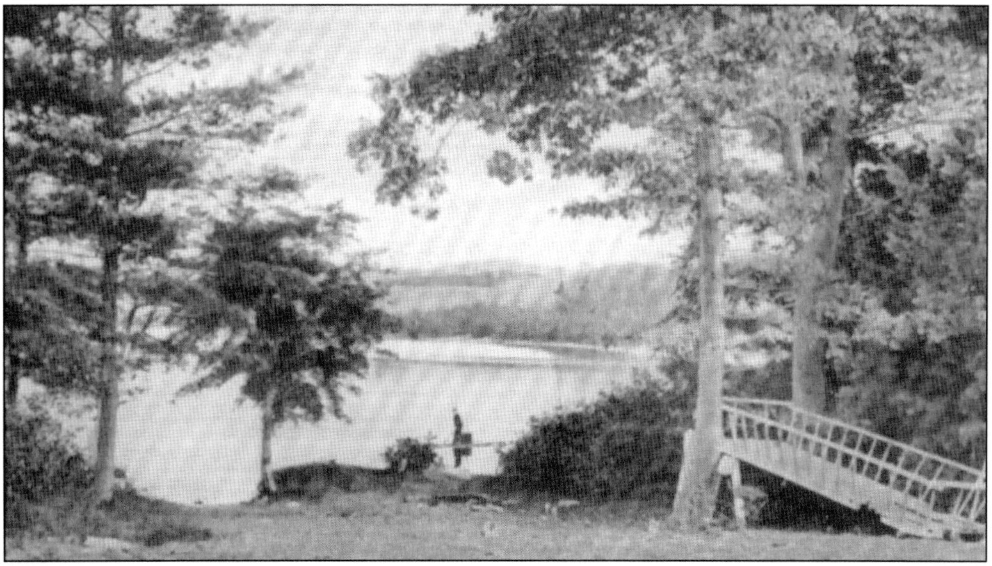

Crescent Lake (148 Acres), Wolfeboro. This natural lake is well secluded in the landscape of Wolfeboro. The best fishing is for pickerel, yellow perch, bass, and horned pout.

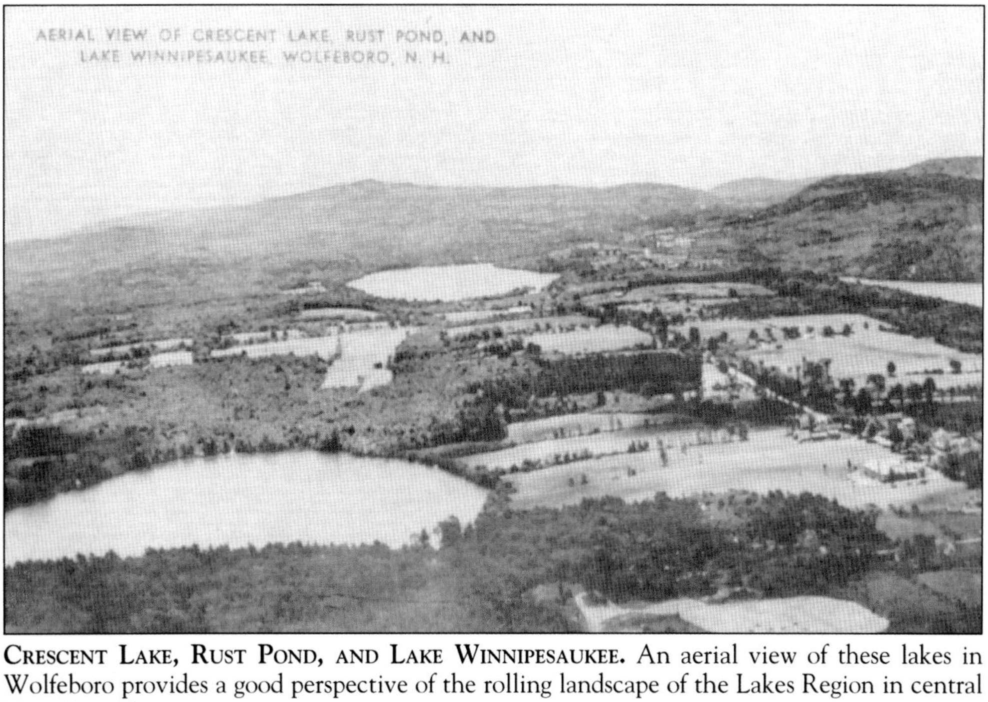

Crescent Lake, Rust Pond, and Lake Winnipesaukee. An aerial view of these lakes in Wolfeboro provides a good perspective of the rolling landscape of the Lakes Region in central New Hampshire.

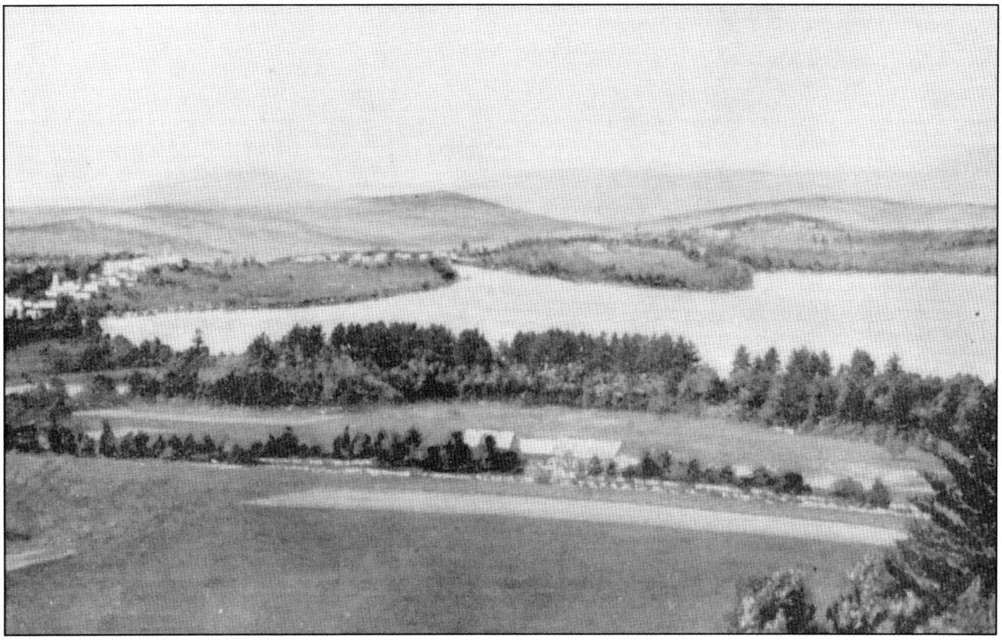

Crystal Lake (Brook Pond), Canaan. This 28-acre lake is surrounded by beautiful natural scenery and is fast becoming a popular summer colony in its own right. The lake abounds with good fishing, as do other waters in the vicinity, featuring smallmouth bass, pickerel, and horned pout.

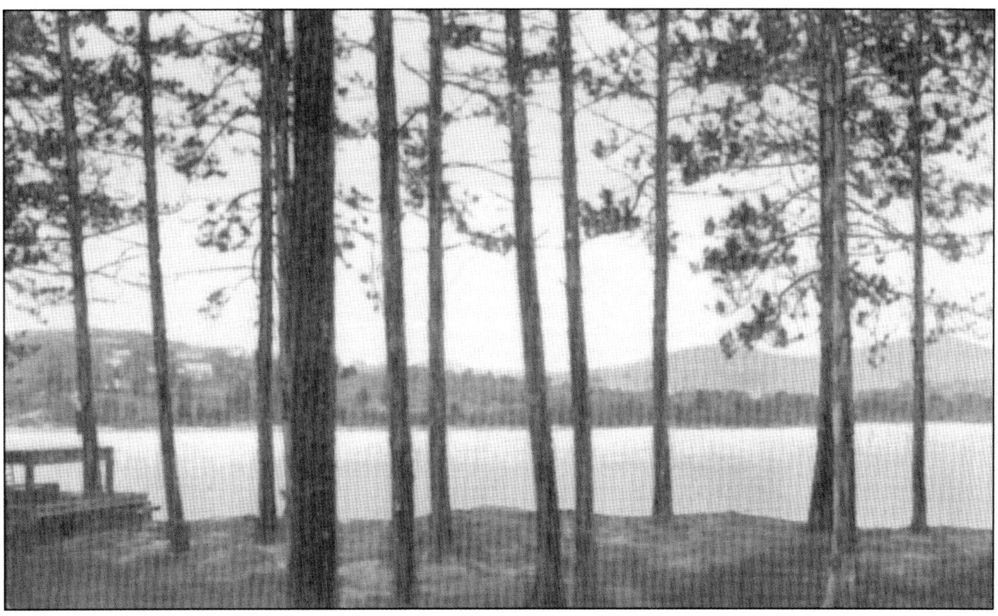

Crystal Lake (441 Acres), Gilmanton. This natural pond, raised by damming, is stocked with mixed sizes of smallmouth bass, horned pout, white and yellow perch, golden shiners, chain pickerel, and smelt.

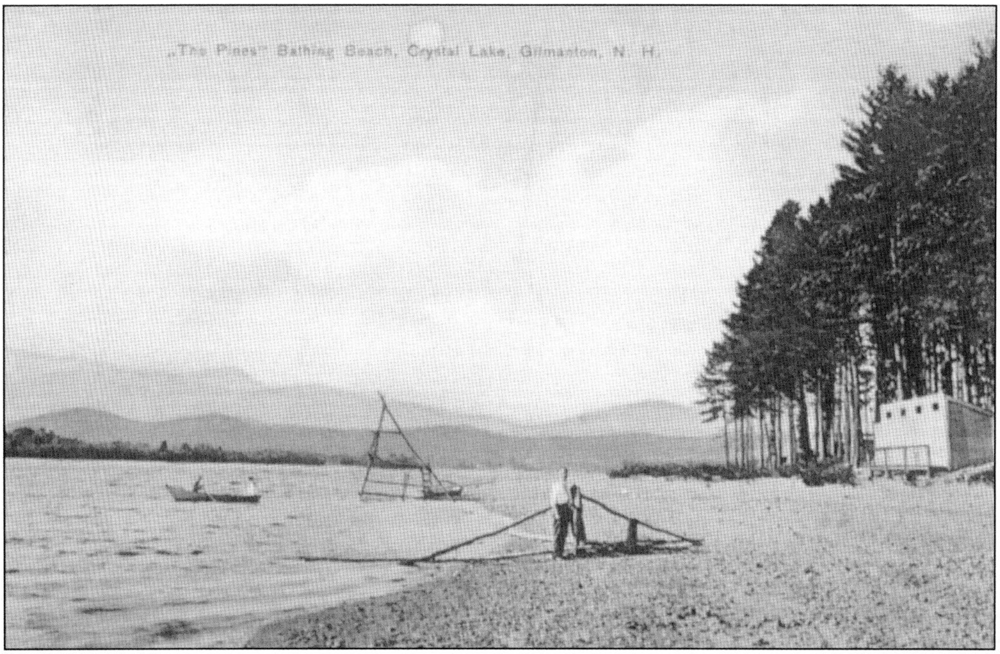

CRYSTAL LAKE, GILMANTON, 1911. The Pines is a popular bathing beach for vacationers and natives alike.

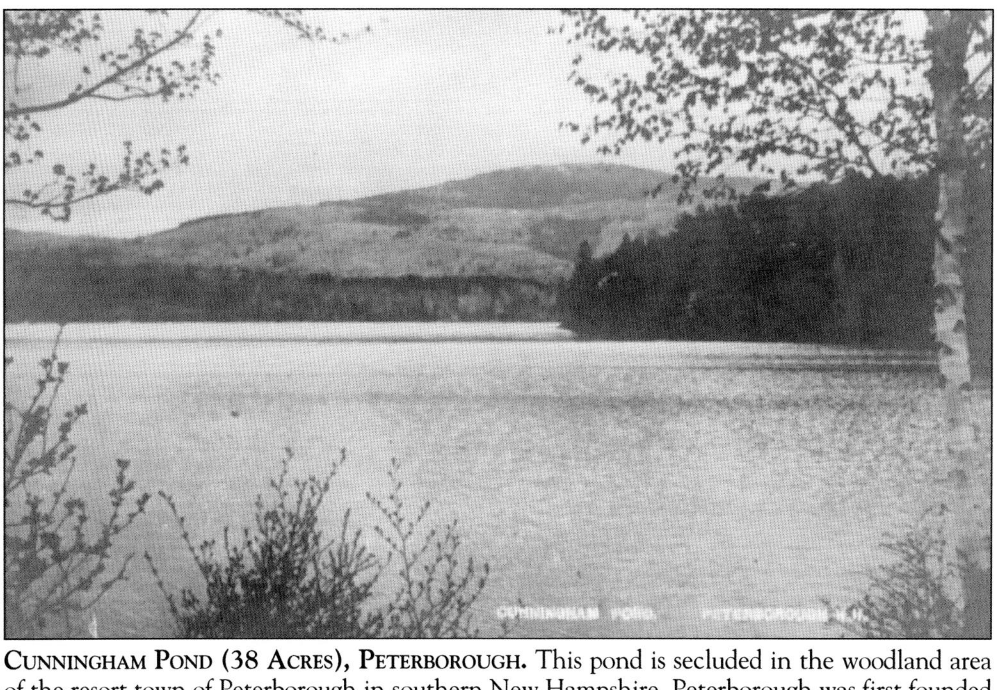

CUNNINGHAM POND (38 ACRES), PETERBOROUGH. This pond is secluded in the woodland area of the resort town of Peterborough in southern New Hampshire. Peterborough was first founded in 1739, but it was not until 1749 that the first permanent settlement was made. Since then, Peterborough and its scenic lakes and ponds have become a major attraction in this region.

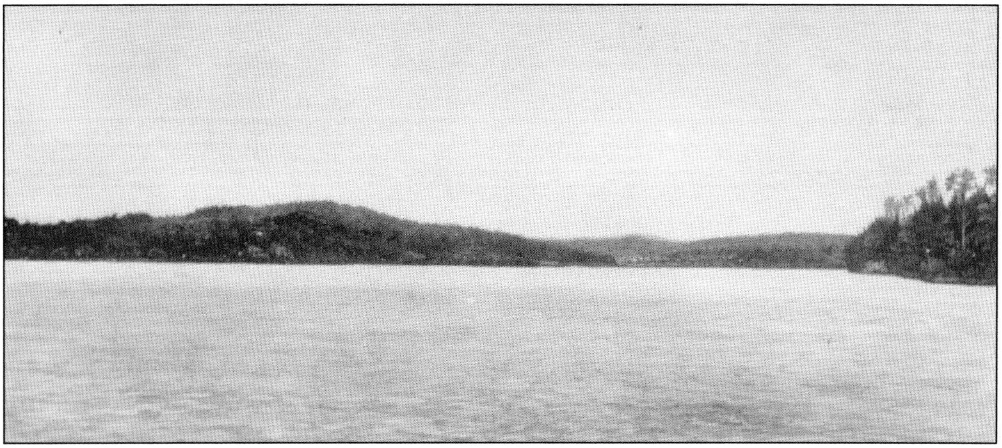

The Diamond Lakes, Stewartstown. These lakes have become quite famous for trout fishing. The area is as wild and romantic a spot as any sportsman could desire. It is also a well-known hunting ground for deer and other wildlife. No brief description can do justice to this superior fishing and hunting region.

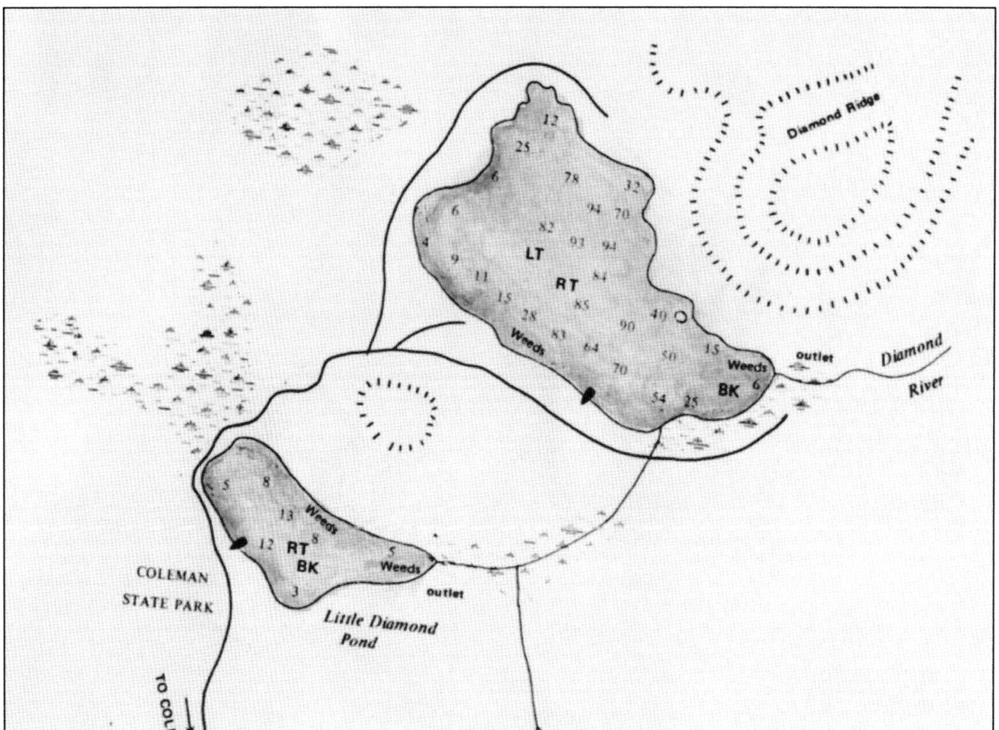

A Map of the Diamond Lakes, Stewartstown, Coos County. Both of these bodies of water offer good trout fishing and are accessible with state launching sites. This lake is very popular for ice fishing for both lake trout and rainbow trout.

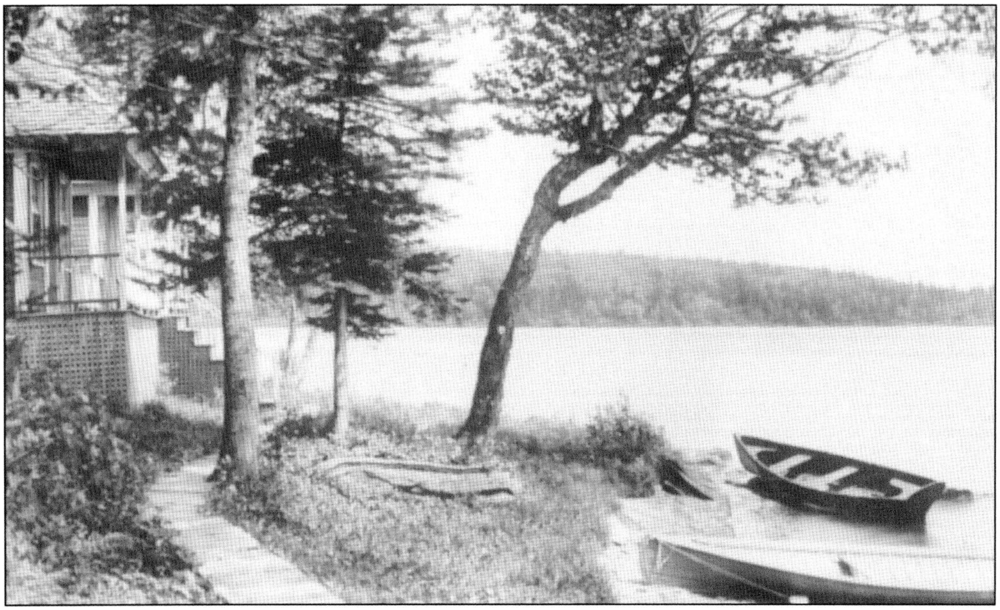

Diamond Lake (Big), 179 Acres, Stewartstown. Only lake trout are found in Big Diamond Pond.

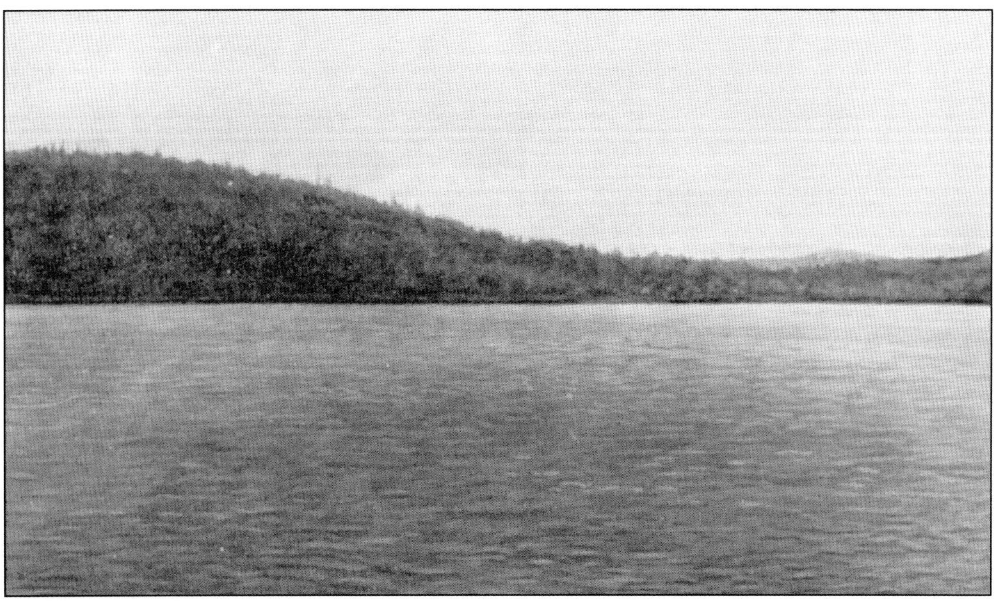

Diamond Lake (Little), 53 Acres, Stewartstown. This lake is near Diamond Lake and has become a favorite for fishing, hunting, and general camping for the outdoorsman.

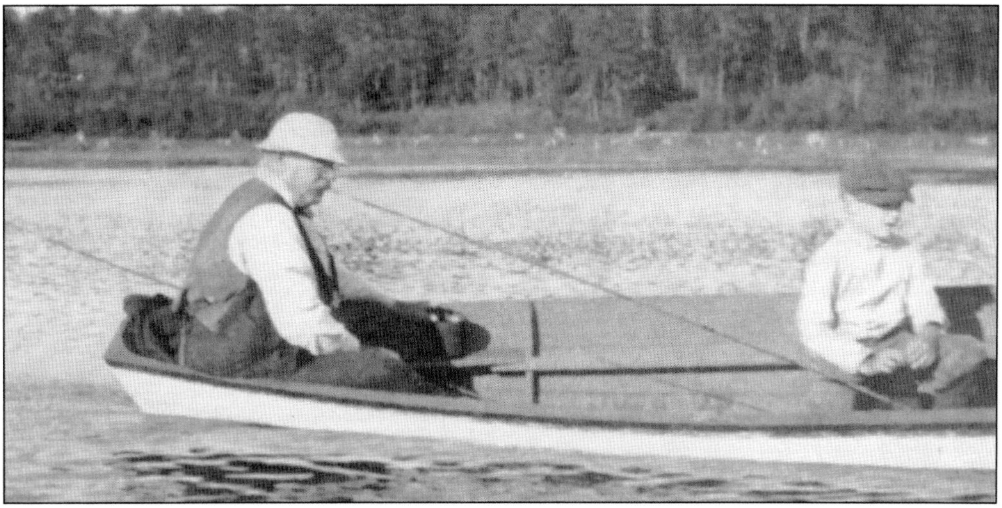

Duncan Lake (114 Acres), Ossipee. Pres. Grover Cleveland and his son, Richard Cleveland, spend a day fishing in Duncan Lake in the early 1900s. Fishing is very good in this lake with pickerel, horned pout, and white and yellow perch all plentiful in their proper season.

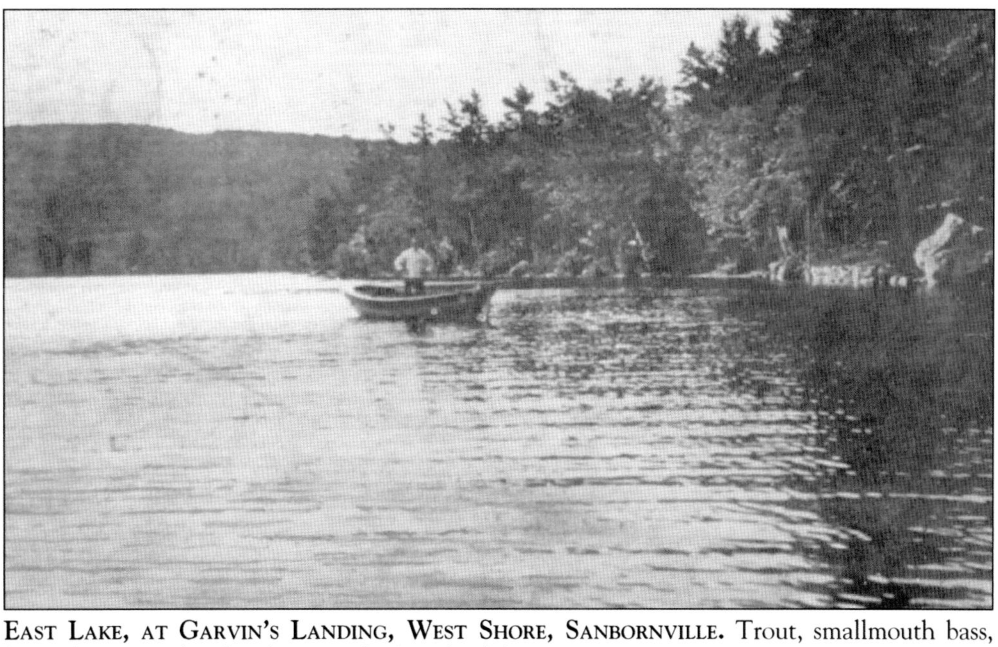

East Lake, at Garvin's Landing, West Shore, Sanbornville. Trout, smallmouth bass, horned pout, and pickerel are stocked in this lake.

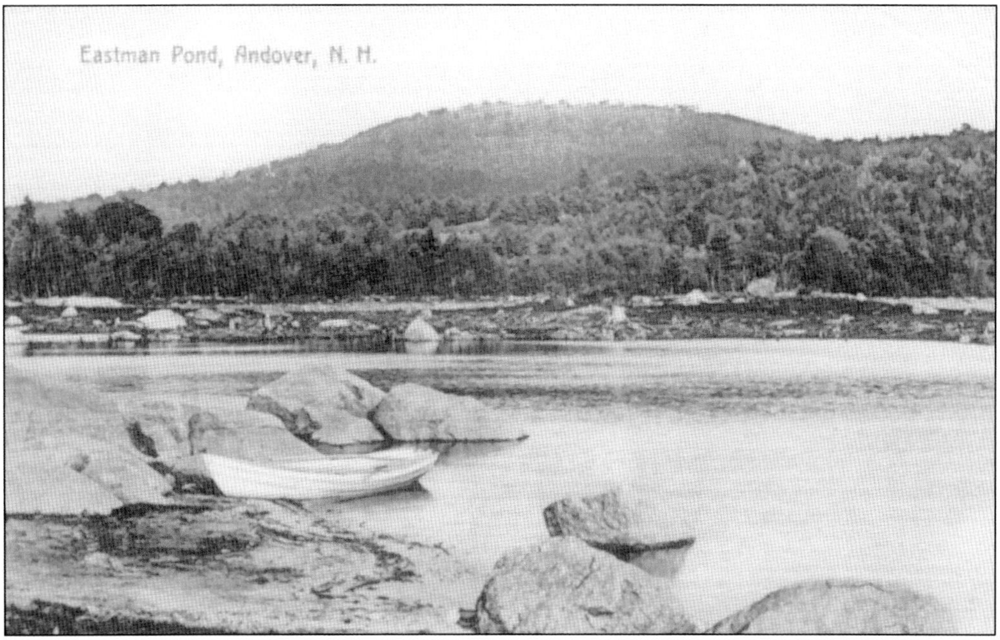

EASTMAN POND (142 ACRES), GRANTHAM, ANDOVER, 1910. This natural pond is a watershed for the Connecticut River. Fishing is fairly good, as the lake is stocked with shiners, pickerel, and yellow perch.

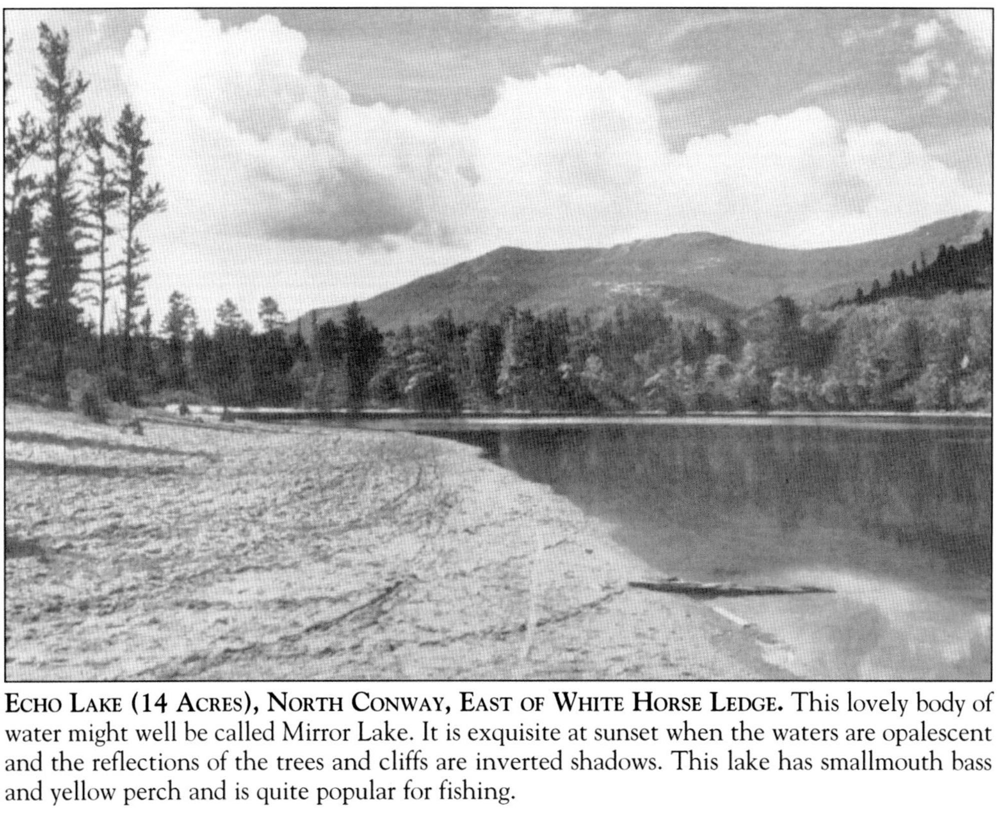

ECHO LAKE (14 ACRES), NORTH CONWAY, EAST OF WHITE HORSE LEDGE. This lovely body of water might well be called Mirror Lake. It is exquisite at sunset when the waters are opalescent and the reflections of the trees and cliffs are inverted shadows. This lake has smallmouth bass and yellow perch and is quite popular for fishing.

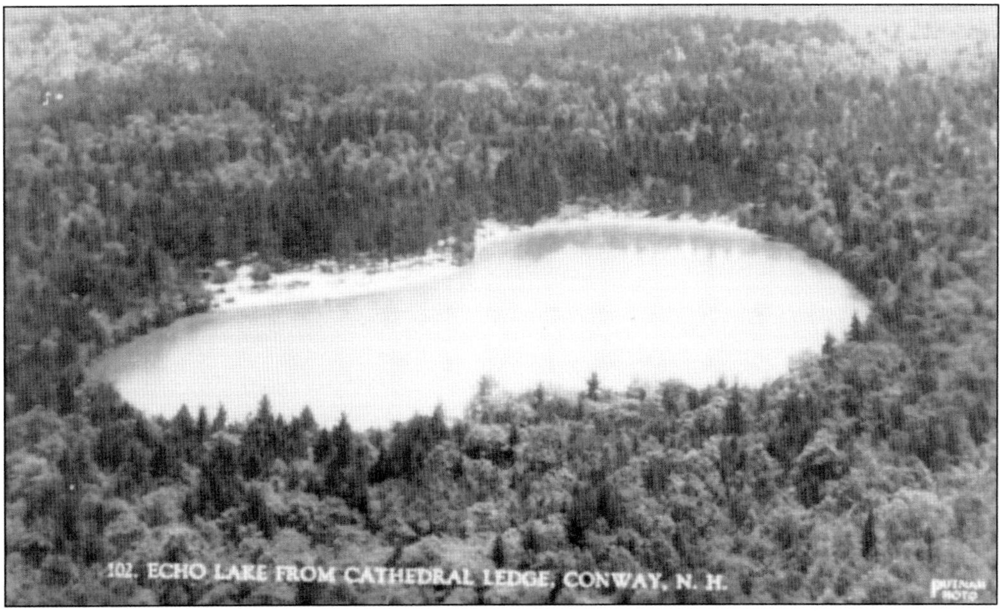

Echo Lake, from Cathedral Ledge, Conway. In *The White Hills* (1859), Thomas Starr King writes, "An evening spent there when the full rising moon silvers 'The Ledges,' and burnishes the bosom of the lake, and sheds its beams among it dark pine fringes, to slip slowly down the stately columns of the larger trees, will long be remembered as a sweet midsummer night's dream."

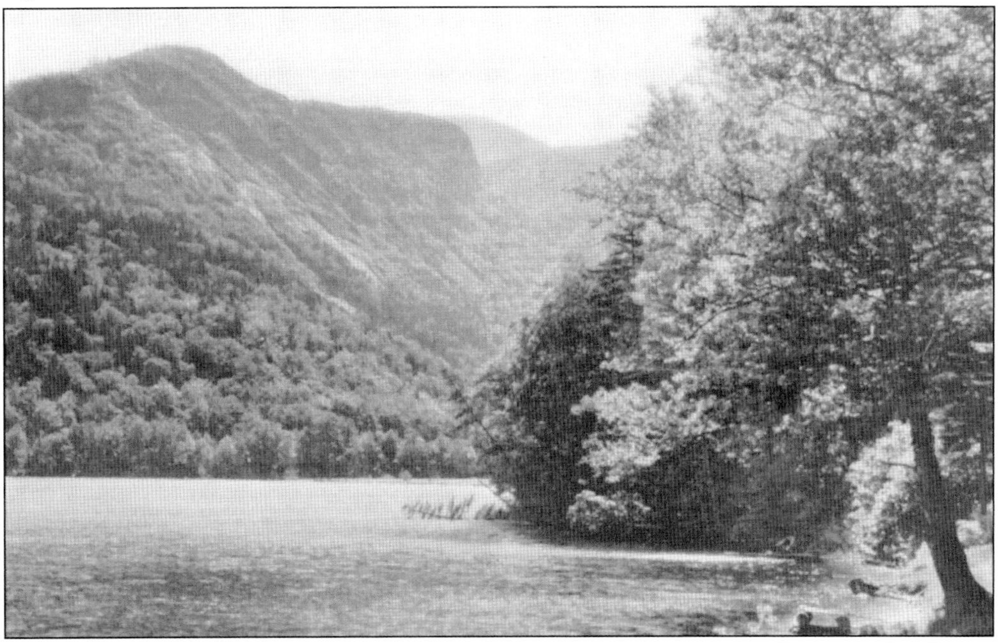

Echo Lake (28 Acres), with Eagle Cliff and Mount Lafayette Framing Its Body, Franconia Notch. This lake lies beneath the sheer and castellated granite walls of Eagle Cliff, which rise 1,500 feet above this small tarn. It is environed on the north and east by low, rocky Bald Mountain and on the west by massive Profile (Cannon) Mountain. The scene would be almost savage without the lake, the name of which indicates the acoustic effect found here.

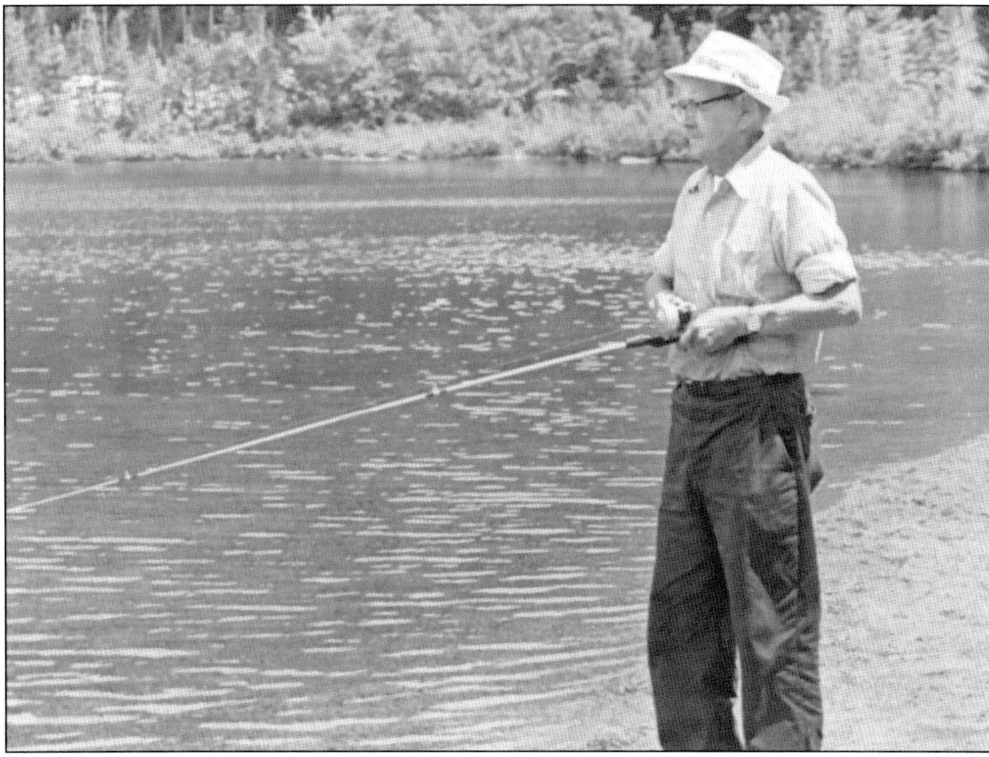

ECHO LAKE, FRANCONIA NOTCH. Gordon St. Lawrence of Littleton (above) takes advantage of the good trout fishing in this lake. On a still day, an ordinary shout will echo three or four times around the cliffs, while the shot of a gun will resound as though it were a whole battery. Toward evening the lake is worth visiting more for its echoes of color than of sound and becomes "a sweet and perennial symbol of purity and peace." (Thomas Starr King, *The White Hills*, 1859).

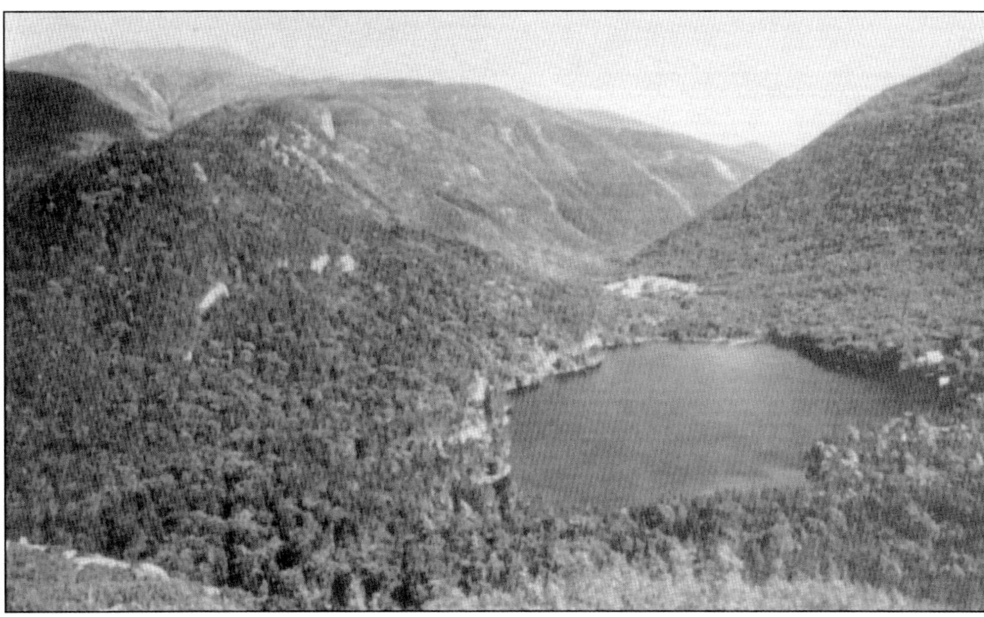

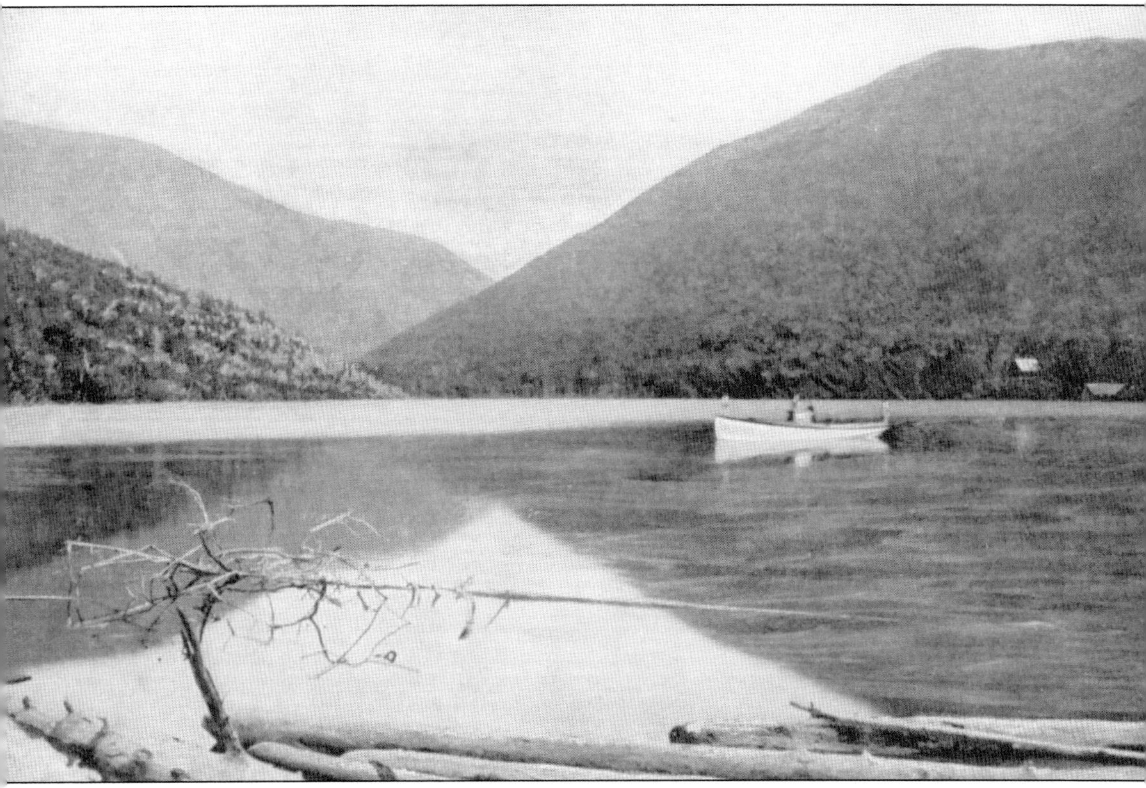

ECHO LAKE, FRANCONIA NOTCH, ANOTHER VIEW. This little lake is one of the sources of the Ammonoosus River. Echo Lake is very popular for swimming, hiking, and brook trout fishing.

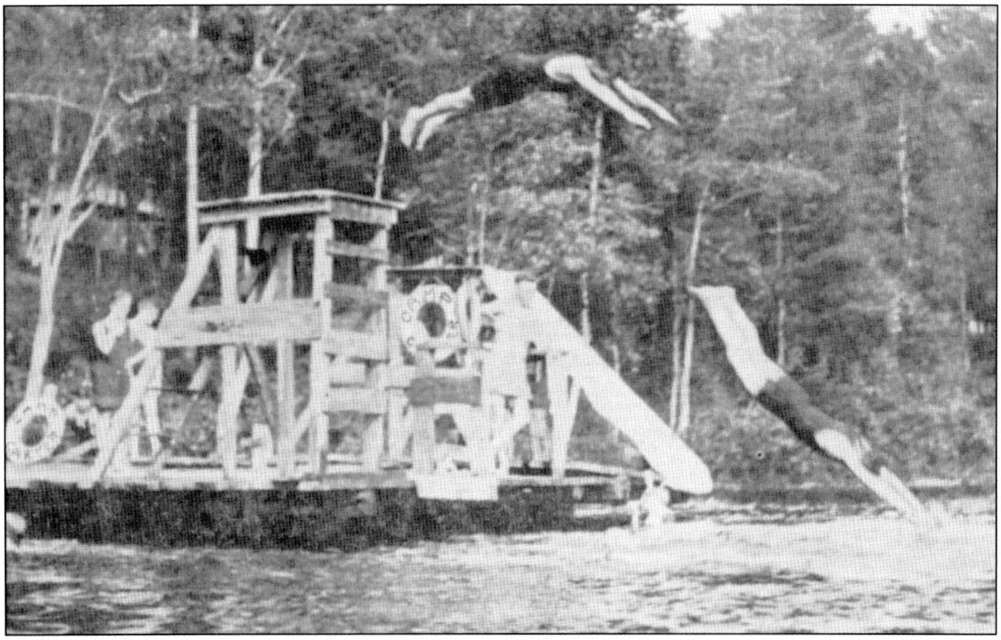

Elbow Pond (61.8 Acres), Andover. This action photograph shows Camp Carter in Andover in 1922. On a hot summer day, nothing is more refreshing than a plunge into the cool waters of Elbow Pond. Lying at the very foot of Ragged Mountain, the pond is well fed by clear mountain brooks and streams.

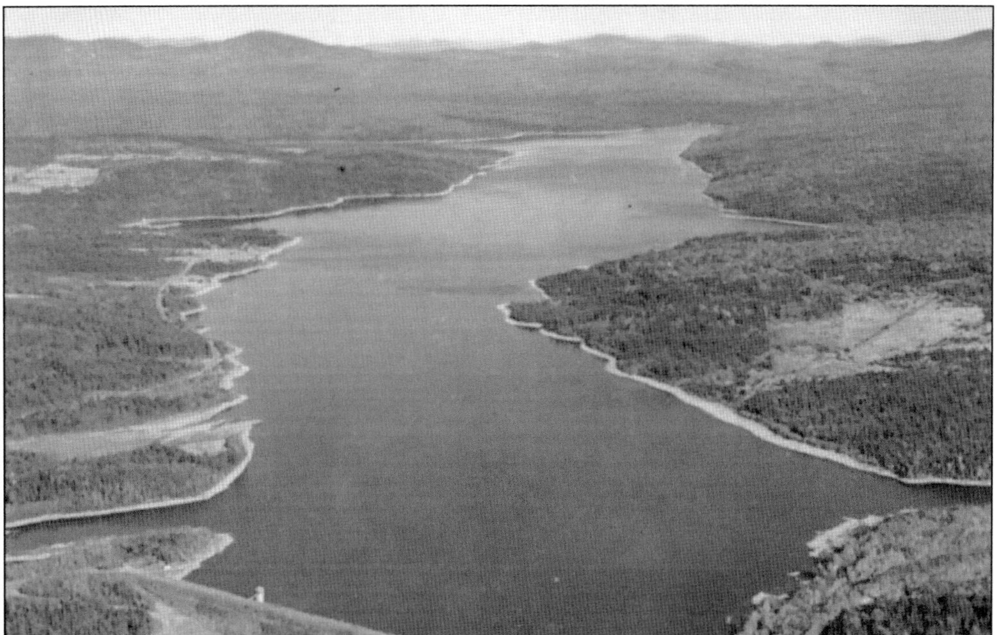

Francis Lake (2,081 Acres), Clarksville. Although this is a man-made lake, it has the same unspoiled charm of the other lakes in the Connecticut Lakes region of New Hampshire. Well known for fishing, Lake Francis offers rainbow trout, brown trout, lake trout, salmon, and pickerel.

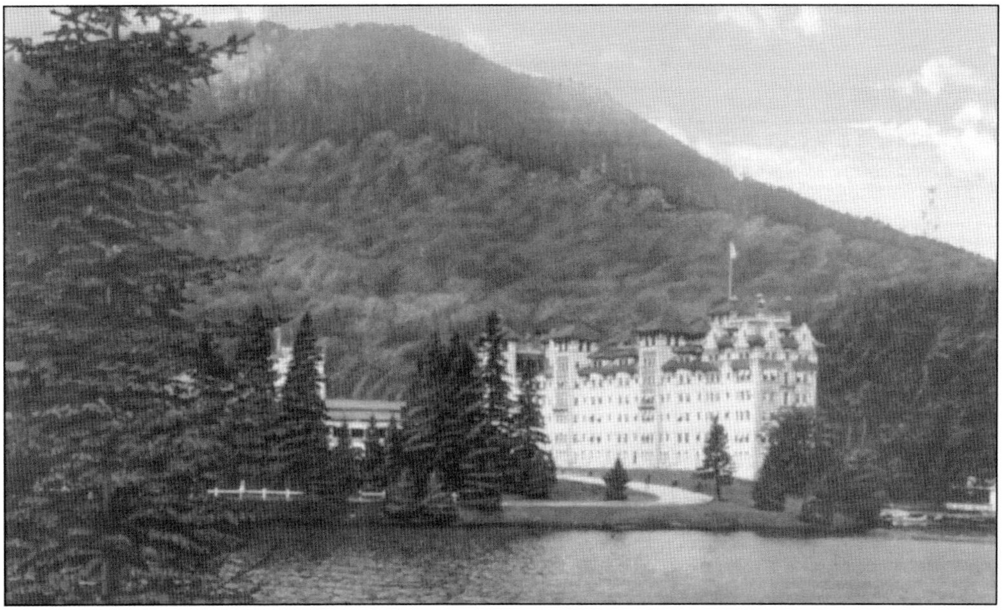

Gloriette Lake (36.7 Acres), Dixville Notch. This lake is part of the beautiful landscape of the Balsam's five-star resort in the rustic setting of Dixville Notch.

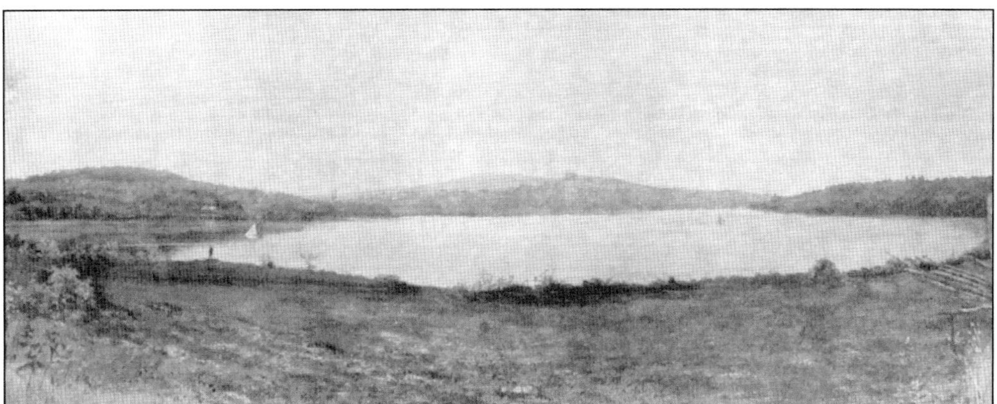

Granite Lake (227.8 Acres), Nelson and Stoddard. Featured in this lake are rainbow trout, lake trout, smallmouth bass, pickerel, and horned pout.

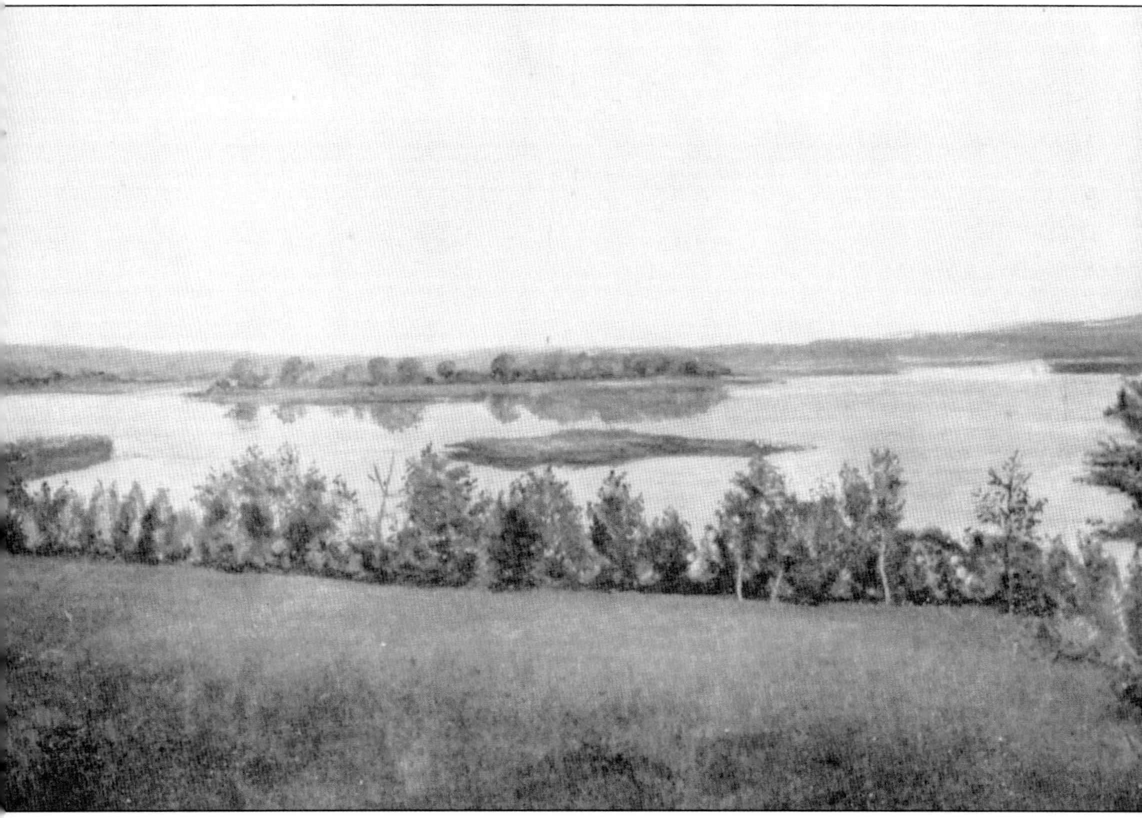

Great Bay, Portsmouth. Great Bay, connected with the Atlantic Ocean at Portsmouth, is in the southern part of the state. This expanse of water is dotted with numerous islands and surrounded by fine cultivated farms and extensive estates. An attractive feature of New Hampshire's water scenery, Great Bay is also a very good fishing ground. In 1975, a fisherman caught a prizewinning bluefish, weighing 21 pounds and measuring 39 inches long. In 1980, another fisherman pulled from the Dover area of the bay a striped bass weighing 60 pounds and measuring 51 inches.

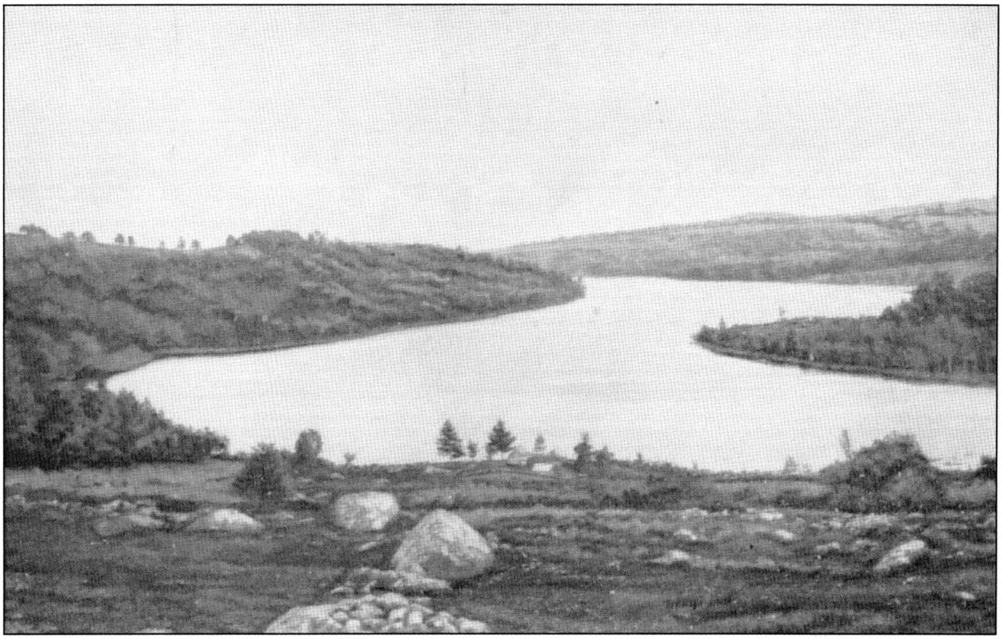

Gregg Lake (195 Acres), Antrim. Its irregular outline and wooded shores make it attractive to the tourist, and the black bass and pickerel lure the sportsmen. The outlook from Holt's Hill, where this view was taken, is grand and extensive. For those in search of rest and solitude, the town of Antrim has much to recommend it.

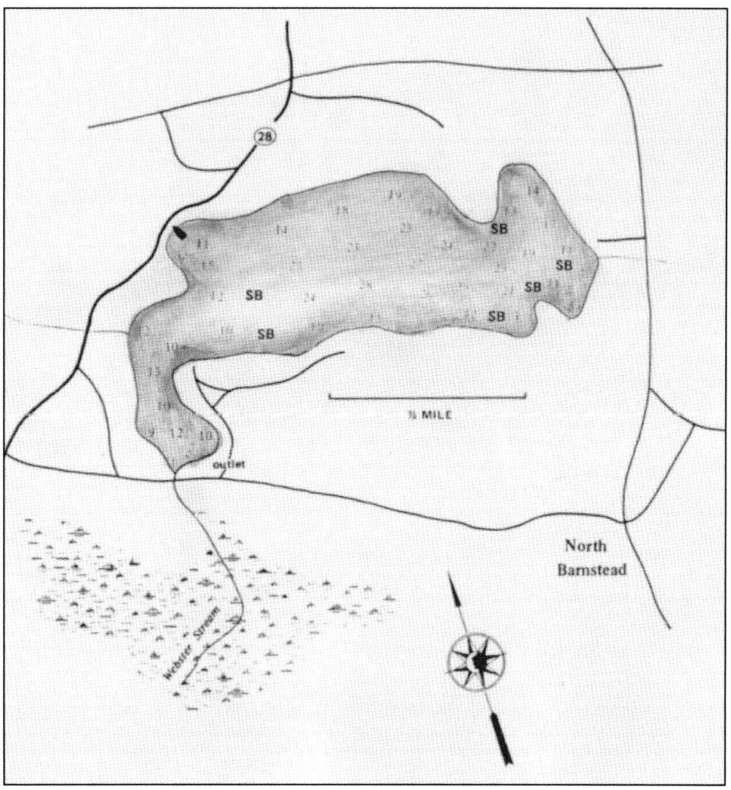

A Map of Half-Moon Lake (280 Acres), Alton and Barnstead. This pleasant body of water has attracted a small summer colony and provides boating and bathing. Stocked are pickerel, white and yellow perch, bass, and horned pout.

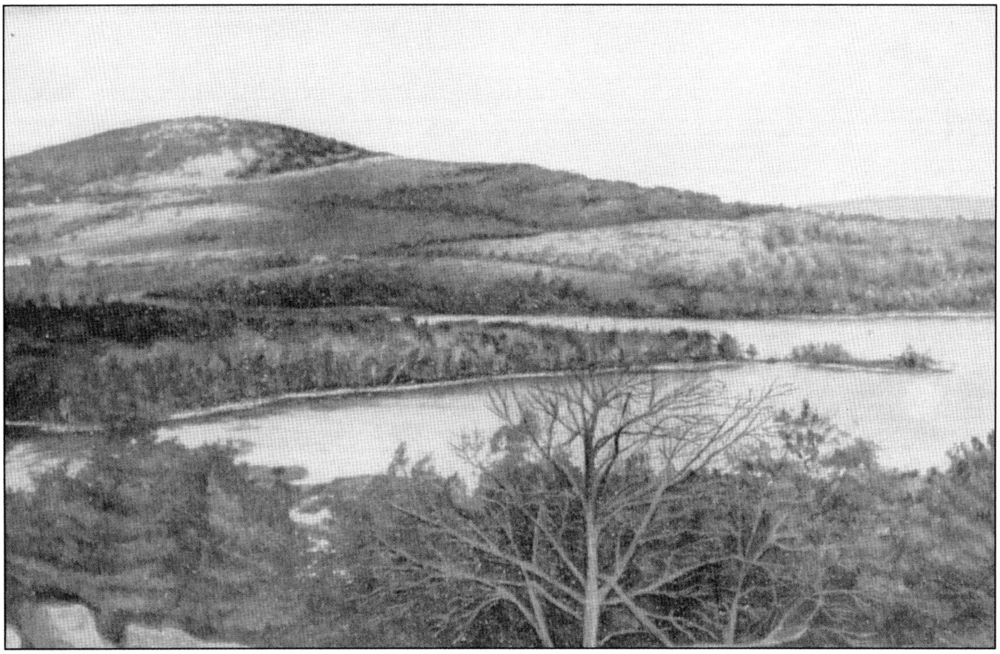

HALF-MOON LAKE (130 ACRES), WASHINGTON. This little-known lake, with Lovell Mountain in close proximity, affords facilities for most recreation. As the tide of summer travel sets more strongly toward remoter hills, the lake no doubt will be discovered. Today, the area enjoys a most enviable reputation as a quiet summer retreat. This natural pond is reported to contain suckers, minnows, sunfish, horned pout, pickerel, and yellow perch.

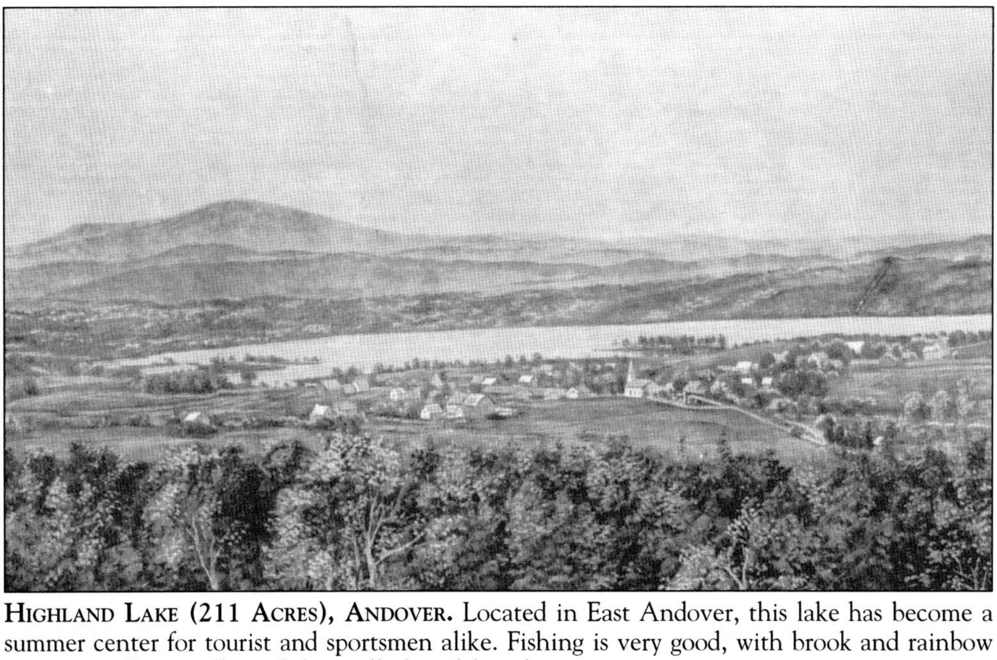

HIGHLAND LAKE (211 ACRES), ANDOVER. Located in East Andover, this lake has become a summer center for tourist and sportsmen alike. Fishing is very good, with brook and rainbow trout, as well as smallmouth bass, all plentiful in their proper season.

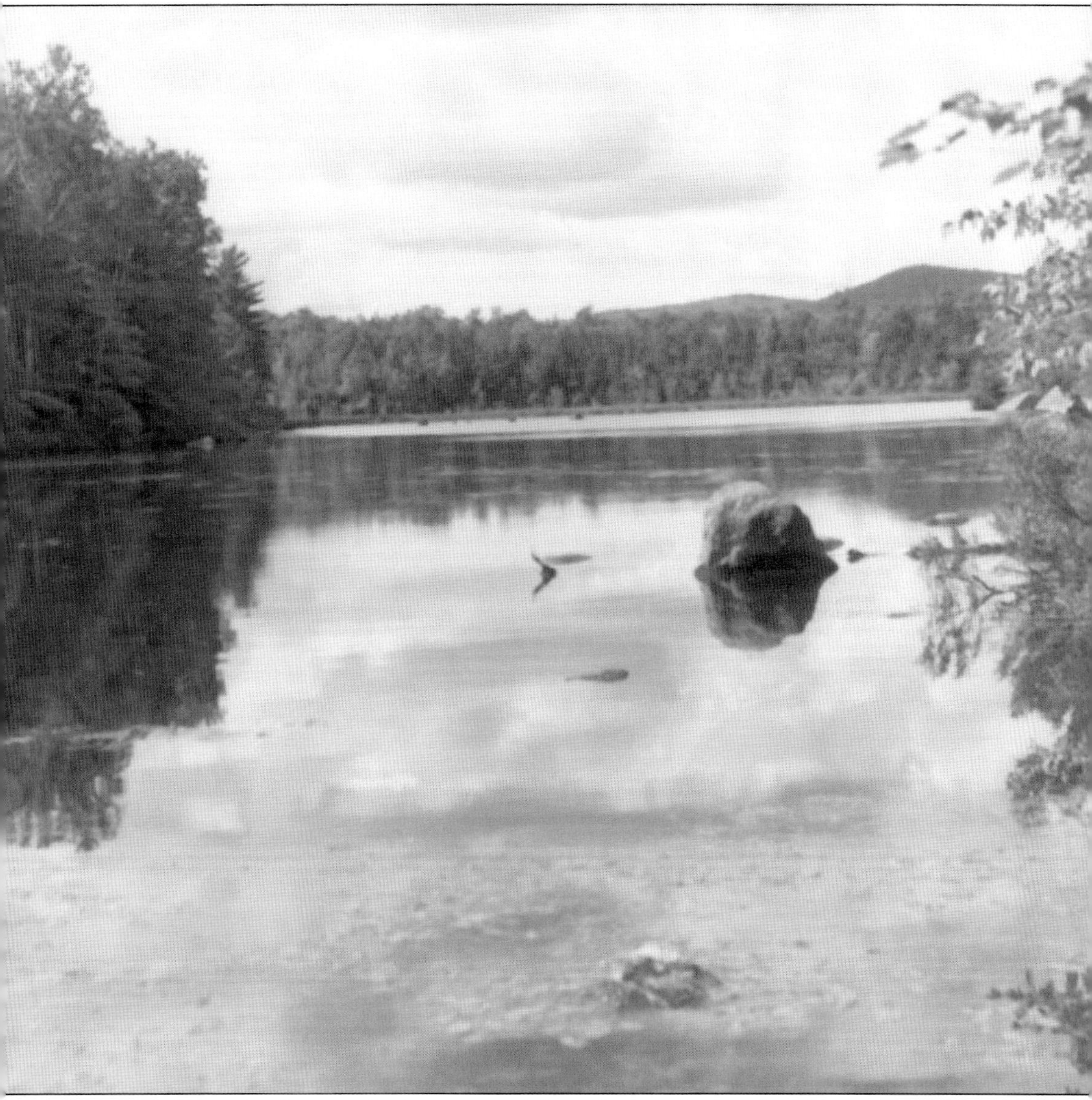

HIGHLAND LAKE (712 ACRES), STODDARD. This pleasant body of water is slowly being developed as a cottage settlement. The small community is located on a commanding height of land between the Merrimack and Connecticut Rivers. According to local lore, the rain falling on one side of a house here runs into the Merrimack, and rain falling on the other side runs into the Connecticut. For the fisherman, smallmouth and largemouth bass, pickerel, horned pout, and white perch are quite plentiful.

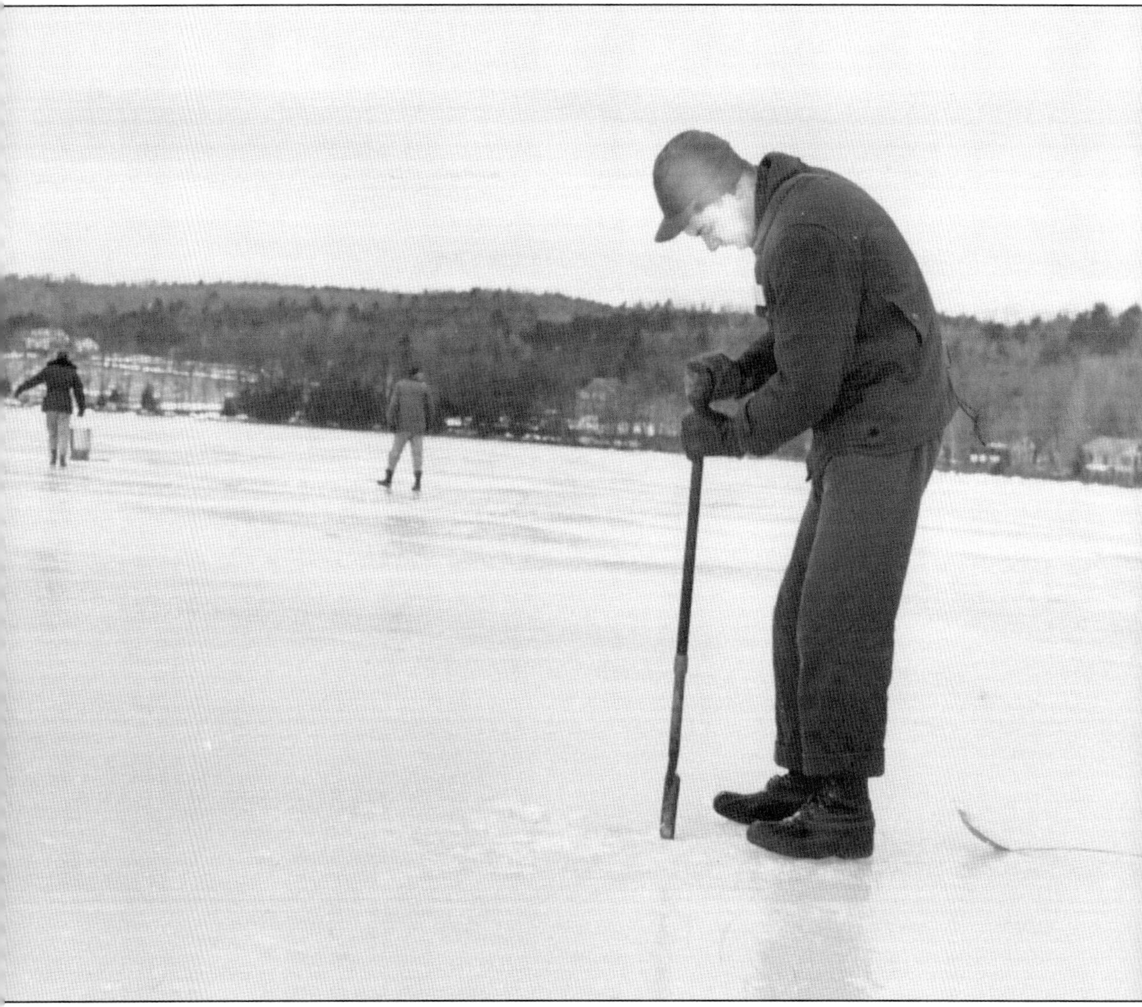

JENNESS POND (237 ACRES), NORTHWOOD. Ice fishing is very good on Jenness Pond, but after you get on the ice, the next step is to get through it. Featured fish are smallmouth and largemouth bass, pickerel, and horned pout.

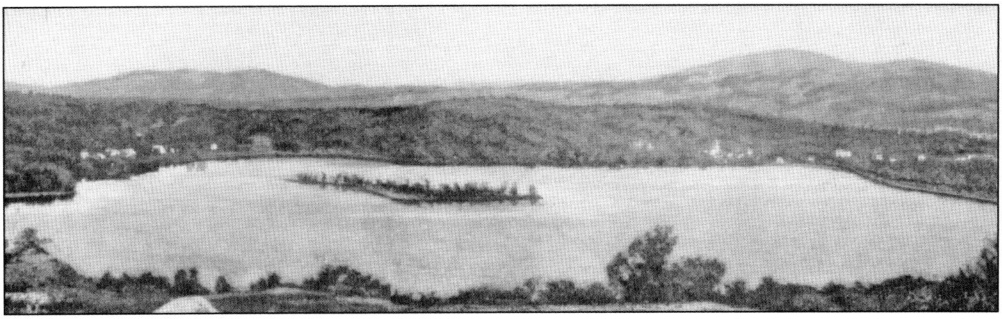

KEYSER LAKE (143 ACRES), SUTTON. In the vicinity of this lake can be found all the comforts and attractions for a summer retreat. Trout streams and game from the wooded hills and mountains make it desirable for the sportsman. It is reported to have been stocked with mixed sizes of smallmouth bass, horned pout, chained pickerel, and yellow perch.

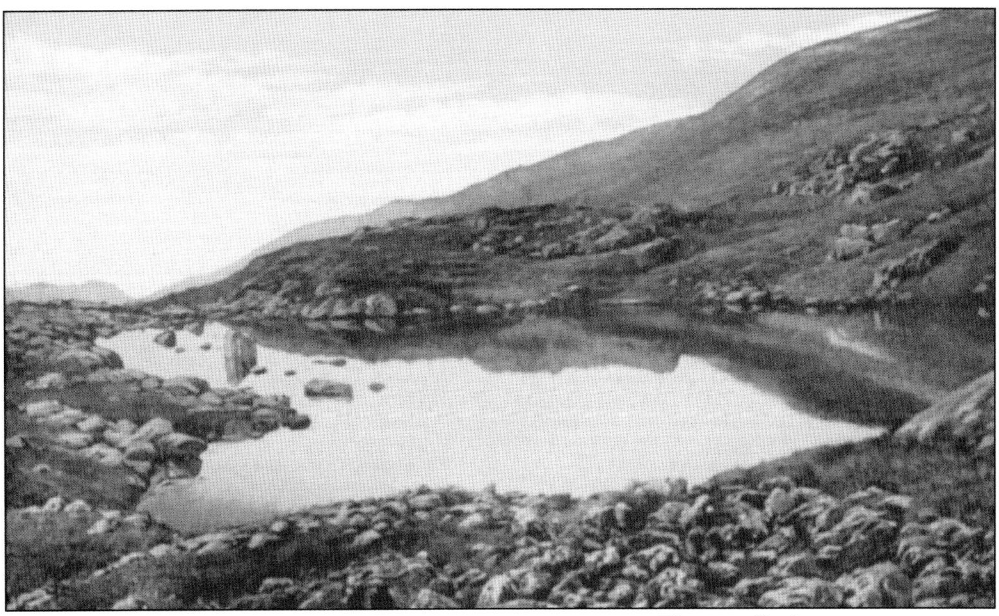

LAKE OF THE CLOUDS (1.5 ACRES), MOUNT WASHINGTON. This small alpine tarn serves as the source of the Ammonoosuc River. It is located a short distance from the summit of Mount Washington, in a small bowl on the northwest side of the ridge near the low point between Mount Washington and Mount Monroe. There are two of these lakes: the larger of them, often called the Lower Lake, is at an elevation of 5,025 feet; the much smaller one, called Upper Lake, has an elevation of 5,050 feet and an area of just under half an acre.

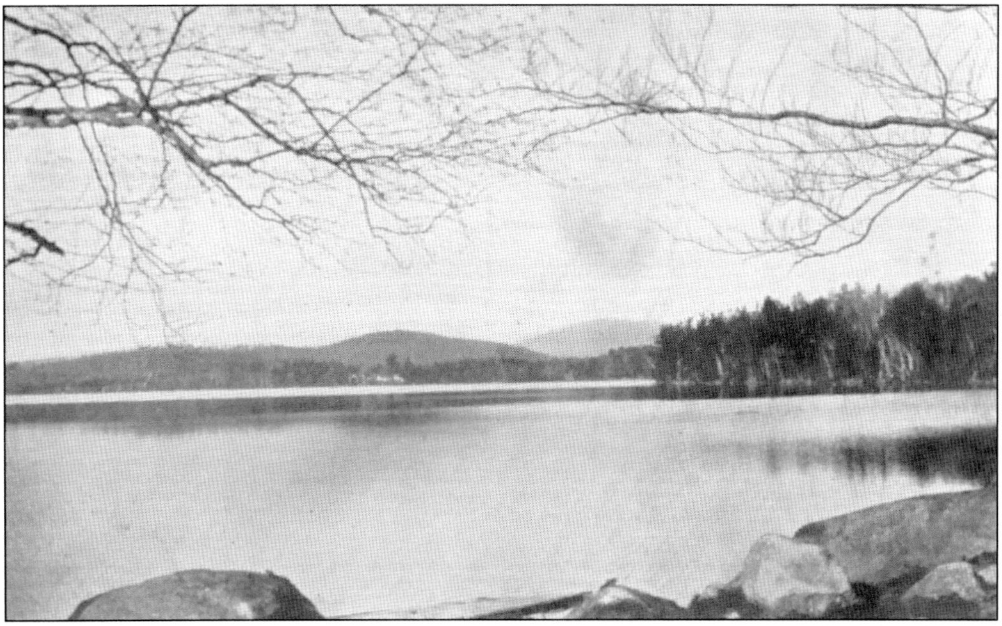

Laurel Lake (155 Acres) with Monadnock Mountain, Fitzwilliam. This lake, located is the southern part of the state, was also known as South Pond. The scenic little community attracts many visitors and anglers who enjoy the out-of-doors.

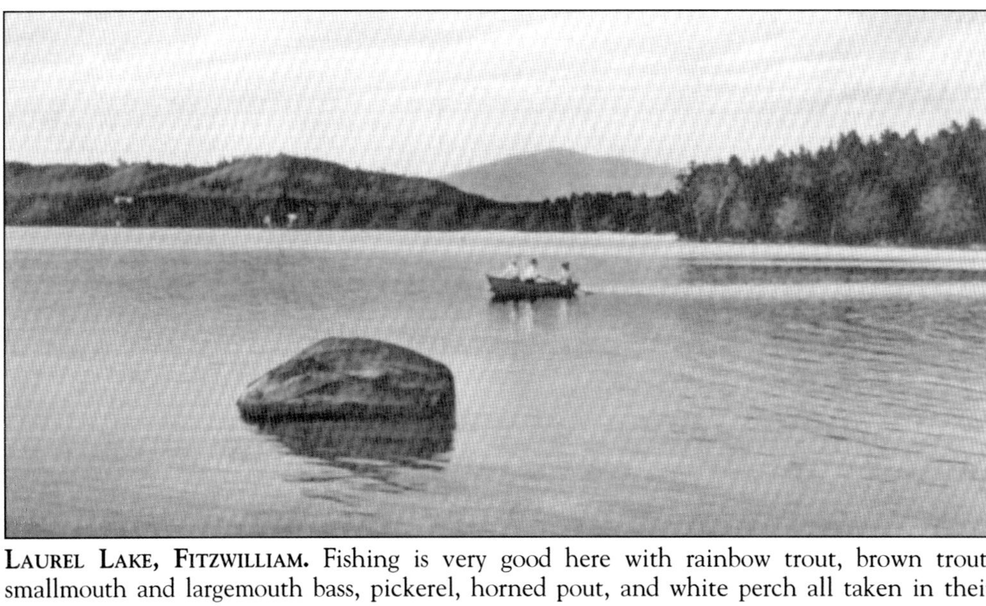

Laurel Lake, Fitzwilliam. Fishing is very good here with rainbow trout, brown trout, smallmouth and largemouth bass, pickerel, horned pout, and white perch all taken in their proper season.

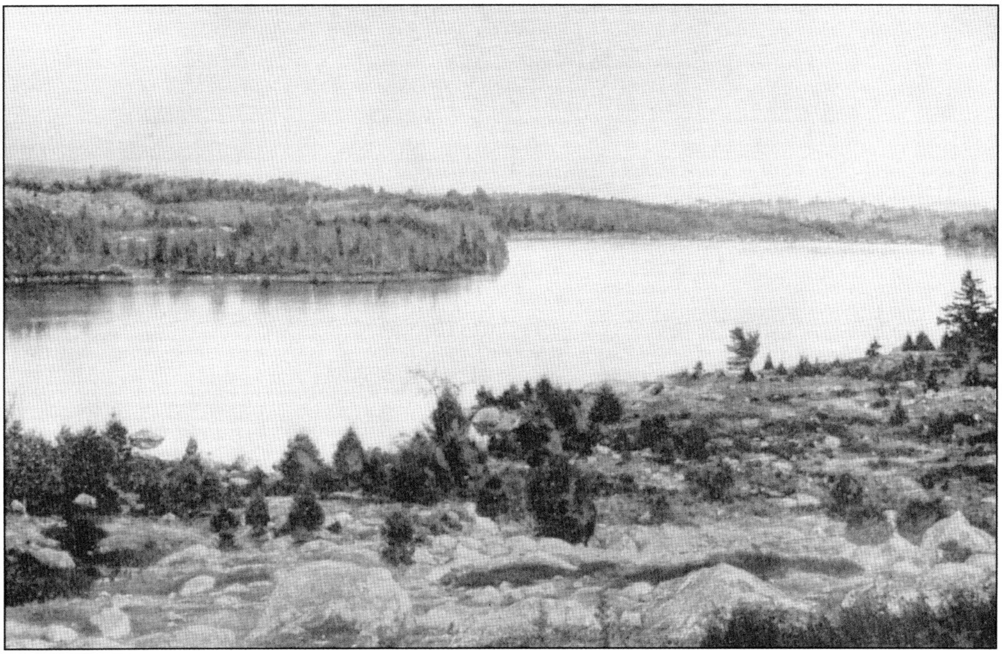

Loon Lake (156 Acres), Hillsboro. This is one of those charming lakes for which the hilly sections of New Hampshire are so famous. Its resources for comfort and pleasure are unbounded, and the surrounding country is most picturesque.

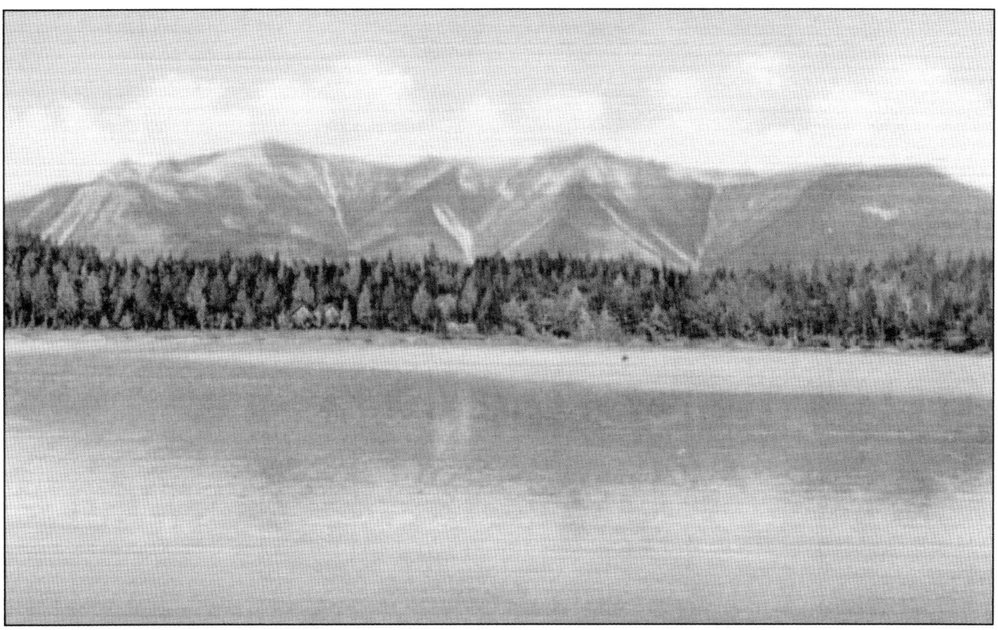

Lomesome Lake (27 Acres), Lincoln. This lake is also known as Tamarock Pond. In the distance are the majestic peaks of the Franconia Range of the White Mountains. For the fishermen, trout are well stocked in this pond.

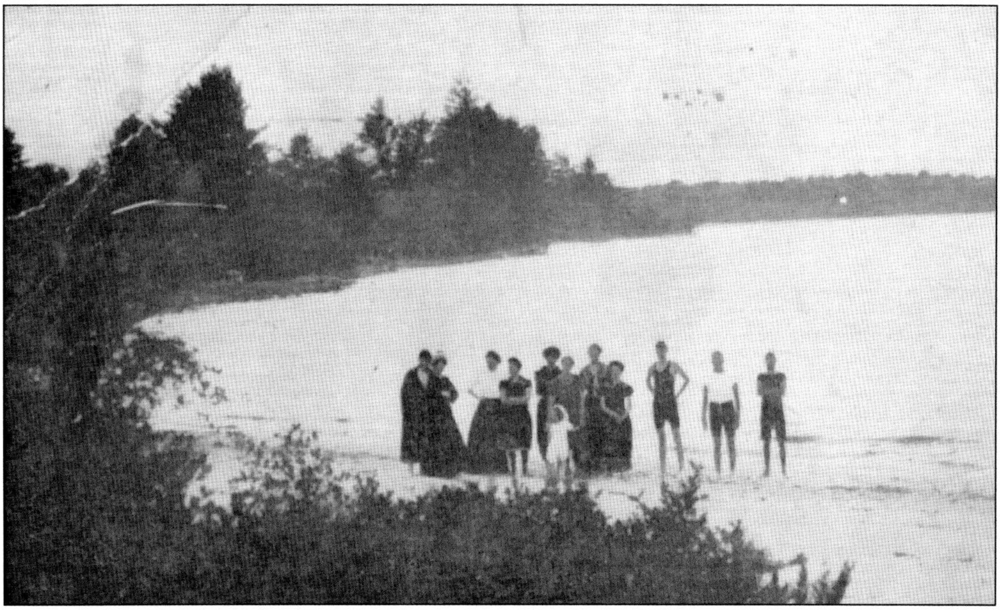

LONG POND (LAKE KANASATKA) 371 ACRES, MOULTONBORO. This charming lake, located one mile east of Center Harbor at the foot of Red Hill, is a popular summer retreat for both bathing and fishing.

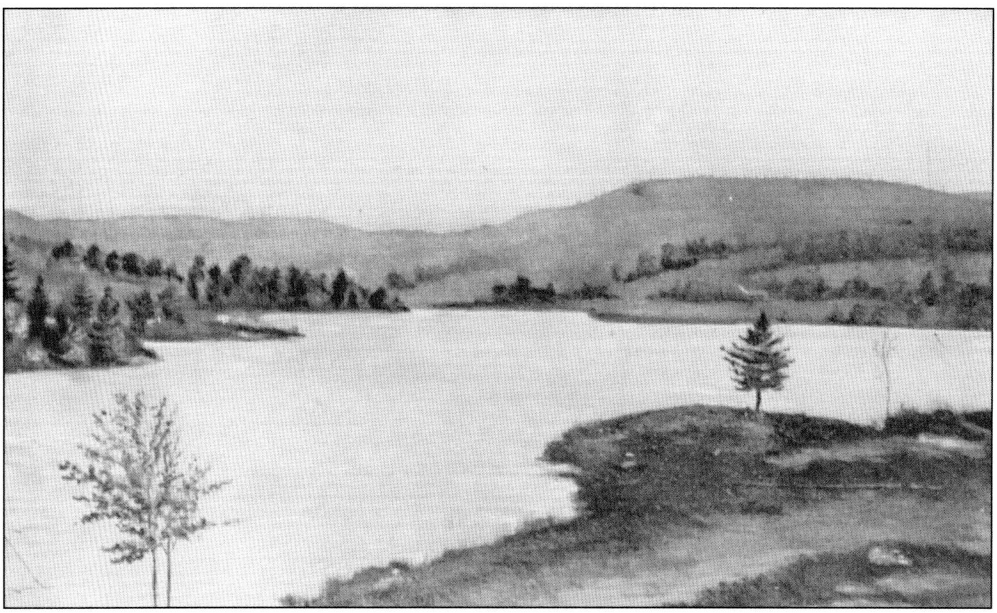

LONG POND (LAKE KANASATKA), MOULTONBORO. The waters of this lake empty into Lake Winnipesaukee by way of a stream between the Second and Third Moultonboro Necks. Lake Kanasatka is well stocked with lake trout, pickerel, white and yellow perch, bass, and horned pout.

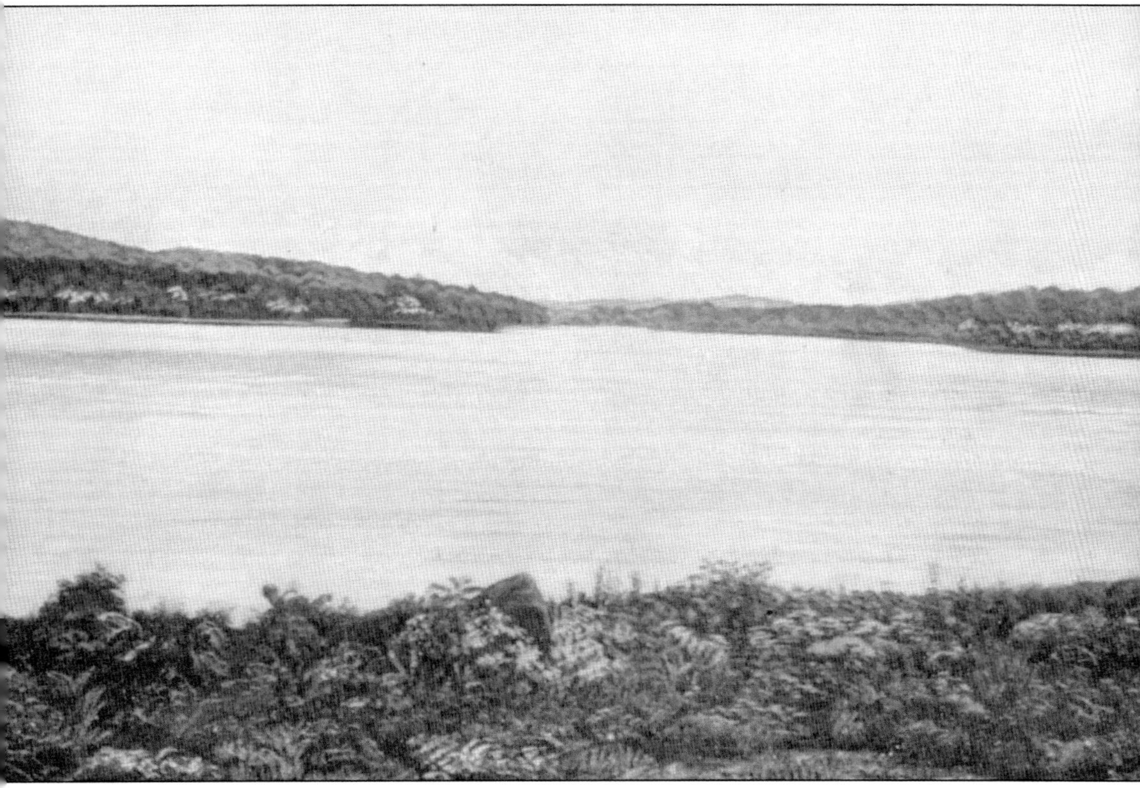

LOVELL LAKE (538 ACRES), WAKEFIELD. This lake is located in the vicinity of fine farms, luxuriant forests, and has already become a popular summer resort. Fishing is quite good and features pickerel, white and yellow perch, bass, and horned pout.

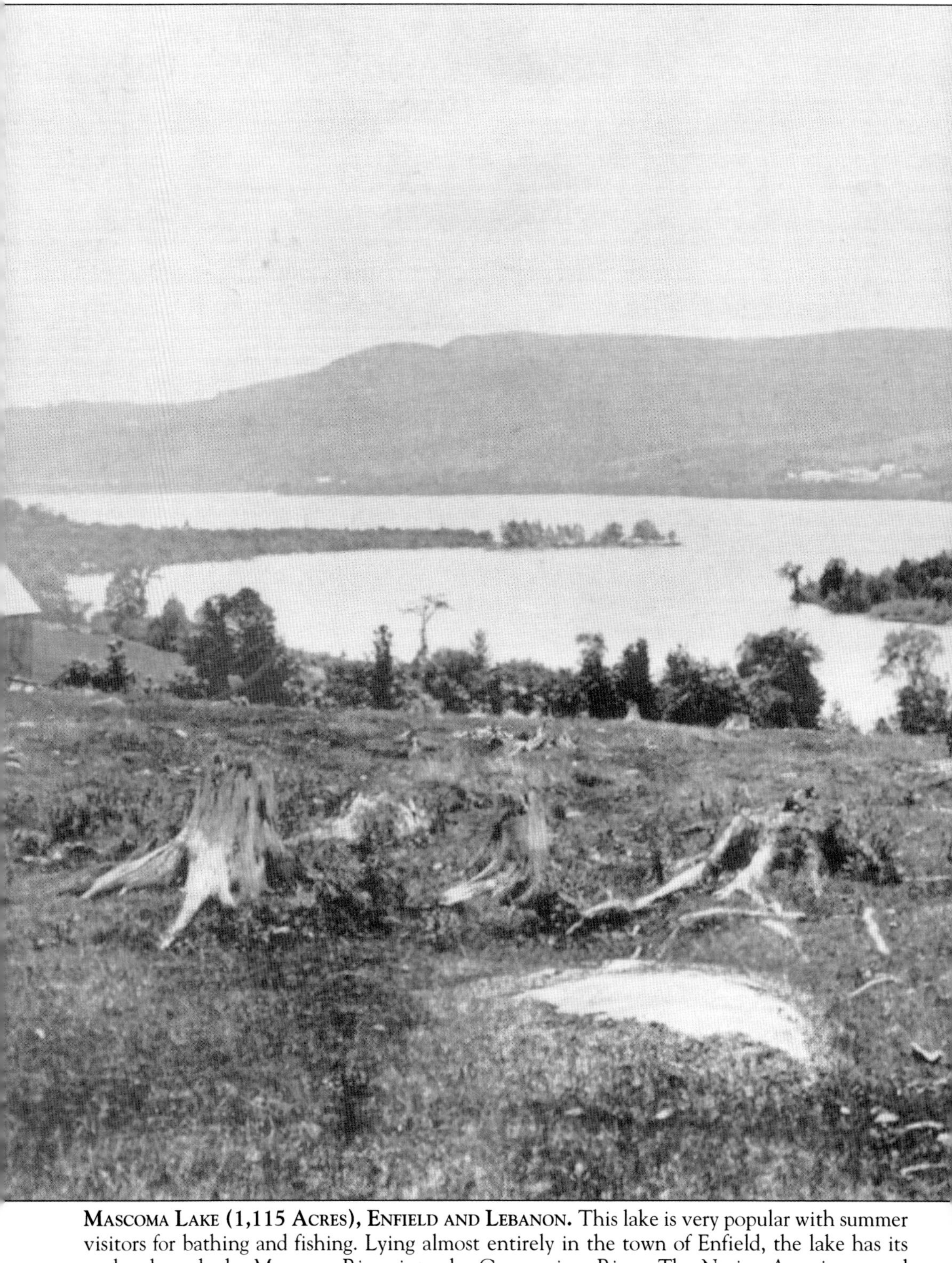

MASCOMA LAKE (1,115 ACRES), ENFIELD AND LEBANON. This lake is very popular with summer visitors for bathing and fishing. Lying almost entirely in the town of Enfield, the lake has its outlet through the Mascoma River into the Connecticut River. The Native American word

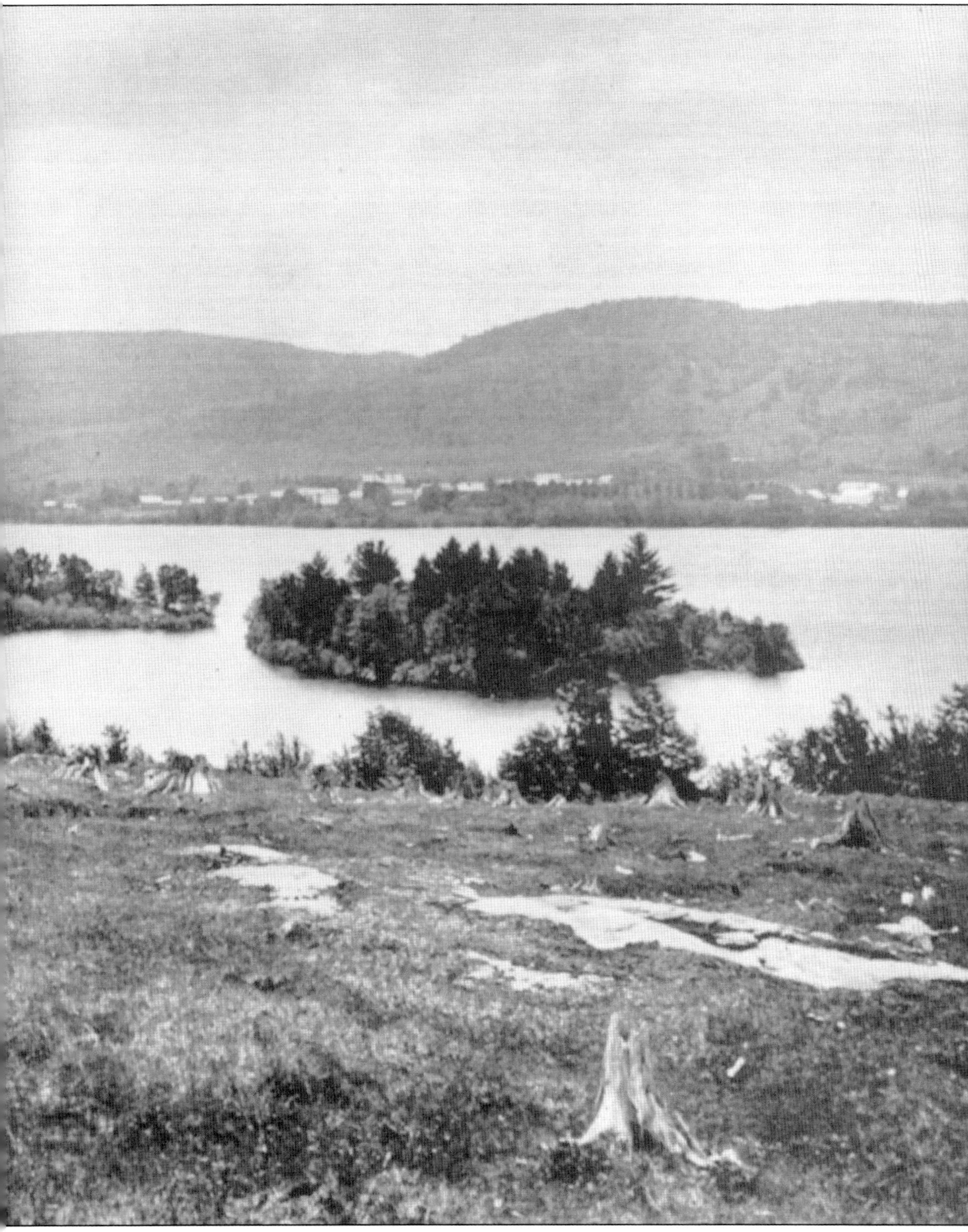

Mascoma means "fish water." Indeed, fish abound in this lake, with rainbow trout, brown trout, smallmouth and largemouth bass, pickerel, horned pout, white perch, and rock bass.

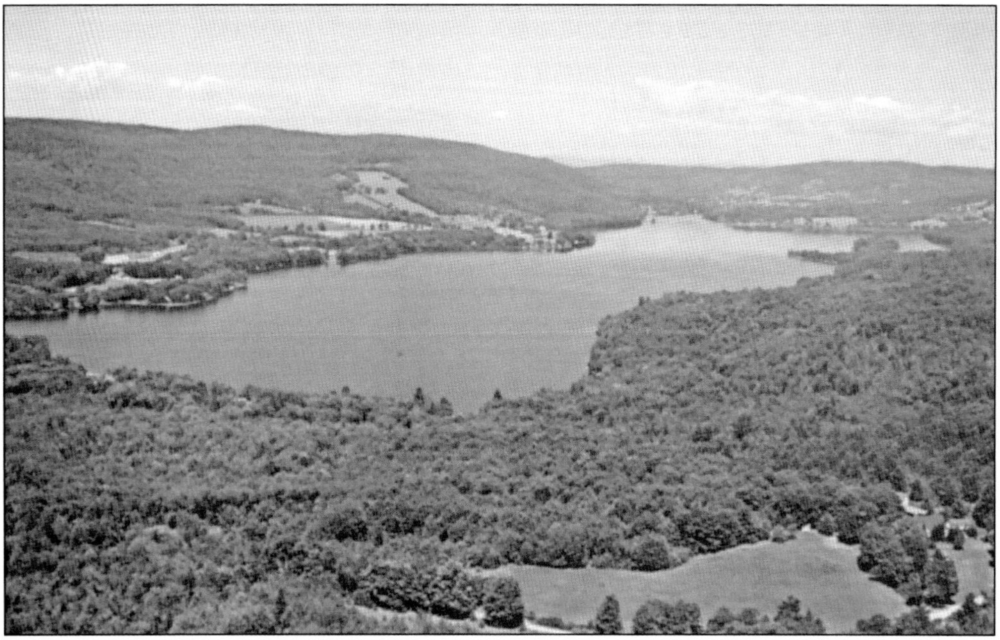

Mascoma Lake, Enfield and Lebanon. This 4-mile-long lake, attractively circled by hills and mountains, is the center of a popular resort area in western New Hampshire. Cottages have sprung up around its shores, and nearby is the historic Shaker settlement in Enfield.

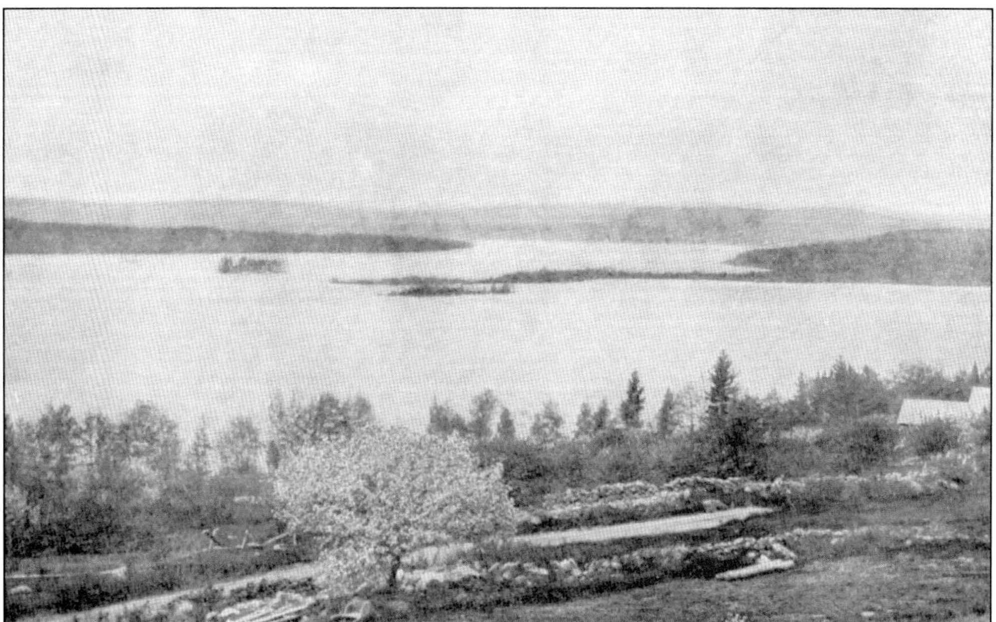

Massabesic Lake (2,900 Acres), Auburn and Manchester. This large body of water is surrounded by low hills and pleasantly dotted with islands. It is the source of the Manchester water supply. Its shores are a popular spot for summer visitors.

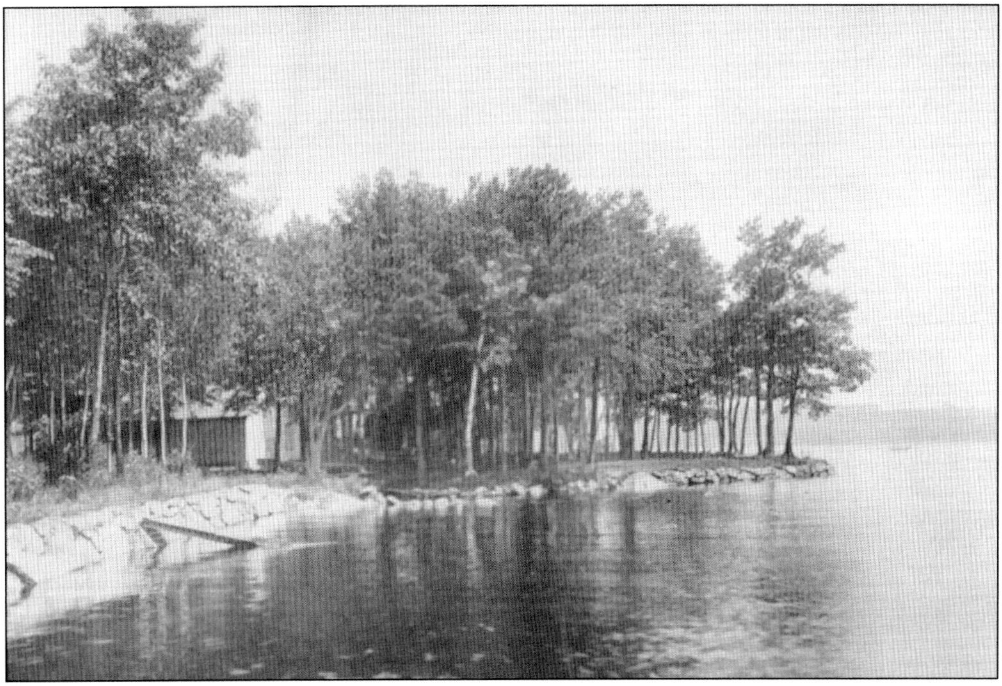

Massabesic Lake, Kimball's Point, Auburn and Manchester. The name of this lake is a variation of the Native American word *Massapeseag*, meaning "great water." A tale related in 1860 by 84-year-old William Graham of Auburn provided another derivation for the name. According to Graham, "Indians plenty round the great pond." Deacon Leach of the Presbyterian Church in Cheshire sold rum in those days. One little Indian came out from great island, called Deer Island, wanted some "occupee." "Who for?" said the deacon. "Massa be sick, want it for him." Later legend went further and gave Massa a grave on an island in the lake.

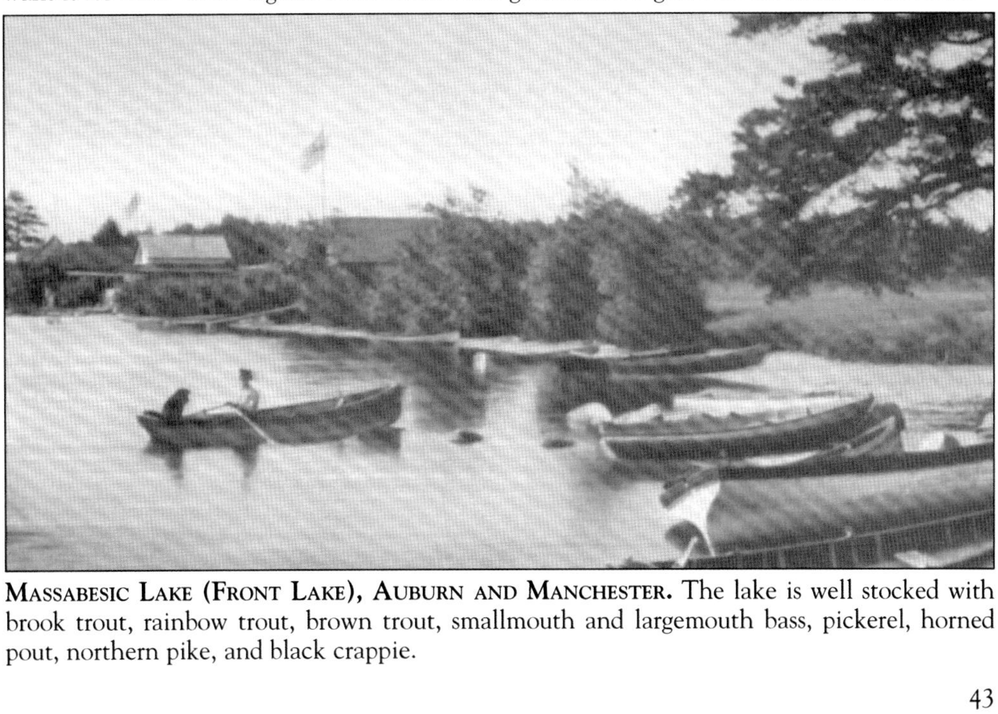

Massabesic Lake (Front Lake), Auburn and Manchester. The lake is well stocked with brook trout, rainbow trout, brown trout, smallmouth and largemouth bass, pickerel, horned pout, northern pike, and black crappie.

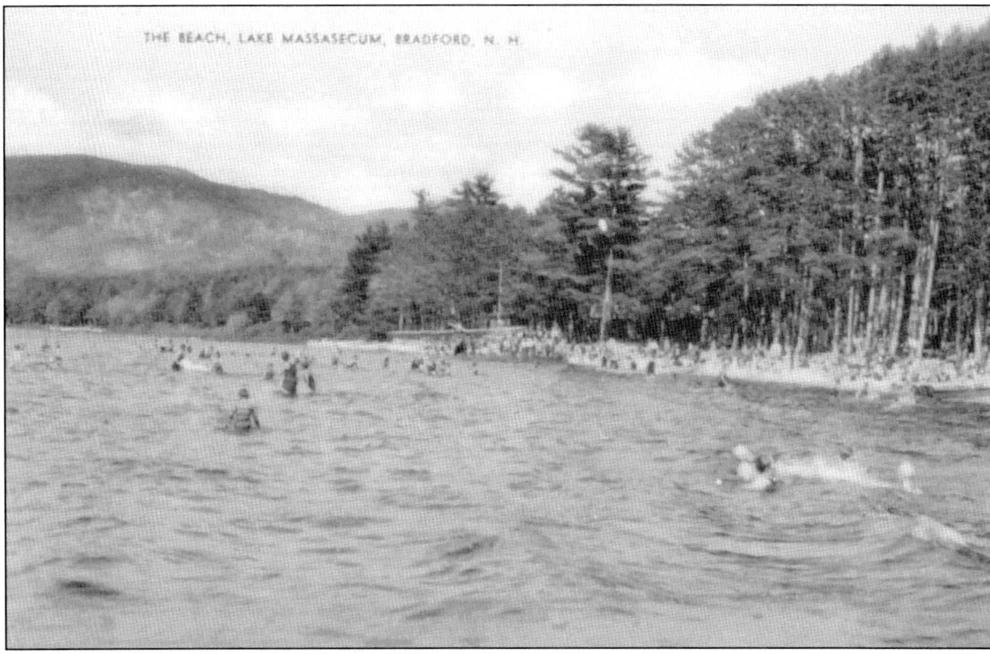

MASSASECUM LAKE (401 ACRES), BRADFORD. This secluded bathing beach, framed by a cool pine grove, embodies the perfect family retreat.

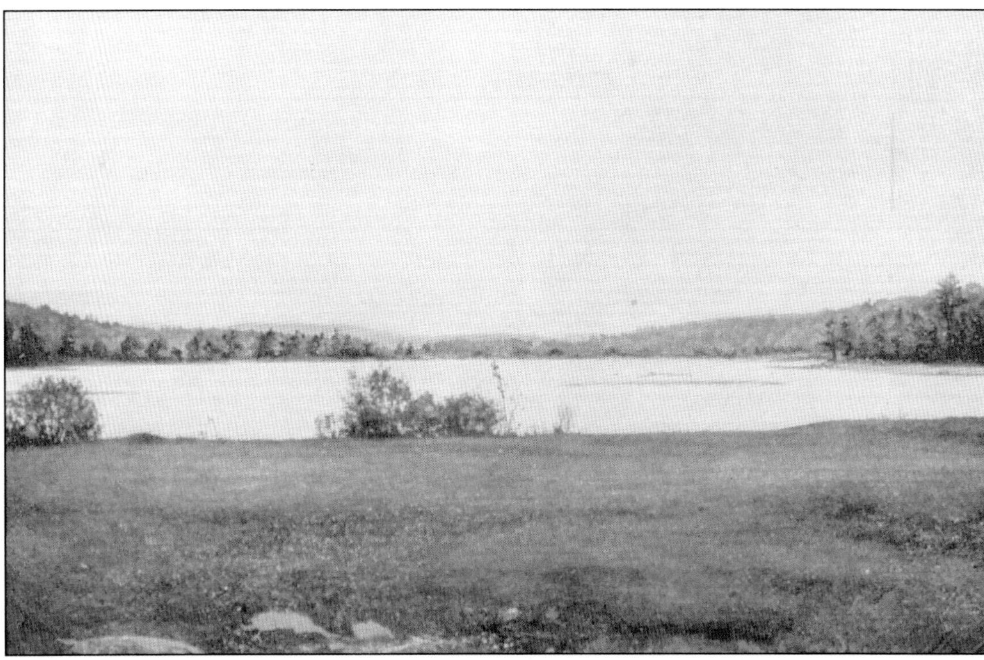

MELLEN LAKE (156 ACRES), WASHINGTON. This lake is about 1.25 miles long, half a mile wide, and is located near Lovell Mountain. Today, this area is becoming well known as a summer retreat. Several cottages occupy the shore of this small body of water.

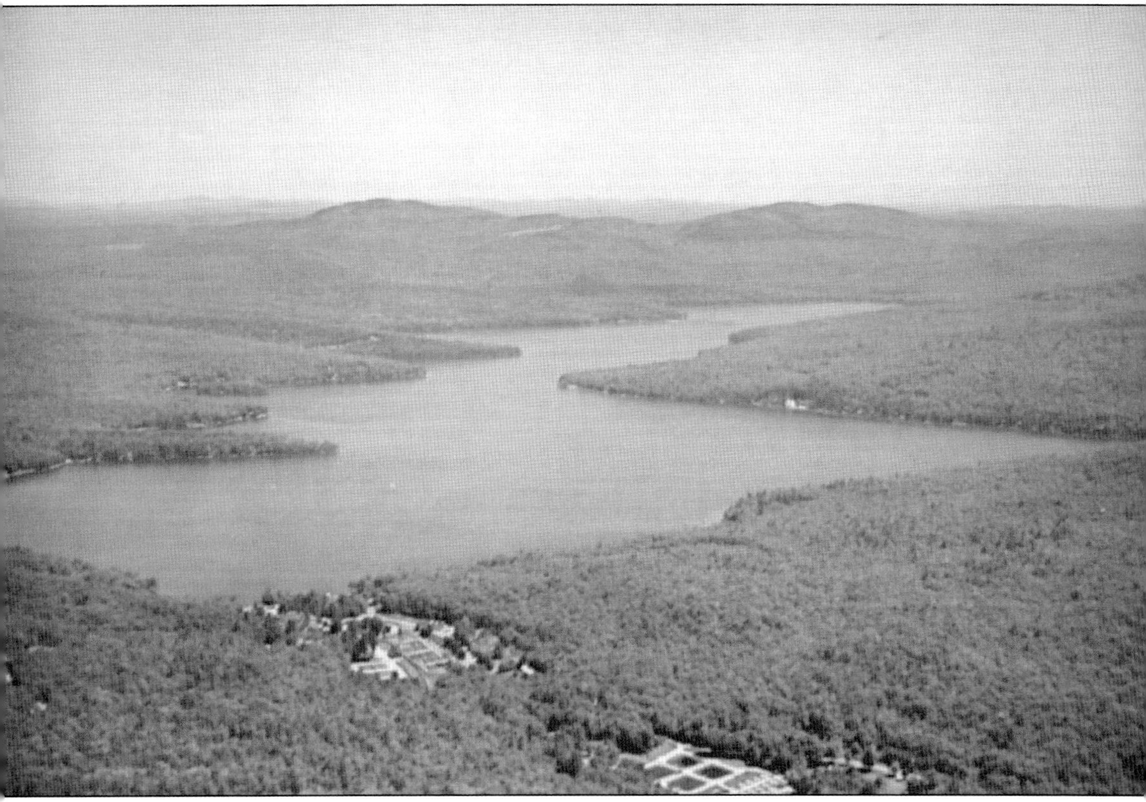

Merrymeeting Lake (1,112 Acres), New Durham. This beautiful lake is gracefully framed by low mountains. Its name dates back to about 1770, when a group of grantees exploring this territory held a meeting and a feast on its shores. Today the lakeshore is clustered with small summer cottages, and its waters are stocked with pickerel, yellow perch, bass, and horned pout.

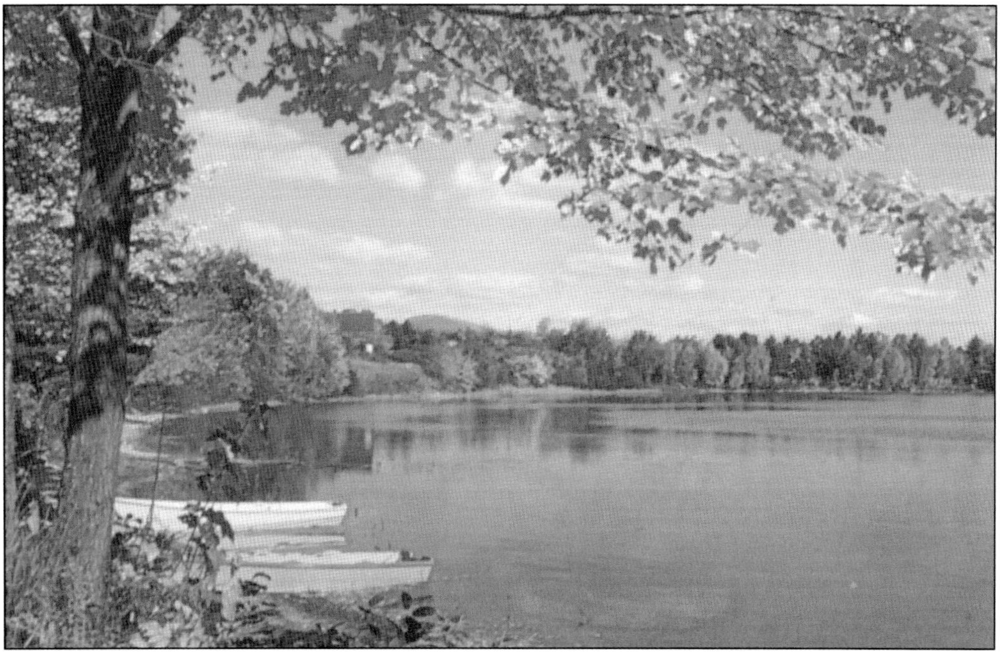

Mirror Lake (377 Acres), Tuftonboro. This very attractive body of water lies in the seclusion of Tuftonboro. Excellent for bathing and fishing, the lake is stocked with lake trout, pickerel, white perch, bass, and horned pout.

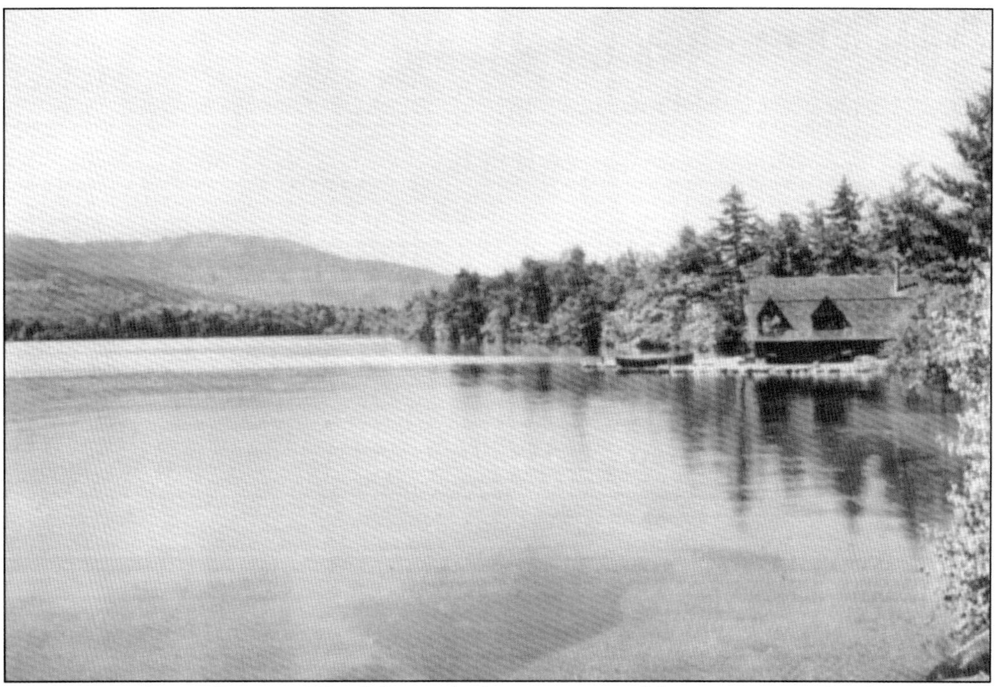

Monadnock Lake, Dublin. This lake, with the mountain of the same name, has become one of the most famous summer resorts in New Hampshire. All elevations overlooking the lake are adorned with elegant homes and plush landscaping, which frame the lake in proper style.

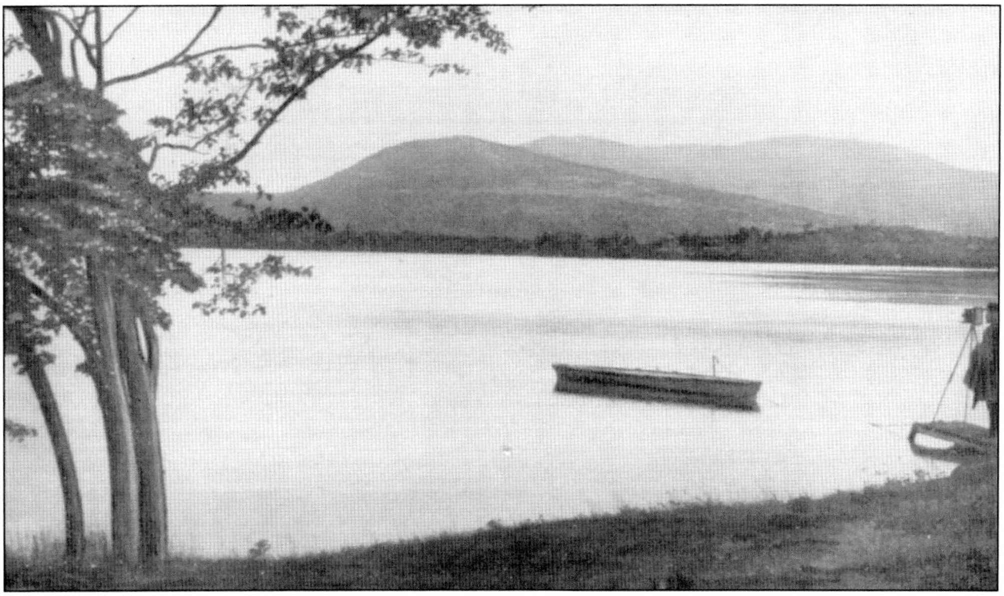

MONADNOCK LAKE, DUBLIN, ANOTHER VIEW. Gleaming like turquoise in a bed of emeralds, Monadnock Lake is surrounded by hills, wooded down to the shore. The lake is fed by mountain springs, which keep the water clear cool. A variety of brook trout is among the fish in its waters.

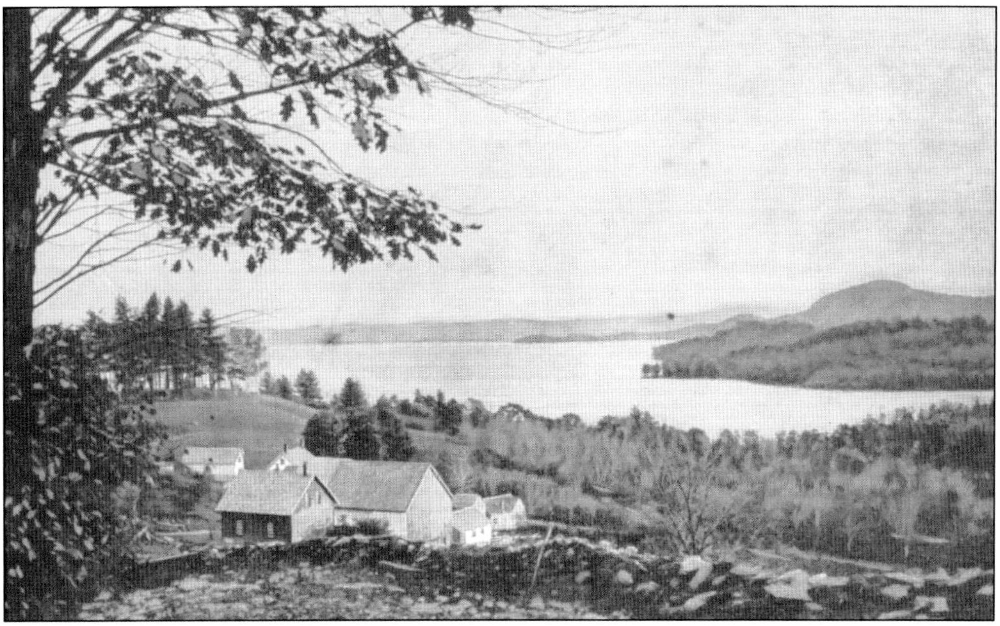

NEWFOUND LAKE (4,106 ACRES), BRISTOL. This long lake of unusual beauty is ringed with rolling hills. Being 6 miles long and 2.5 miles wide gives Newfound the distinction of being the fourth largest lake in the state. From the southern end is an extensive view of the lake, with Mount Tenny at the northern end. Before the early European settlers discover this lake, Algonquin Indians used its shores as camping grounds. The site of Indian workshops, where arrowheads and other implements were made from flint, have been discovered at various points around the lake. The Native American word *Pasquaney* means "place where birchbark for canoes is found."

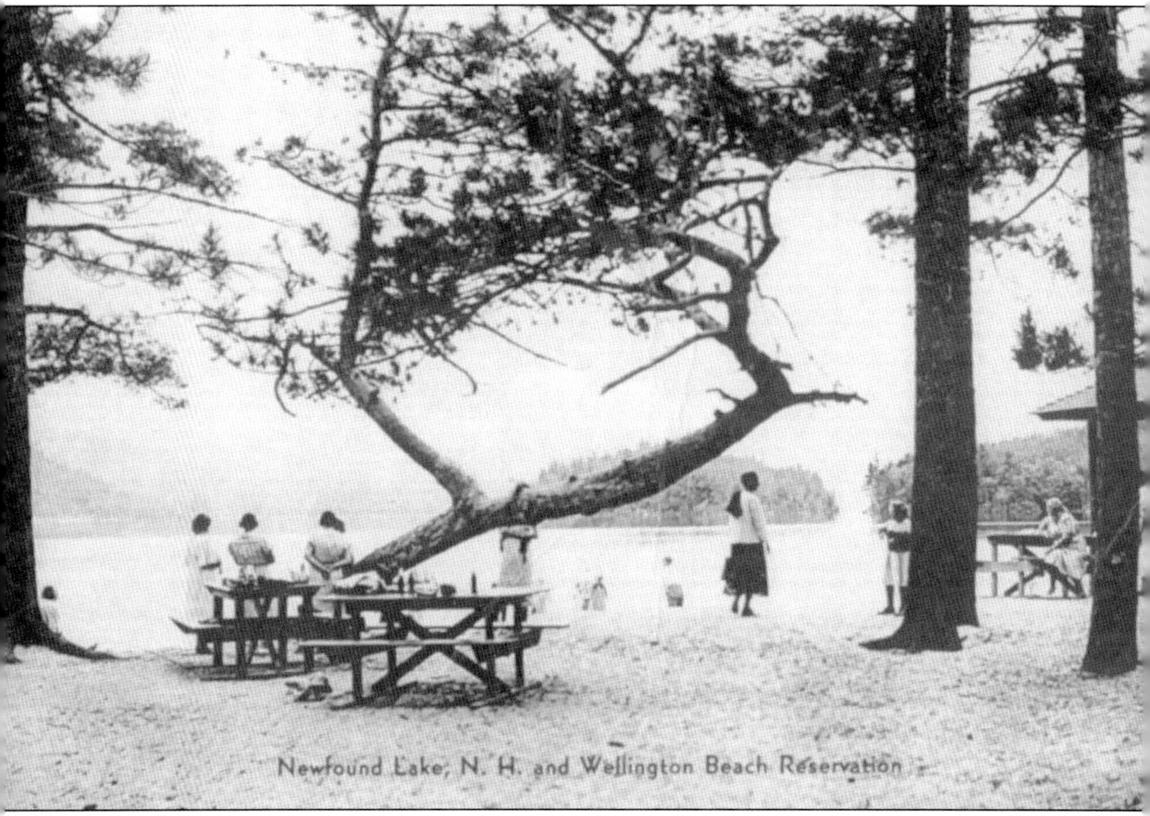

NEWFOUND LAKE AND WELLINGTON STATE PARK, BRISTOL. The beaches on this lake glisten with white sand and attract the bathers of many surrounding towns. In 1735, Capt. John Smith, an early visitor, wrote of "a great pond that Indians say is three days journey around. The land is very full of great hills and mountains, and very rocky." So little legend and history have accumulated around it that it has been called "the hermit of New Hampshire lakes." The confines of the lake, composed mainly of loose till with few rocks and ledges, indicate its formation by glacial erosion.

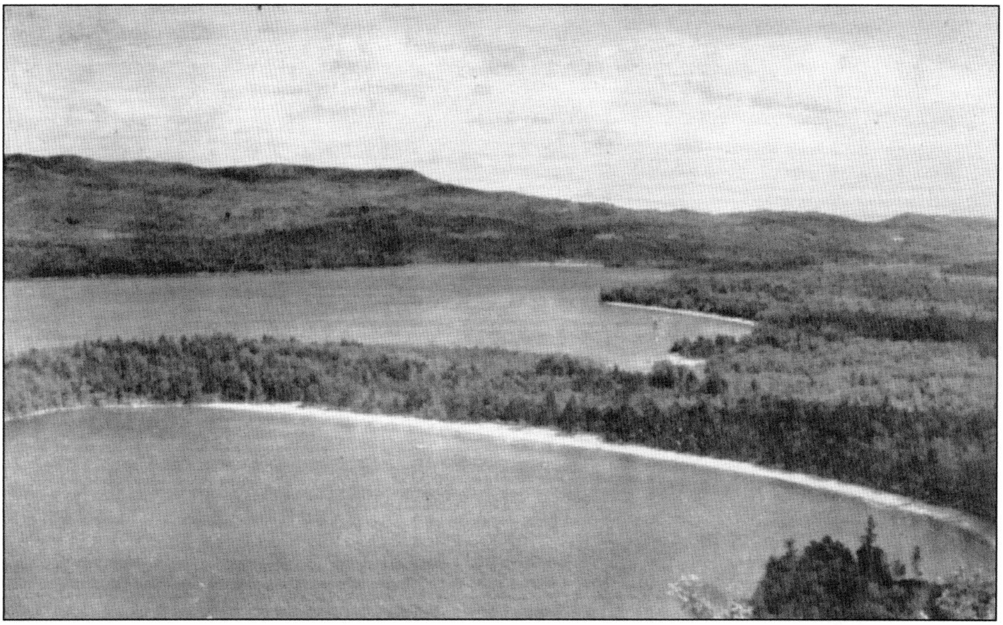

Newfound Lake and Wellington State Park, Another View. In addition to swimming and boating, Newfound Lake also attracts fishermen. Well stocked with fish, Newfound is chiefly known for its lake trout. During the early 19th century, the trout were speared as vast numbers arrived at the spawning beds near the shore. Farmers of the region salted them down in barrels. By 1866, this method of fishing had given way to trolling, following the discovery that the fish could be caught. Well stocked are brook trout, lake trout, salmon, yellow perch, and horned pout. In 1958, a prizewinning lake trout weighing 28 pounds 8 ounces and measuring 39.5 inches was caught here. In 1994, a round whitefish weighing 1 pound 1.44 ounces and measuring 16 inches was caught in this lake. The lake route continues past the Alexandria road junction to the Wellington Beach Reservation, a 97-acre peninsula extending into the waters of Newfound Lake.

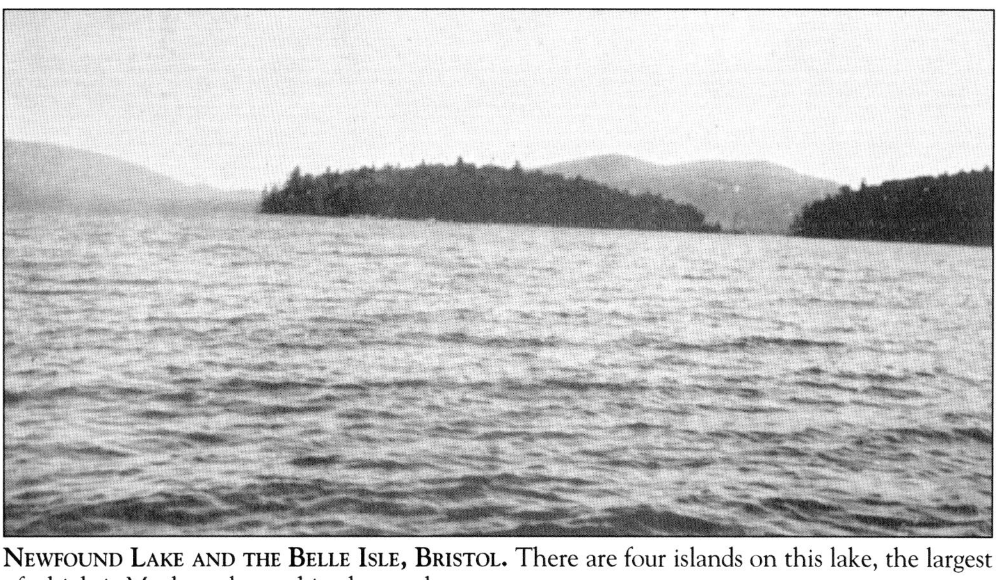

Newfound Lake and the Belle Isle, Bristol. There are four islands on this lake, the largest of which is Mayhew, located in the southern part.

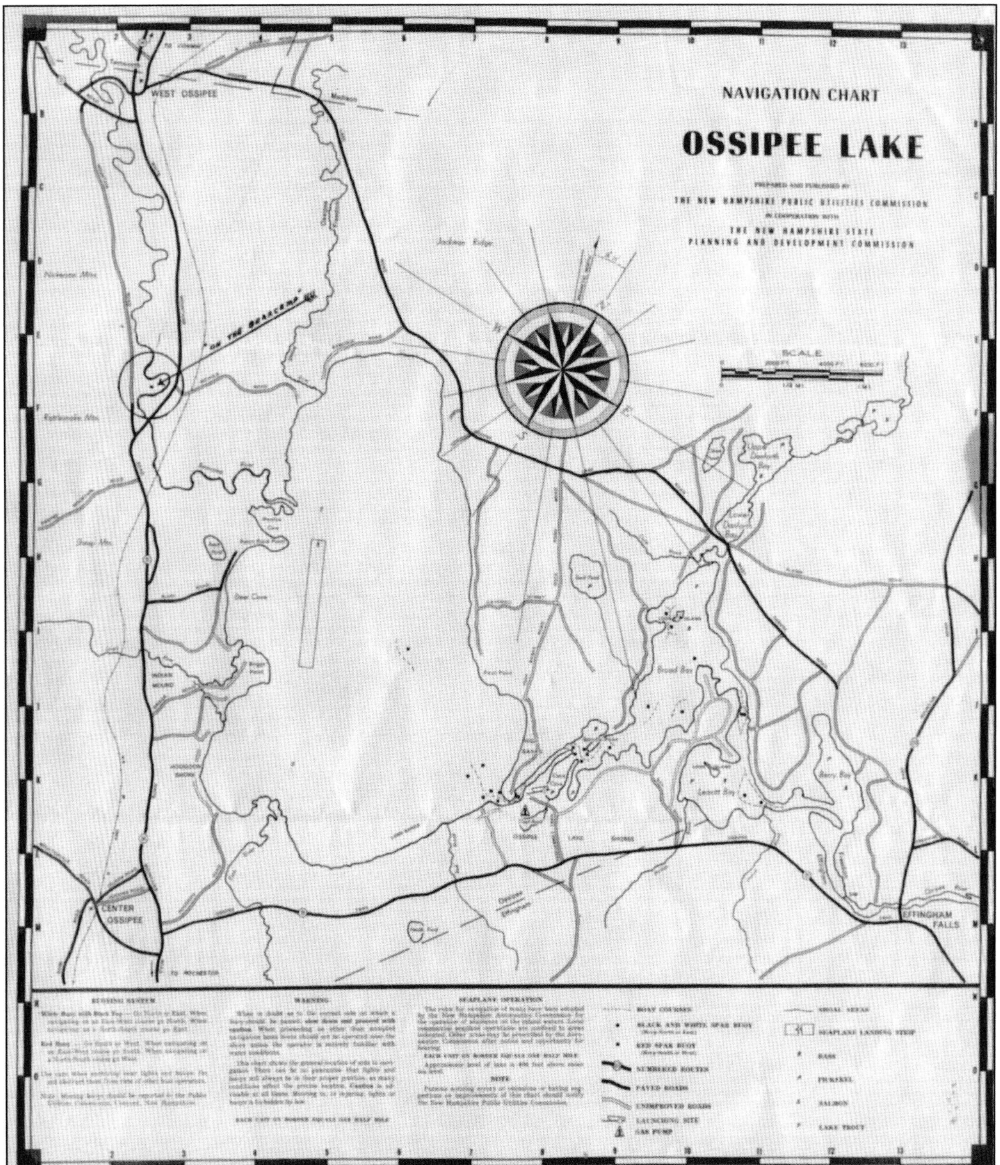

OSSIPEE LAKES NAVIGATION CHART (3,092 ACRES). This navigation chart was prepared in 1967 by the New Hampshire Public Utilities Commission in cooperation with the New Hampshire State Planning and Development Commission.

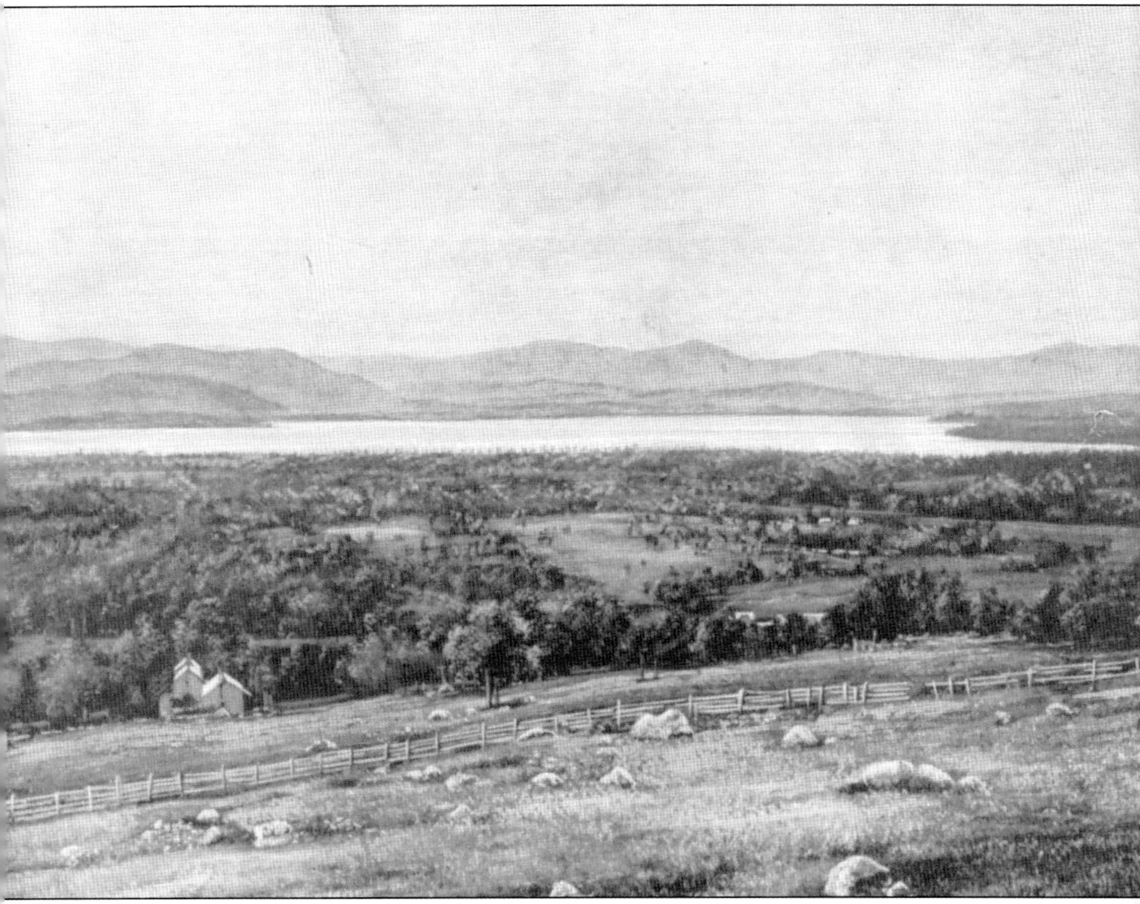

Ossipee Lake, Freedom and Ossipee. This pleasant body of water takes its name from a tribe of Native Americans who made this region their home. With a length of 3.5 miles and a greatest width of 2 miles, its shores are largely bordered by forest. The waters of the Pine, Lovewell's Bearcamp, and Six-Mile Rivers empty into the lake, which is itself emptied by the Ossipee River.

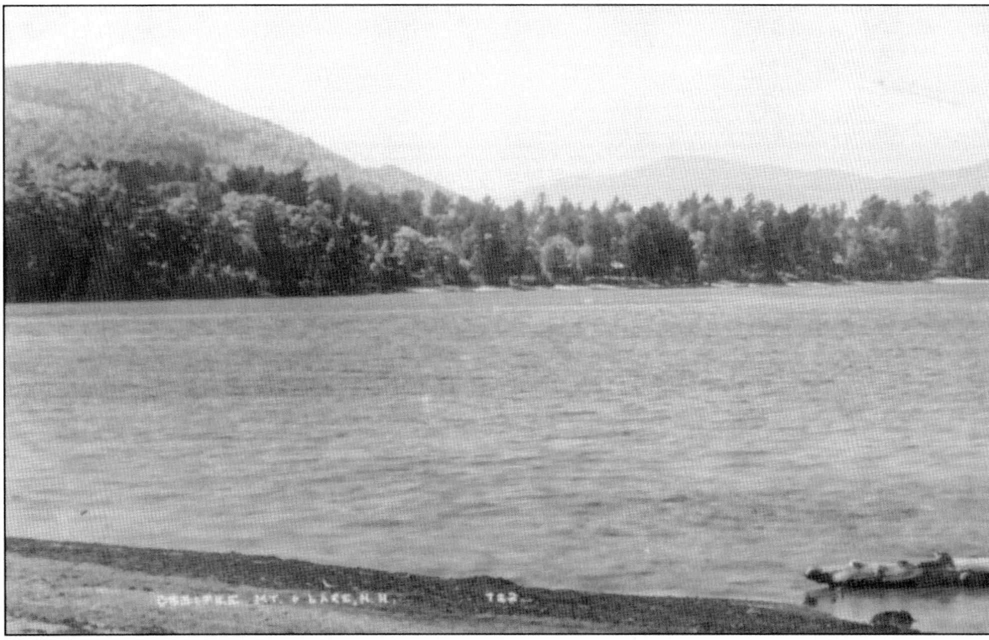

Ossipee Lake, Freedom. No islands dot the surface of Ossipee Lake. Shallower than most New Hampshire lakes, Ossipee's waters are usually transparent. Although not surrounded by hills or mountains, the lake does have a charm that led Harriet Martineau to say, "Lake Ossipee looked what I fancy the wildest parts of Norway to be: a dark blue expanse . . . with pines fringing all its ledges; and promontories bristling with pines, jutting into it."

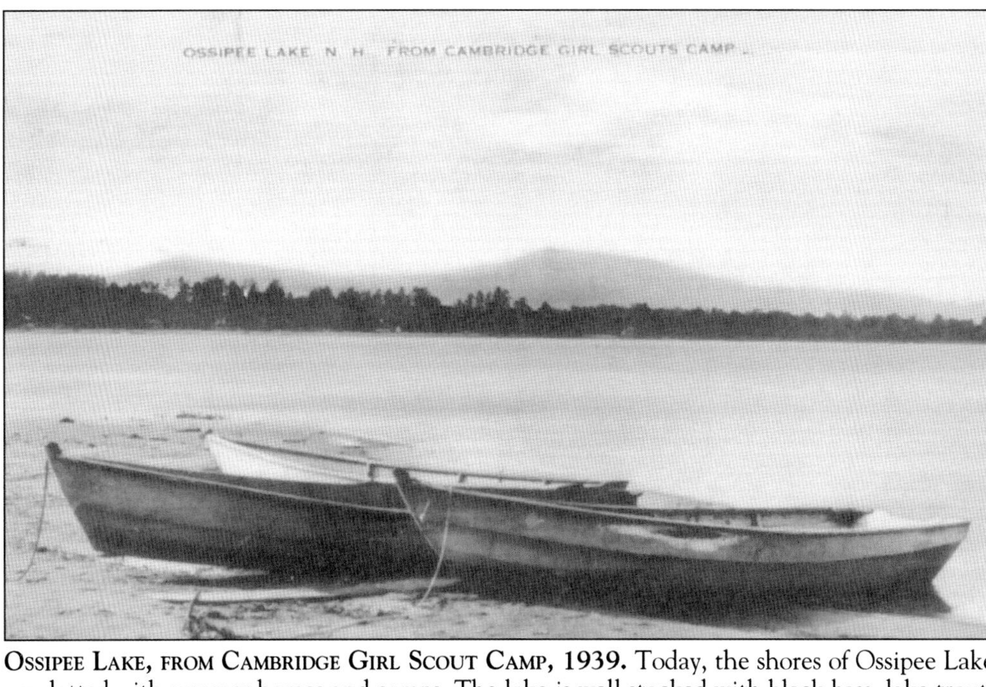

Ossipee Lake, from Cambridge Girl Scout Camp, 1939. Today, the shores of Ossipee Lake are dotted with summer homes and camps. The lake is well stocked with black bass, lake trout, white and yellow perch, horned pout, and huskies.

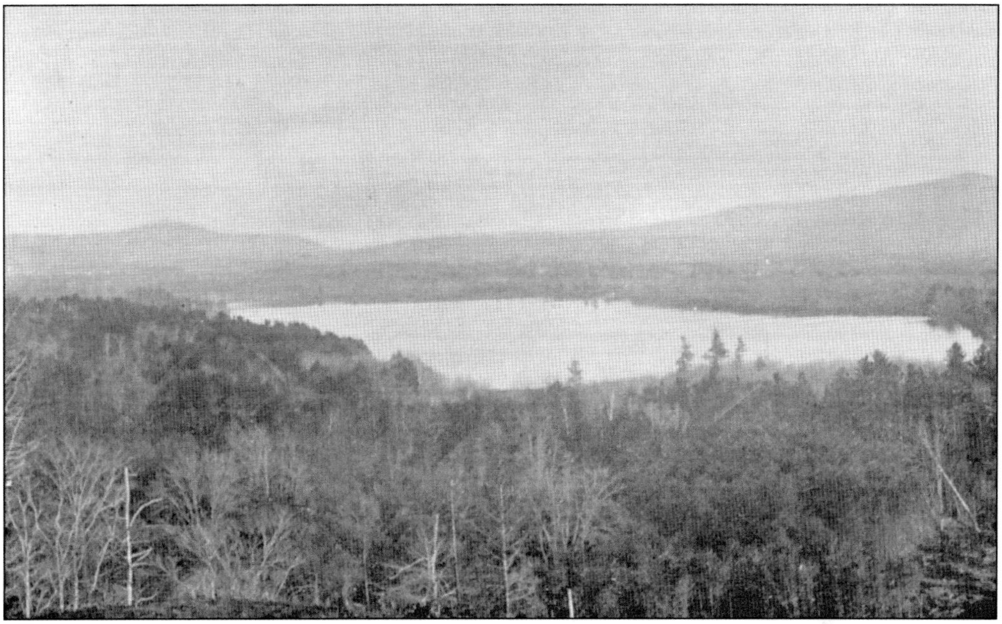

Otter Lake (61.2 Acres) Greenfield. This is a very quiet lake surrounded by dense forest. It is a fine lake for fishing largemouth bass, pickerel, horned pout, and bluegill.

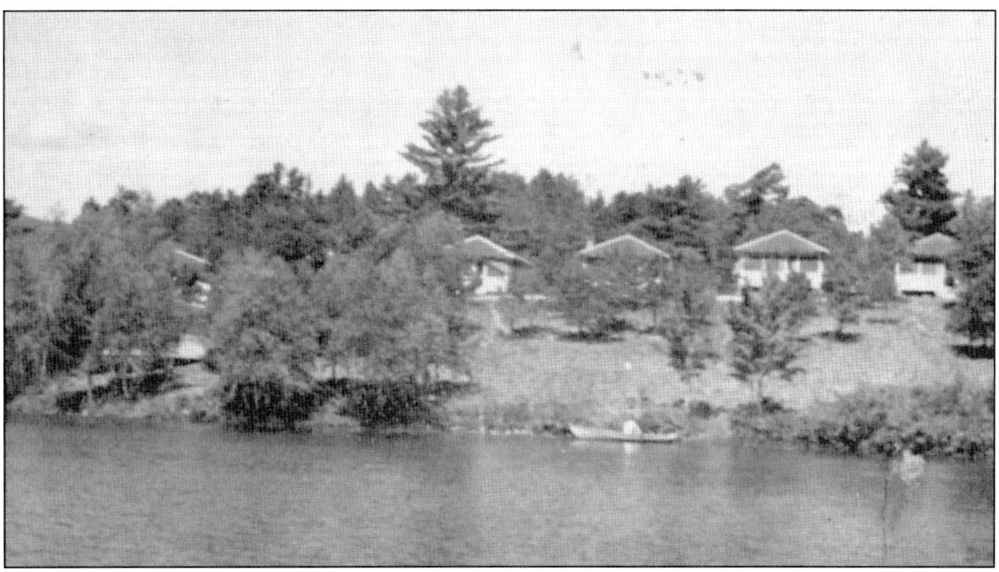

Paquaket Lake (142 Acres), Conway. This is a favorite lake for sportsmen in the North Country.

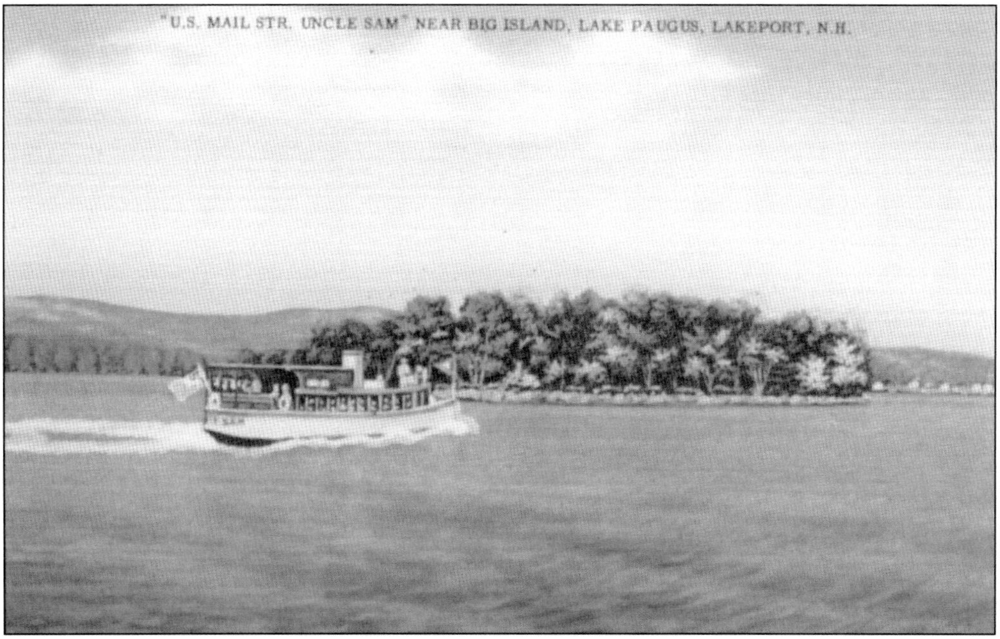

PAUGUS LAKE (BAY) (1,220 ACRES), LACONIA. This lake is named for an Indian chieftain in the Lakes Region. Here we see the U.S. mail boat *Uncle Sam* heading for Big Island in the bay. Fishing is very popular here, with lake trout, pickerel, yellow perch, bass, horned pout, and shad all being taken in their proper season.

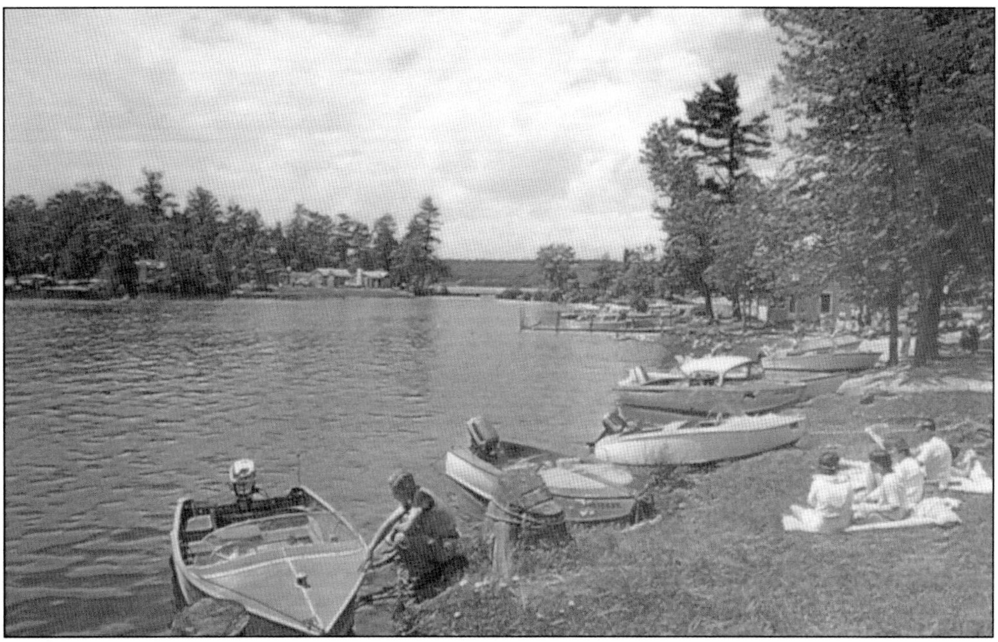

PAUGUS BAY, LACONIA. Pictured is a delightful spot for boating and bathing. Connected to this bay is Opechee Lake (427 acres) in Laconia. This is a natural lake that has been raised by damming in Lakeport. It is a tributary of the Winnipesaukee River, fed by Lake Winnipesaukee by way of Paugus Bay. This lake has been stocked with smallmouth bass, chain pickerel, perch, and lake trout.

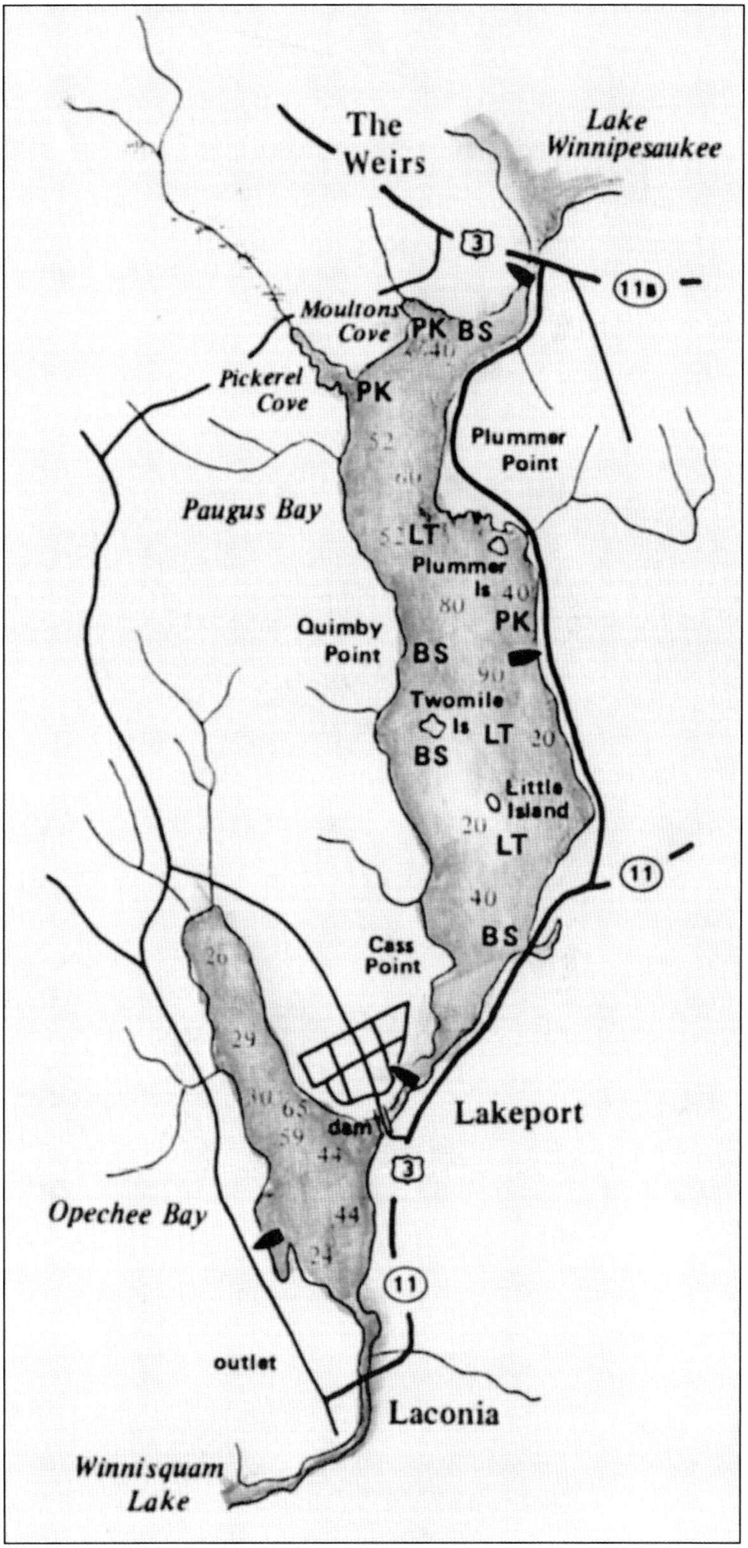

A Map of Paugus and Opechee, Laconia. This map shows Paugus Bay and Opechee Lake in Laconia.

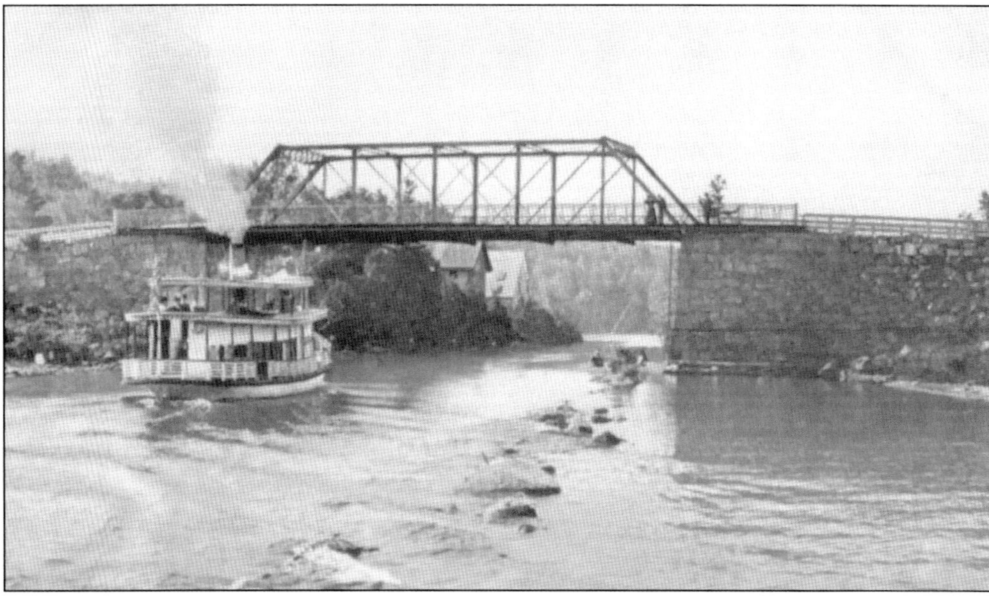

Paugus Bay, Laconia, Another View. Pictured above is the steamer *Belle of the Isle* sailing under the Aquedahtan Bridge (Weirs Bridge) en route to Lake Winnipesaukee, due east of the bridge. Even though Paugus is called a bay, its size would qualify it to be a lake. Below, ice boating was very popular on Paugus Bay during the 1930s and 1940s.

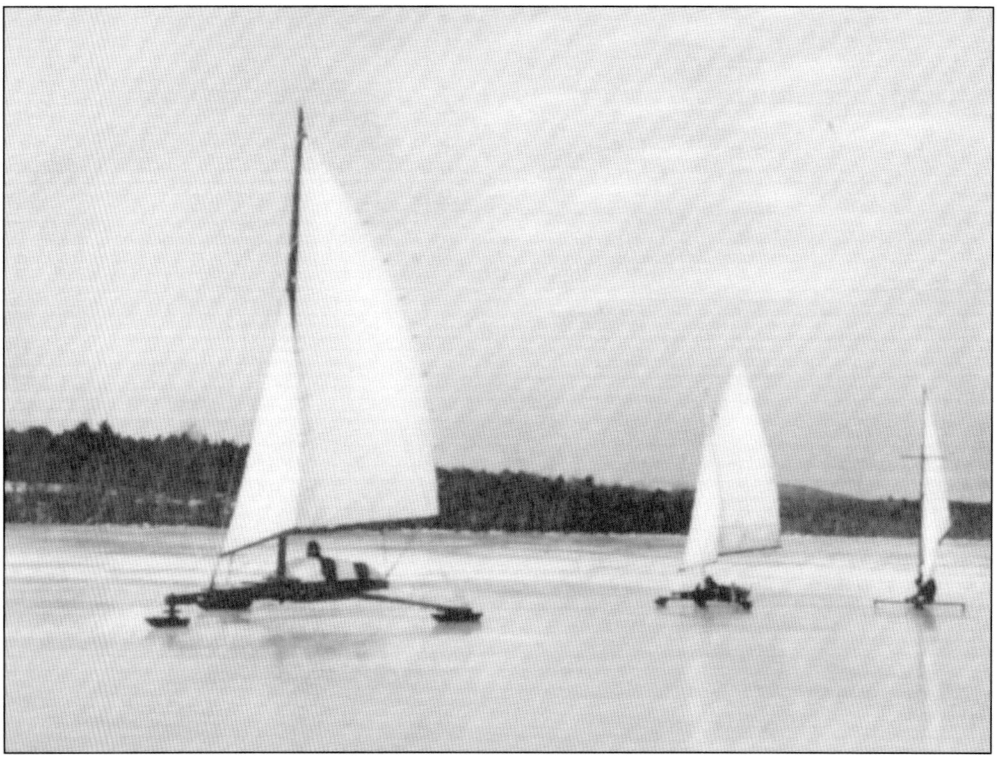

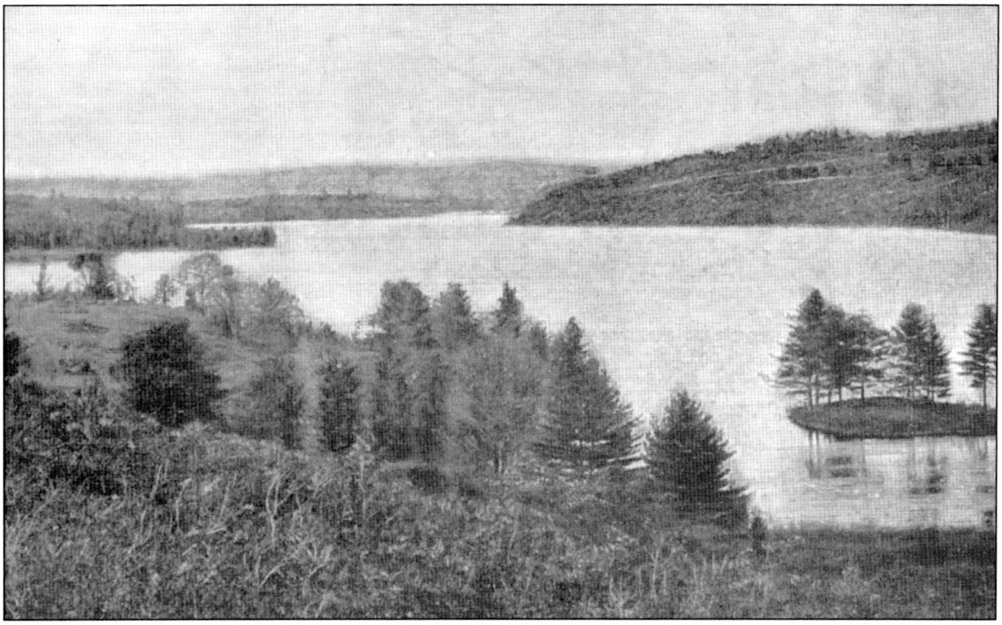

Penacook Lake (360 Acres), Concord. This lake is also known as Long Pond.

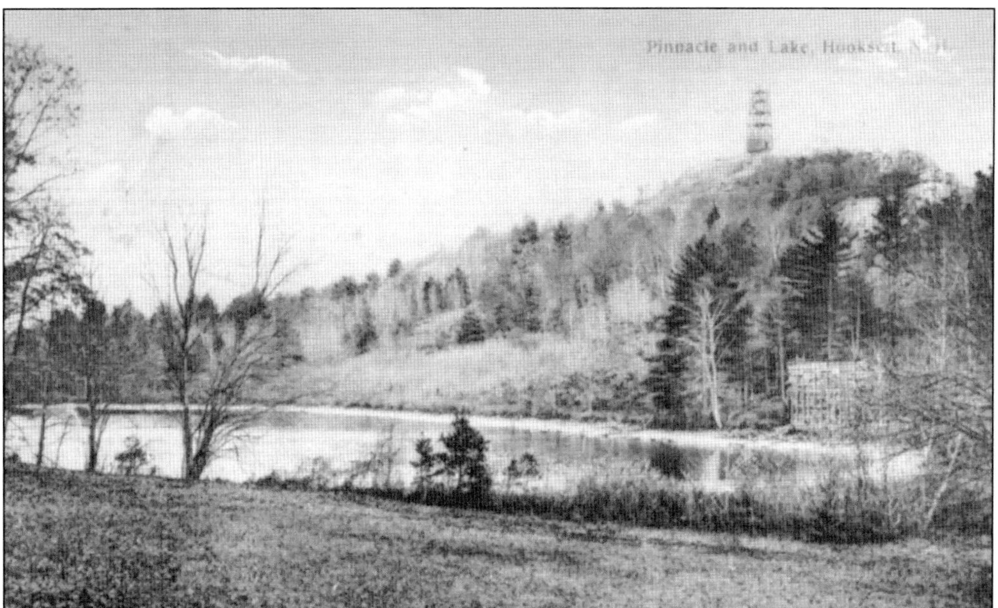

Pinnacle Lake (18.6 Acres), Hooksett. This is a natural body of water raised by damming to its present level. The lake is a water supply for the town of Hooksett. It has been stocked with brook trout, pickerel, perch, and smallmouth bass.

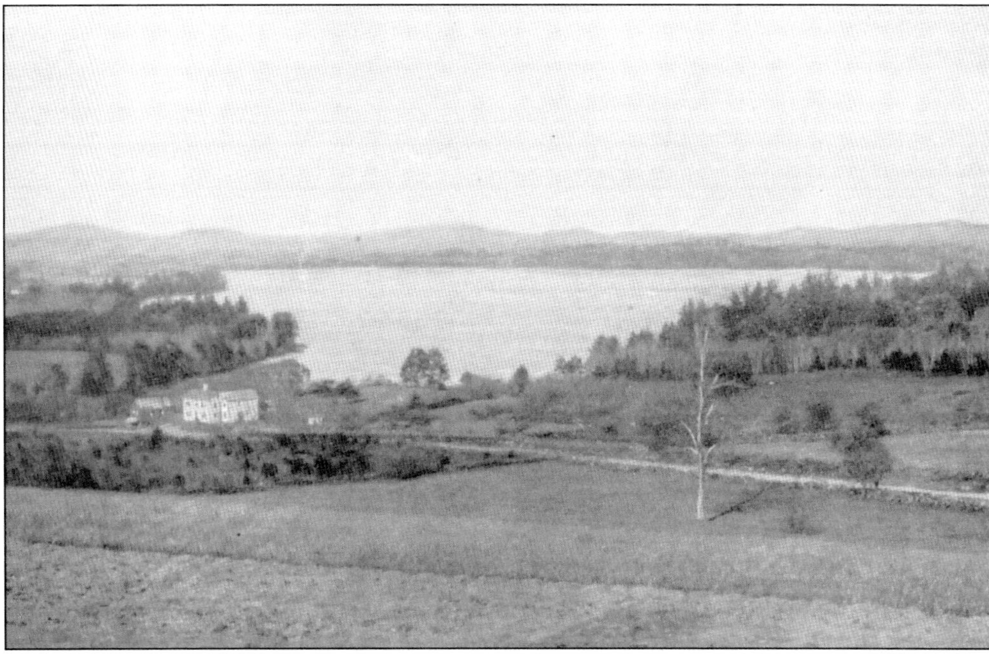

PLEASANT LAKE (493 ACRES), DEERFIELD. This lake, about 3 miles long and a mile wide, is noted for pickerel and black bass fishing. It is surrounded by charming countryside, abounding in uncultivated farmland and quaint cottages.

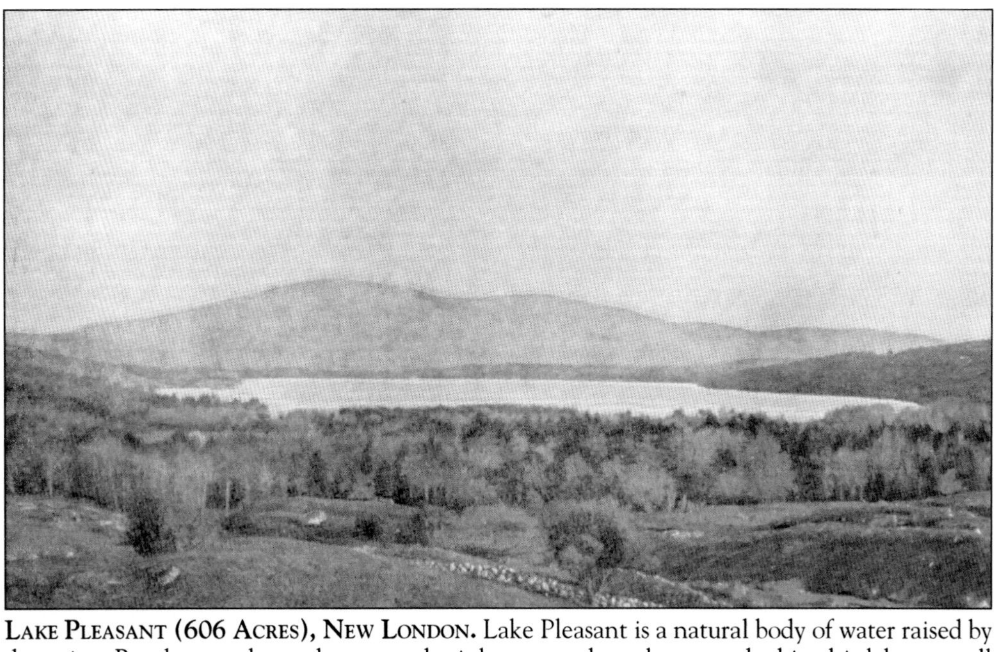

LAKE PLEASANT (606 ACRES), NEW LONDON. Lake Pleasant is a natural body of water raised by damming. Brook trout, horned pout, and rainbow trout have been stocked in this lake, as well as bass and yellow perch.

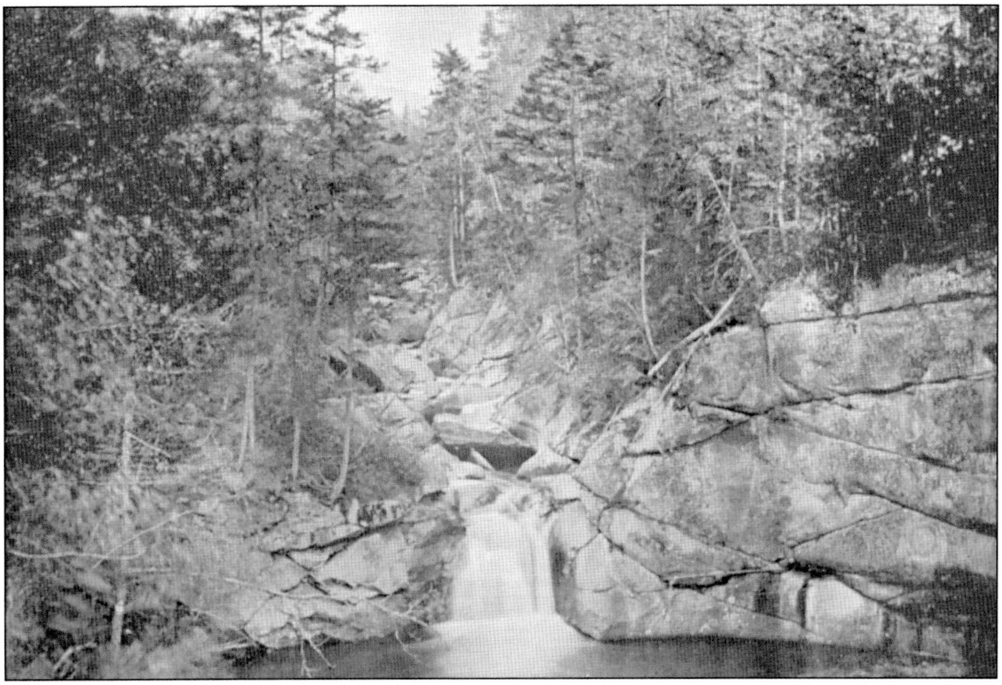

The Pool, Franconia Notch. Located in the Flume area is a great 50-foot-deep pothole. Ledges, 100 feet high, rise above it with alpine flowers and delicate ferns growing on the rocky terraces of the steep black cliffs.

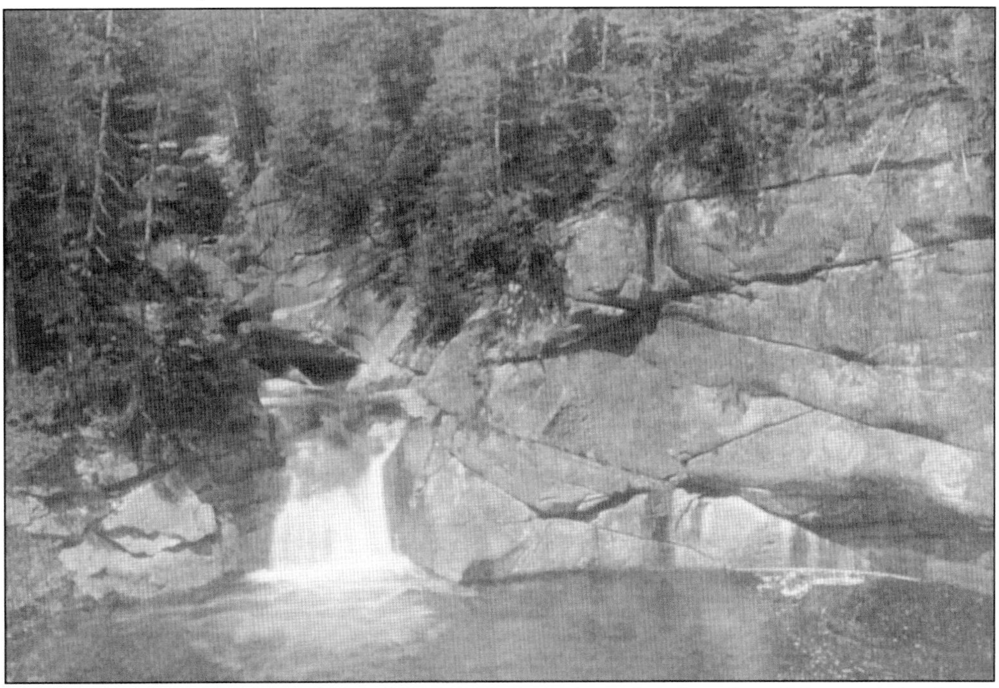

The Pool, a Closer View. The Pool appears to be a gloomy and profound chasm in the forest, where the Pemigewasset River falls into a deep black basin surrounded by high cliffs. The cliffs around this stygian pool create deep shadows, adding to its weirdness and gloom.

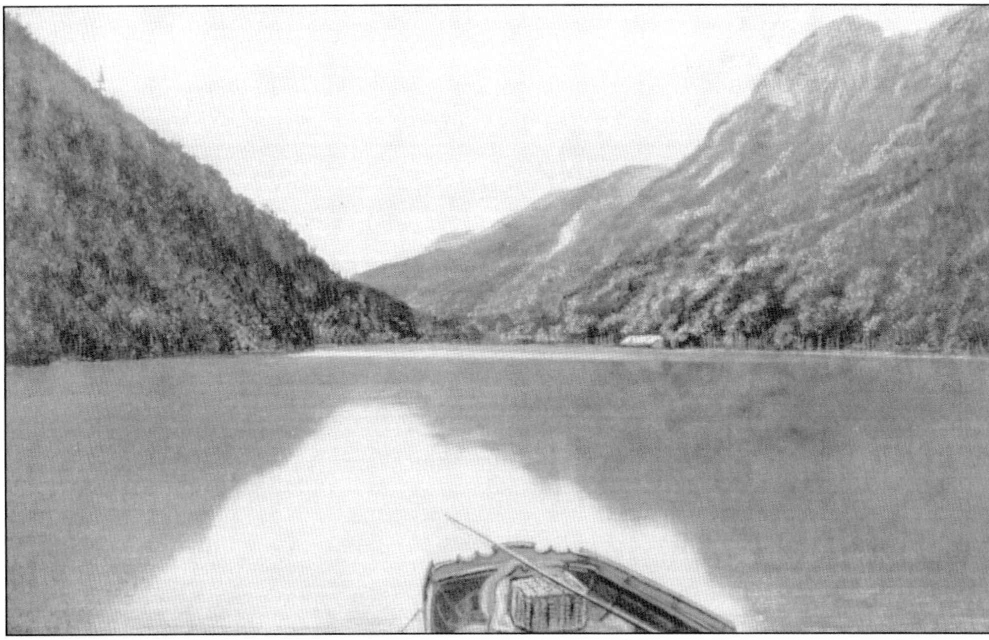

Profile Lake (15 Acres), Franconia Notch. This small body of water was once known as the Old Man's Washbowl. Sheer above its silver surface rises a shoulder of Profile Mountain (Cannon) on which is the stern profile of the Old Man of the Mountain, a striking rock sculpture of a human face, New Hampshire's best-known natural wonder.

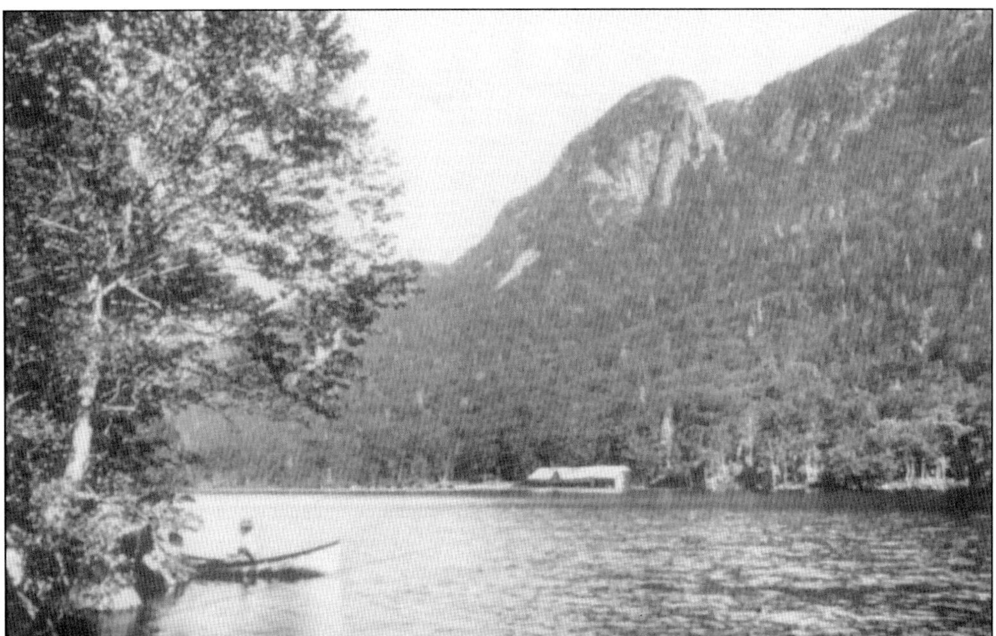

Profile Lake and Eagle Cliff, Franconia Notch. This small lake is also known as Ferrins Pond. Fly-fishing only for brook trout is permitted in this lake.

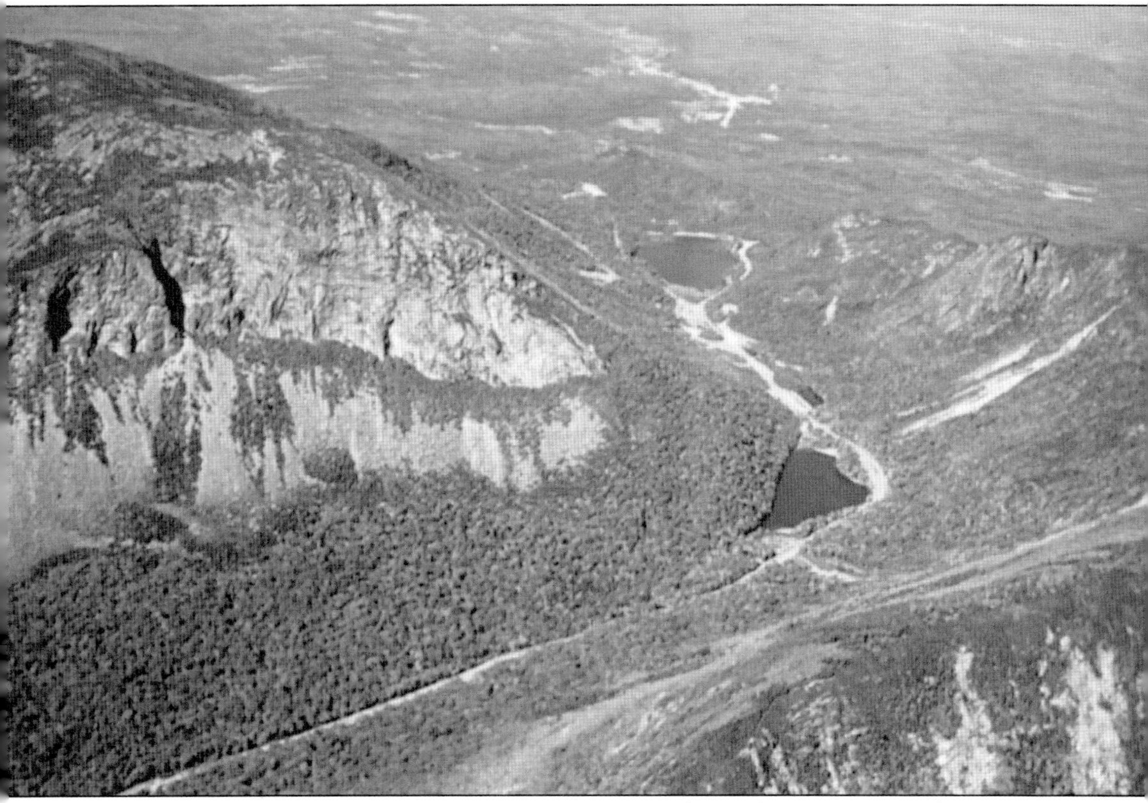

Profile and Saco Lakes, Franconia Notch. Southward, 500 feet along a brook side path from the parking lot, is a fine vantage point on the edge of this lake, where a boulder marker has been placed by the state. About four in the afternoon is the best time to view the massive ledge silhouette against the blue sky—the famous Old Man of the Mountain.

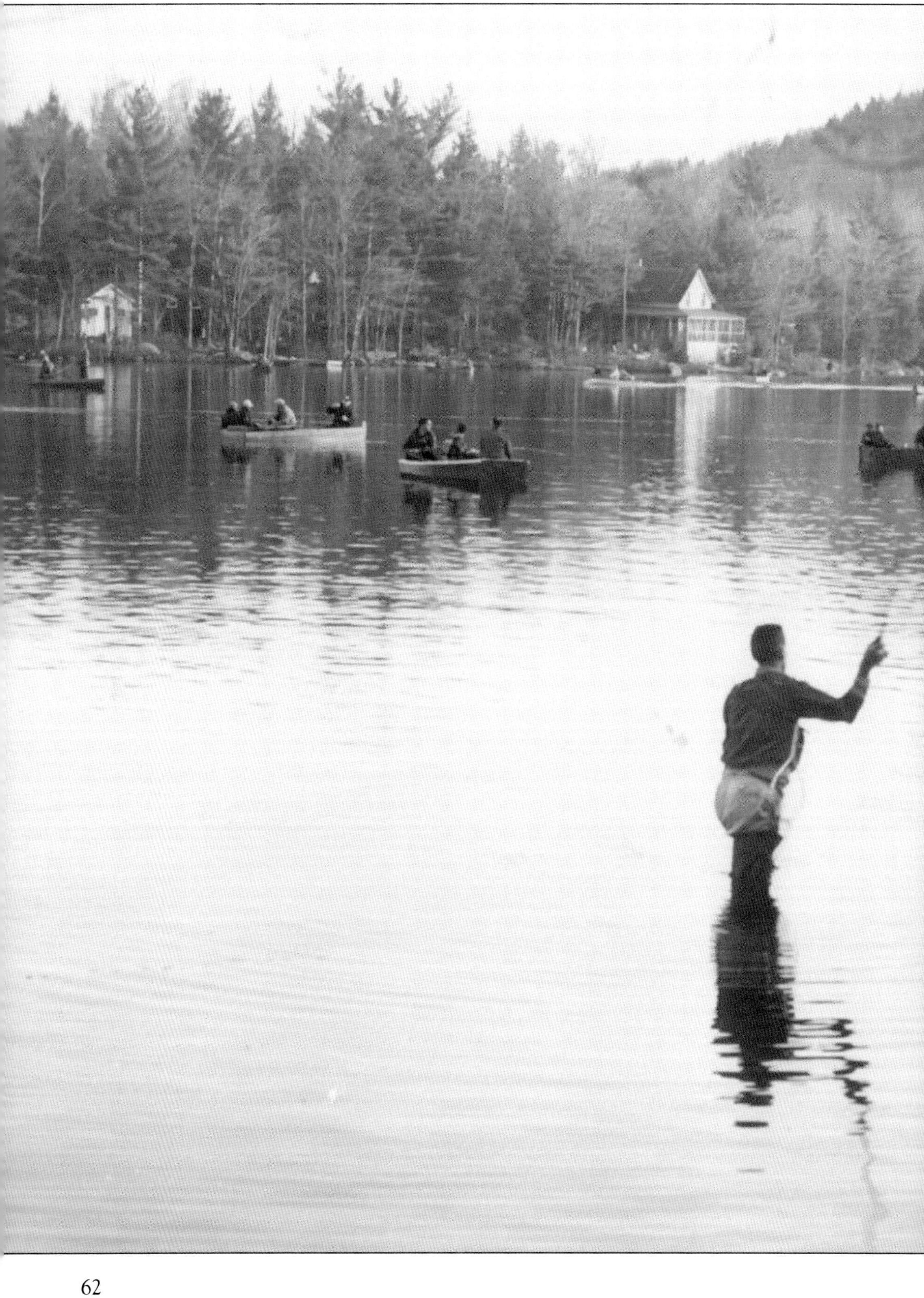

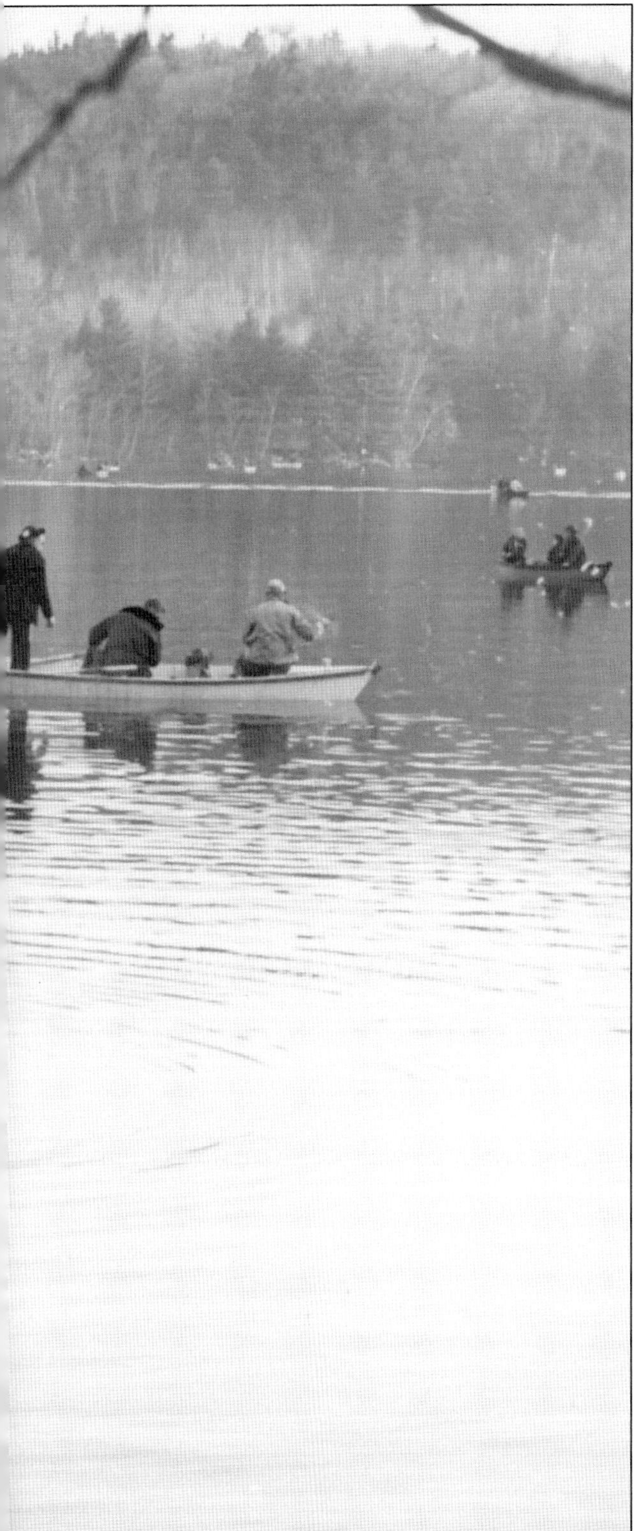

RAND POND (38.7 ACRES), GOSHEN. This small pond attracts many anglers for the first day of trout fishing in May 1955. It is said that brook and rainbow trout are plentiful in this pond.

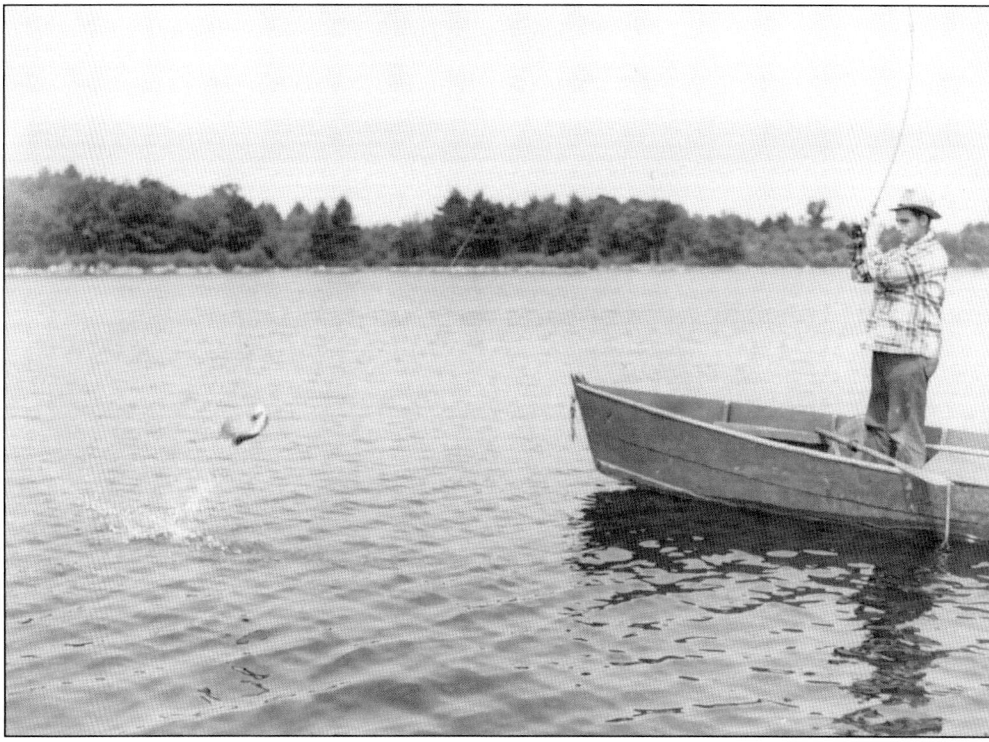

Round Pond (100 Acres), Barrington. This pond is a popular spot for bass fishing. According to the New Hampshire Fish and Game Department, "Bass are one of the fightingest, yet least sought after game fish in the state."

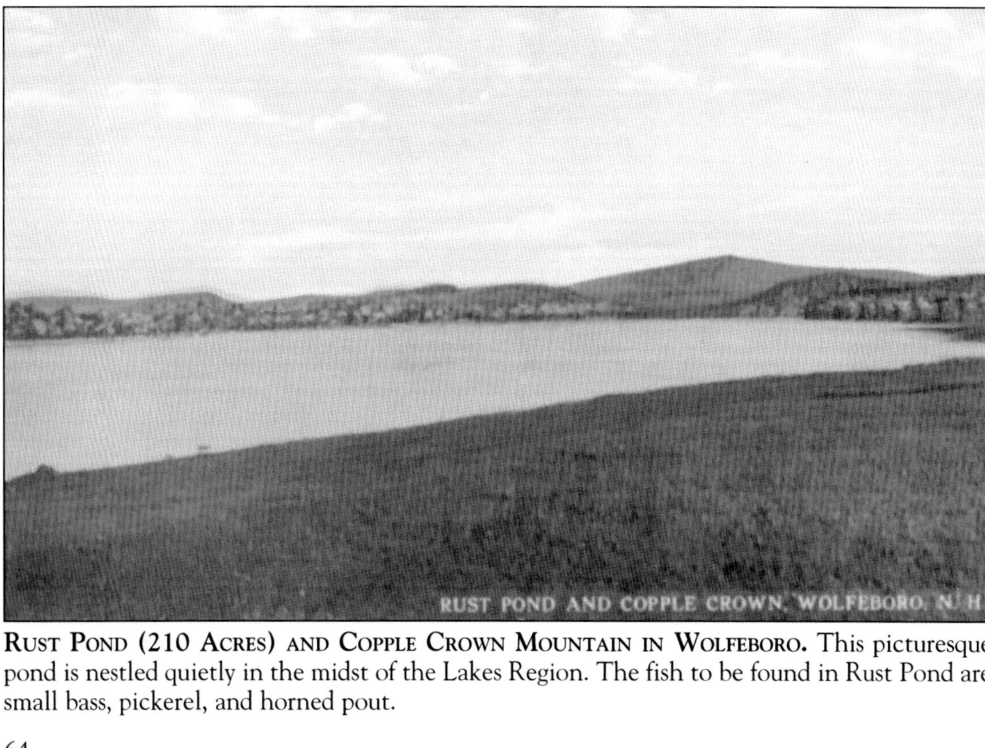

Rust Pond (210 Acres) and Copple Crown Mountain in Wolfeboro. This picturesque pond is nestled quietly in the midst of the Lakes Region. The fish to be found in Rust Pond are small bass, pickerel, and horned pout.

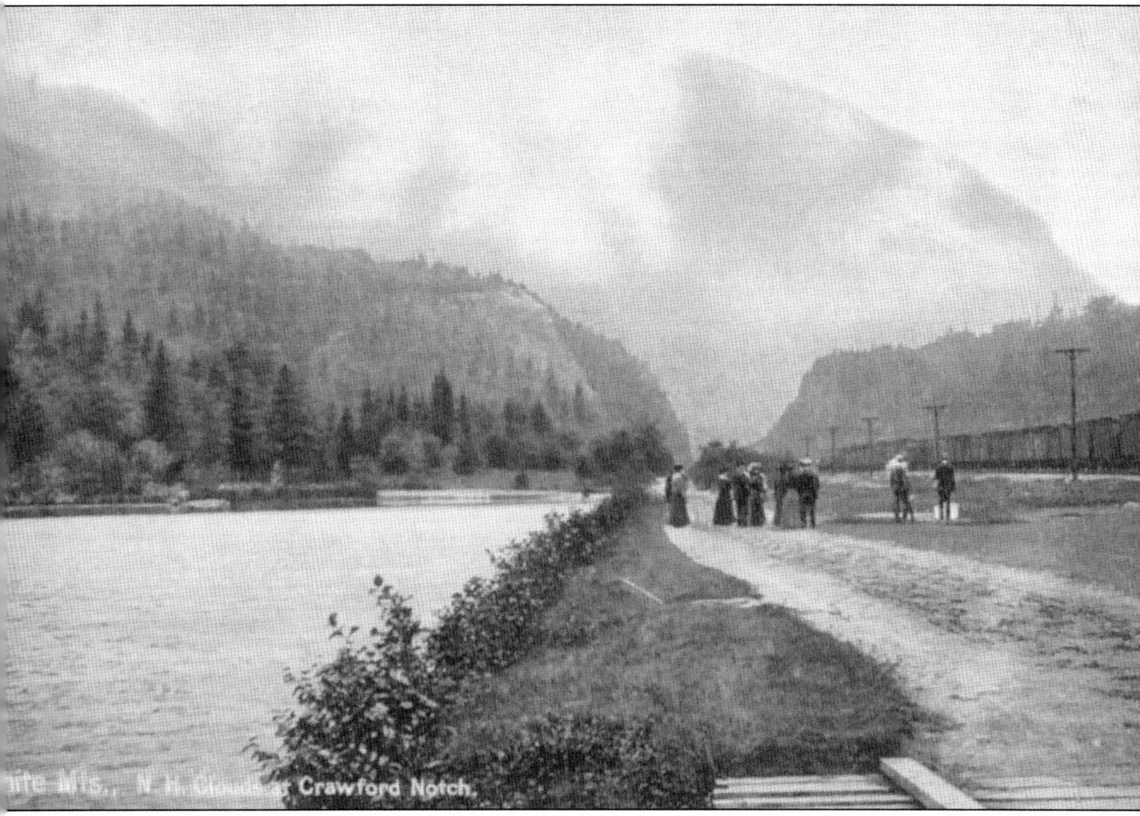

SACO LAKE (6 ACRES), CRAWFORD NOTCH. This body of water is located at the north gateway of Crawford Notch. This sparkling lake is the source of the Saco River and has become a popular spot for fly-fishing enthusiasts and picnickers. Julius H. Ward refers to this lake as "the gem of the Notch."

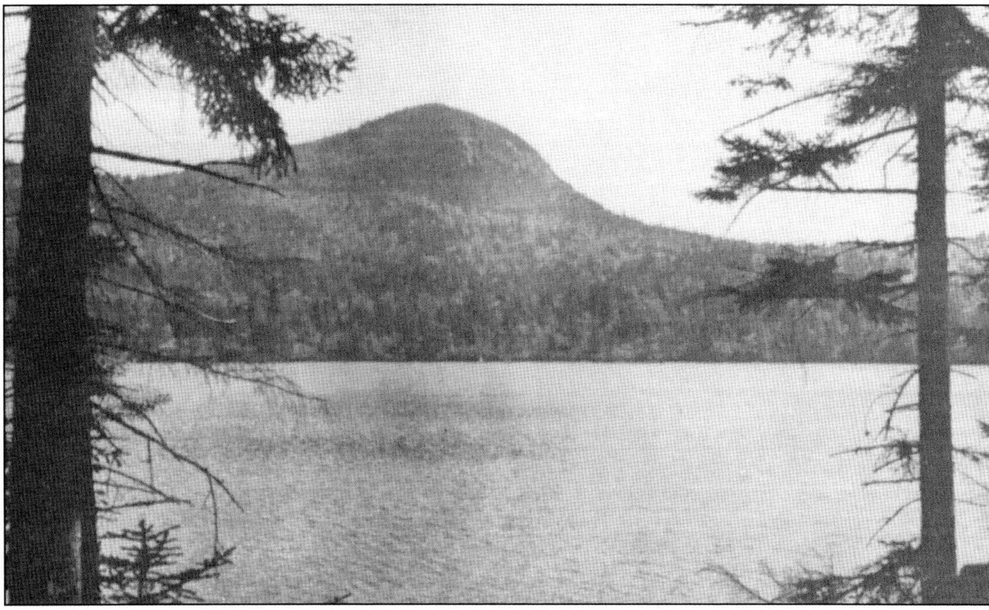

Sawyer Pond (47 Acres), Livermore and Bartlett. From the shore of Sawyer Pond, an open and impressive view of Mount Tremont and Owl's Cliff is available. "By daylight Sawyer Pond was more beautiful— Although, like all small mountain ponds, a little lonely, pitiful, and triste." (J. Brooks Artkinson, *Skyline Promenades: A Potpourri*, 1925.)

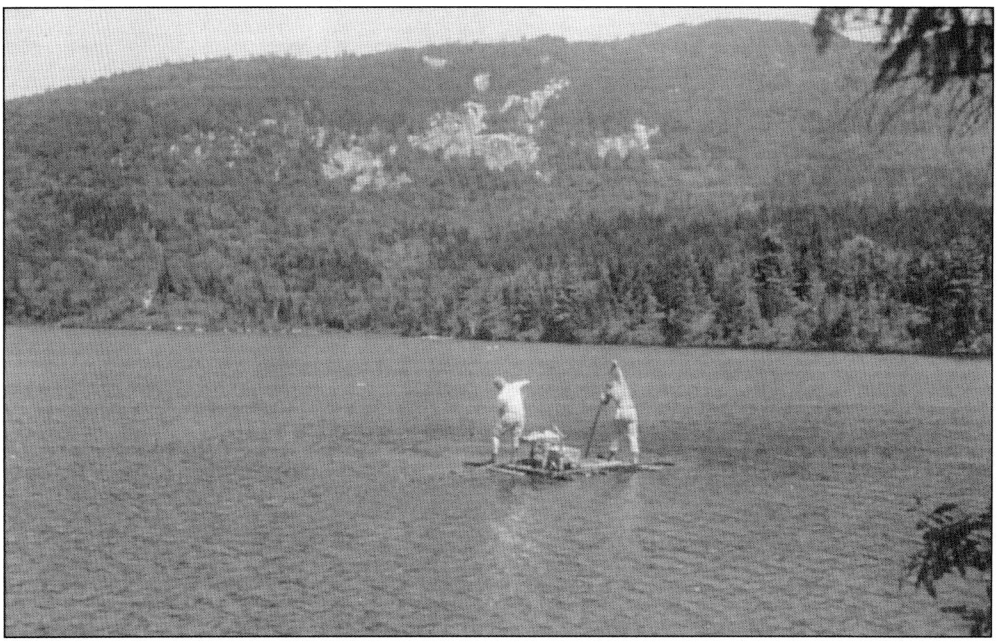

Sawyer Pond, Livermore and Bartlett. This pond, sheltered on all sides by cliffs and mountain peaks, is nestled away from the rush of civilization. It occupies a deep basin left by a retreating glacier. Some 47 acres in size, the lake has crystal-clear water that reaches a depth of more than 100 feet, with an average depth of 44 feet. Biologist Paul Hooper and a helper are shown conducting the August 14–22, 1958 fish census of Sawyer Pond for the U.S. Fish and Wildlife Service. Fishing in this lake is restricted to fly-fishing for brook trout.

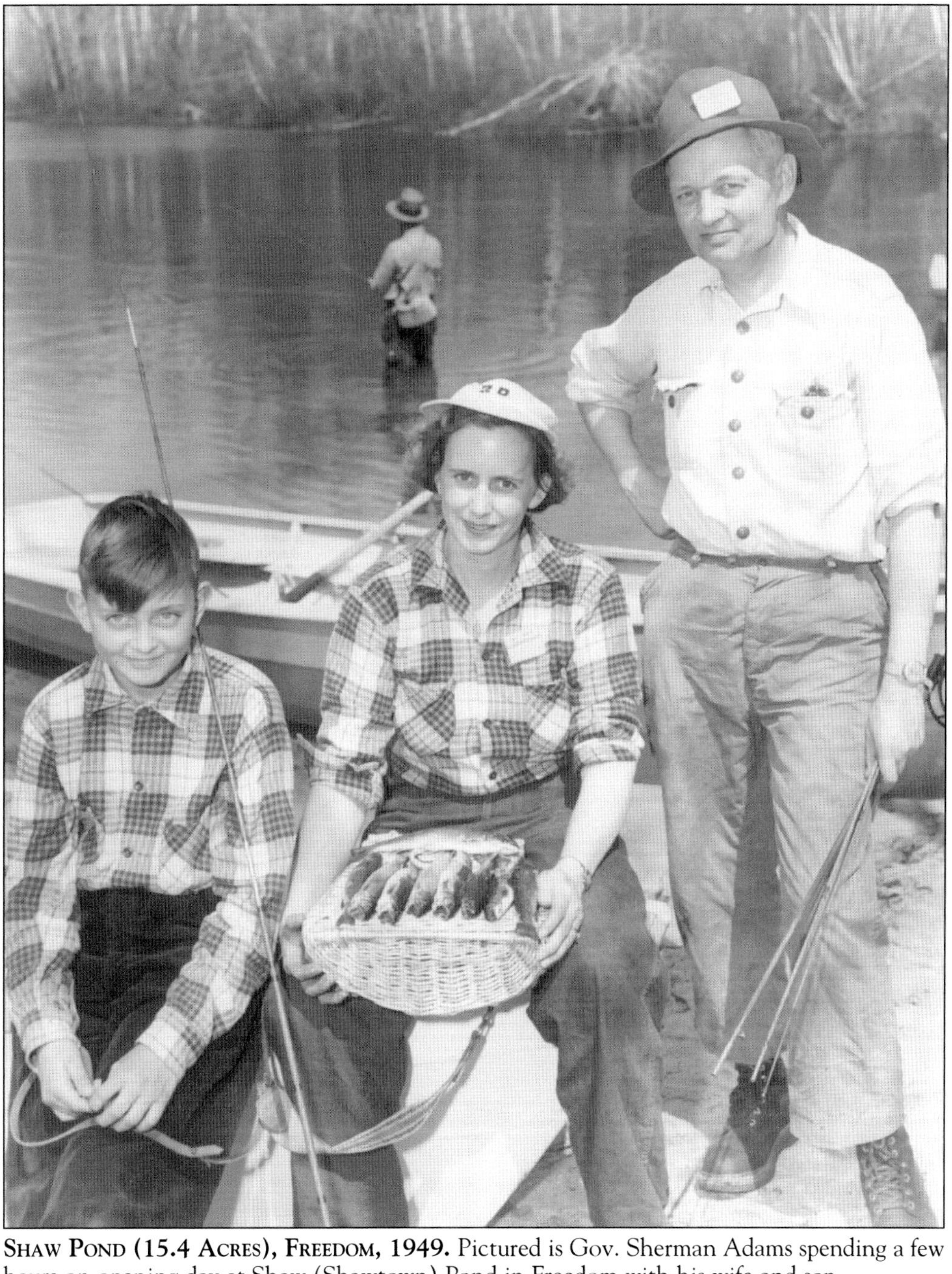

Shaw Pond (15.4 Acres), Freedom, 1949. Pictured is Gov. Sherman Adams spending a few hours on opening day at Shaw (Shawtown) Pond in Freedom with his wife and son.

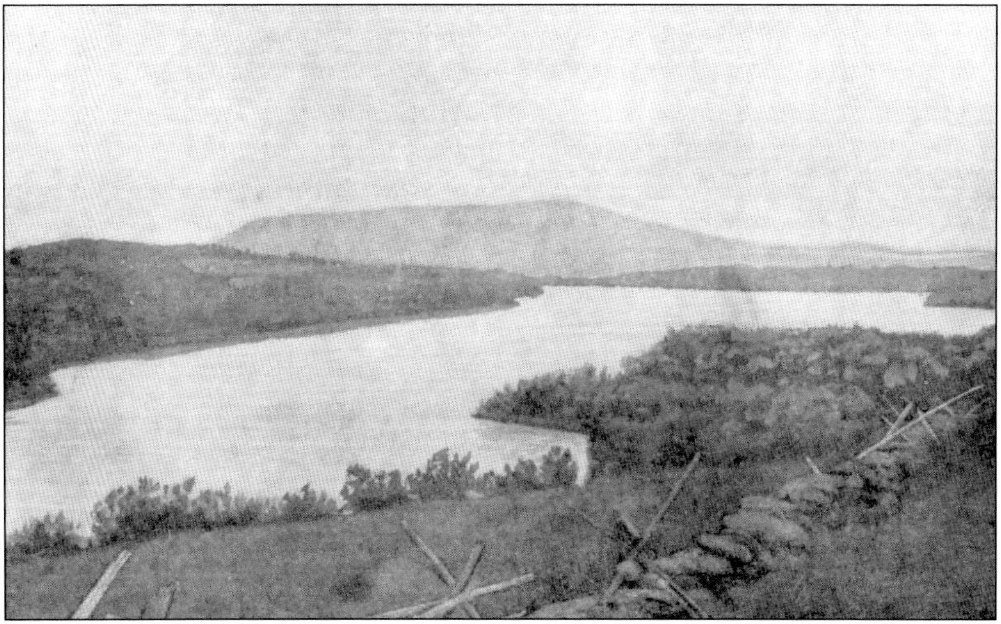

Silver Lake (332.7 Acres), Harrisville. The town of Harrisville originally developed as a small manufacturing center, taking its power from the controlled outlets of its three lakes: Lake Skatutakee, Harrisville Pond, and Silver Lake. This attractive lake is stocked with rainbow trout, lake trout, smallmouth bass, pickerel, and horned pout.

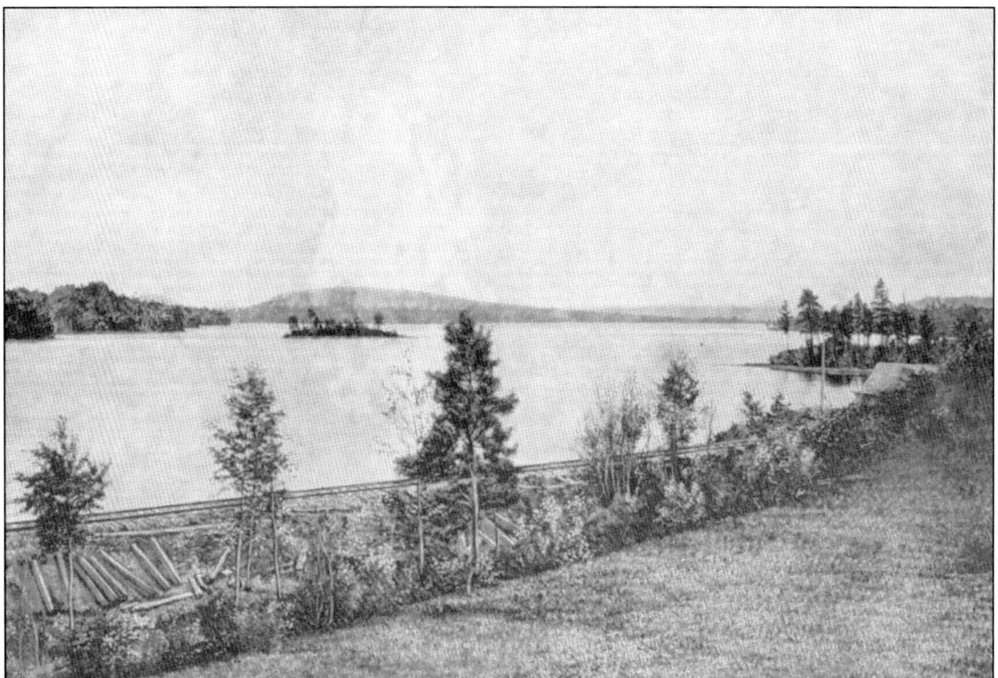

Silver Lake (995 Acres), Madison. This crystalline body of water, with its spacious beaches, is enjoyed by bathers and sportsmen alike. Fishing is quite good here; the lake is stocked with lake trout, salmon, pickerel, yellow perch, bass, and horned pout.

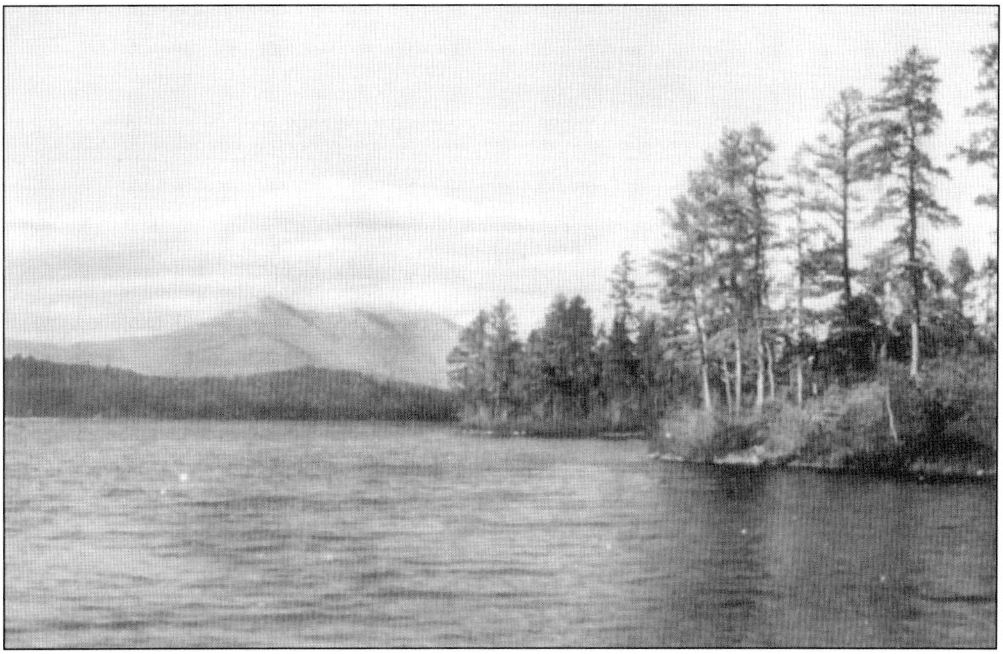

Silver Lake (White Lake), Madison, with Mount Chocorua in the Distance. These shores were favorite grounds for Native Americans, as is evidenced by the many relics found here. Glowing in sunset splendor, streaked with all the hues on the rainbow, the lake is indeed magnificent. As the sun glides down in the west, a ruddy glow tinges Chocorua's pinnacle, while the shadows lurking in the ravine and lake steal darkly up the mountainside and crouch for a final spring upon the summit.

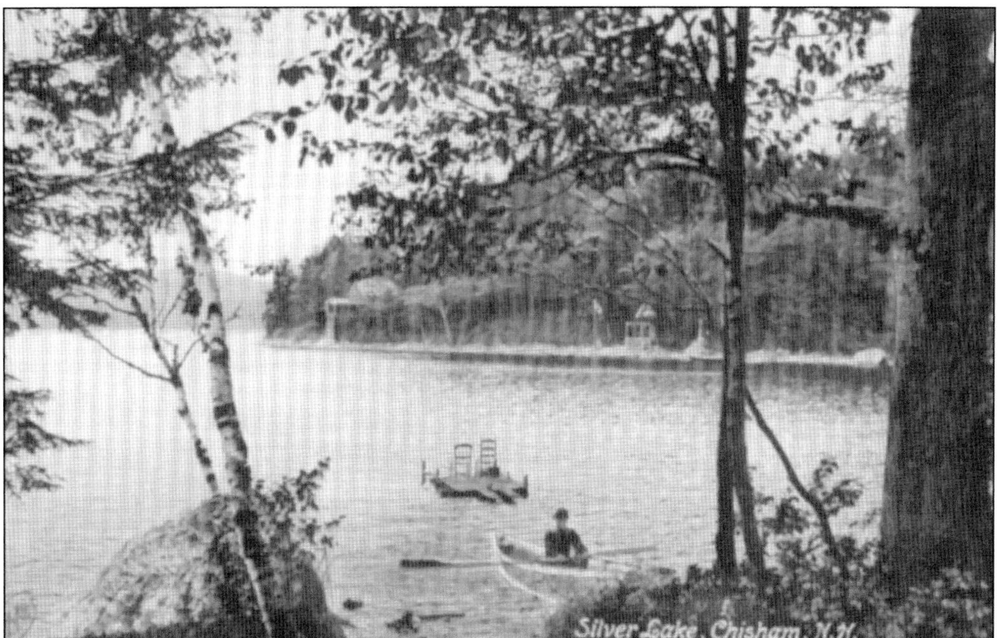

Silver Lake, Chisham. This small restful body of water nestled in the woodland is an ideal spot for campers, boatmen, and fishermen alike.

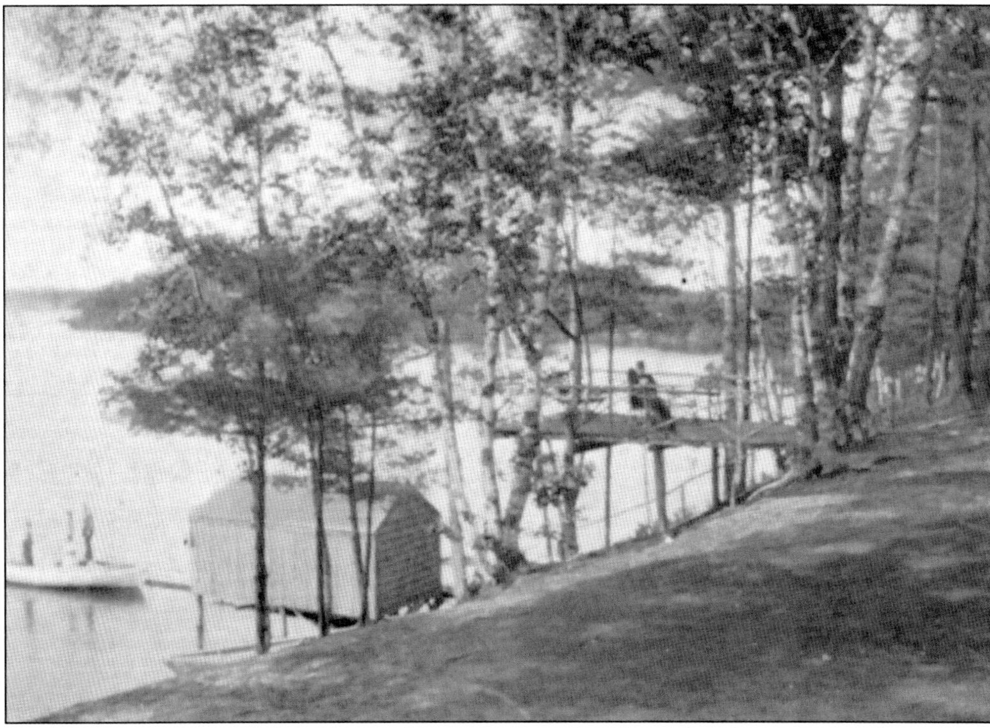

Silver Lake, Newton. This lake is a boatman's paradise, framed with cottages and pines.

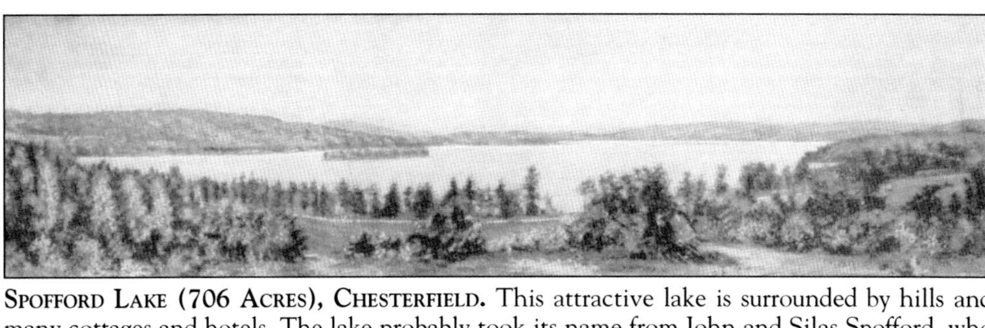

Spofford Lake (706 Acres), Chesterfield. This attractive lake is surrounded by hills and many cottages and hotels. The lake probably took its name from John and Silas Spofford, who were among its grantees. There is a tradition that a man named Spofford lived near the lake at an early date, but the original charter in Chesterfield (1761) gives the outline of the lake with the name Spofford on it.

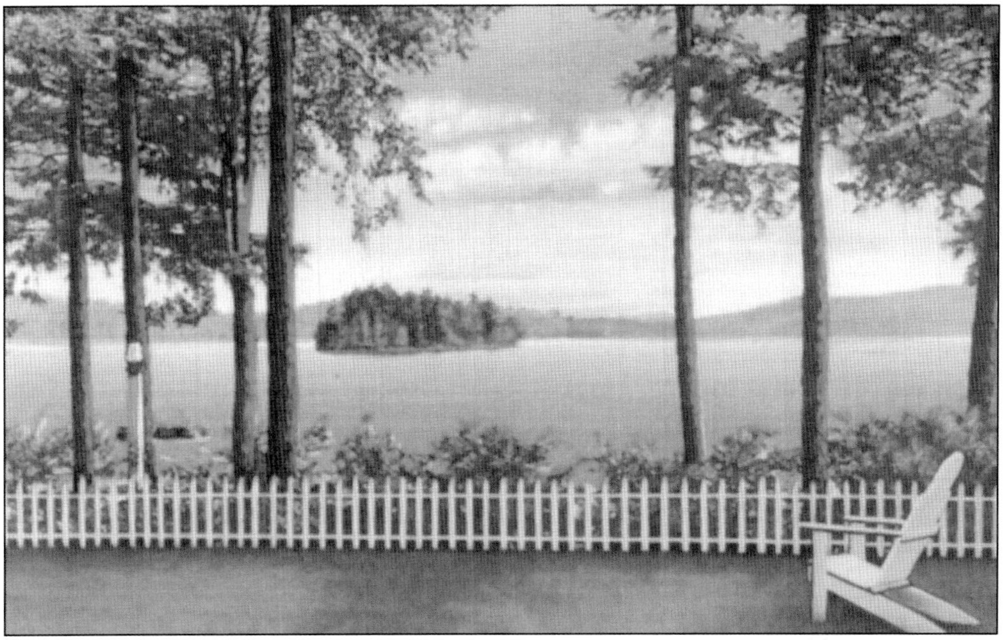

Spofford Lake, Chesterfield. This is one of the numerous small and lovely lakes that appear in southern New Hampshire. Beautiful scenery, good sport, and a delightful climate have made this spot an attractive one. Summer cottages line the shores; rainbow trout, smallmouth bass, pickerel, horned pout, white perch, and northern pike thrive in the waters.

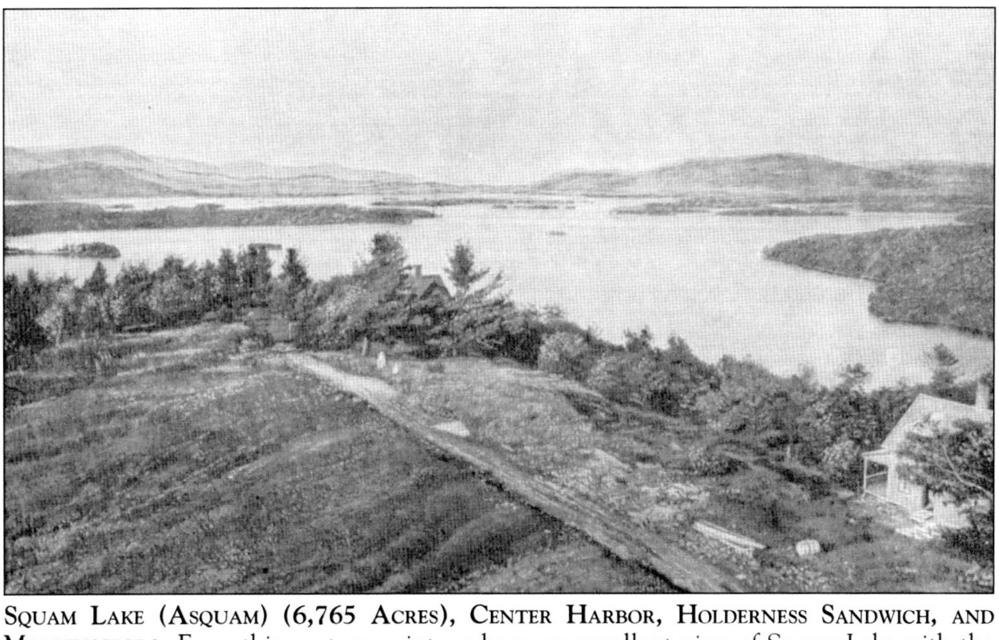

Squam Lake (Asquam) (6,765 Acres), Center Harbor, Holderness Sandwich, and Moultonboro. From this vantage point we have an excellent view of Squam Lake with the Sandwich Mountain Range in the distance. This lake is a natural one raised by a dam on Little Squam Lake. It has an altitude of 562 feet above sea level, an area of 6,765 acres, and lies in three counties and four townships.

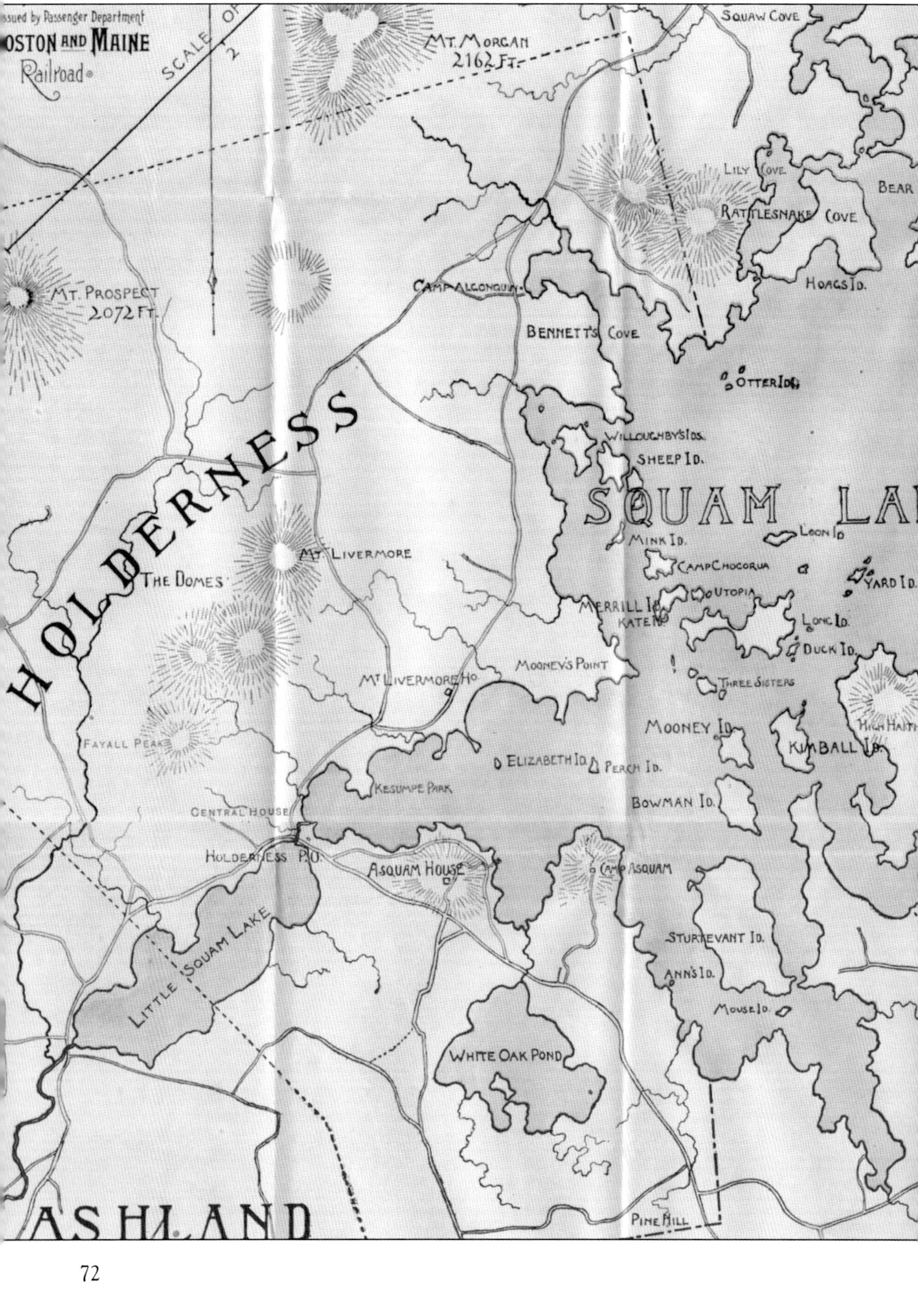

Issued by Passenger Department
Boston and Maine Railroad
Scale of
2
Mt. Morgan 2162 Ft.
Squaw Cove
Lily Cove
Bear
Rattlesnake Cove
Hoags Id.
Mt. Prospect 2072 Ft.
Camp Algonquin
Bennett's Cove
Otter Ids.
Holderness
Willoughby's Ids.
Sheep Id.
Squam Lake
Mink Id.
Loon Id.
Camp Chocorua
Mt. Livermore
The Domes
Utopia
Yard Id.
Merrill Id.
Kate Id.
Long Id.
Duck Id.
Mooney's Point
Mt. Livermore Ho.
Three Sisters
Fayall Peak
Mooney Id.
Kimball Id.
Elizabeth Id.
Perch Id.
Kesumpe Park
Bowman Id.
Central House
Holderness P.O.
Asquam House
Camp Asquam
Little Squam Lake
Sturtevant Id.
Ann's Id.
Mouse Id.
White Oak Pond
Pine Hill
Ashland

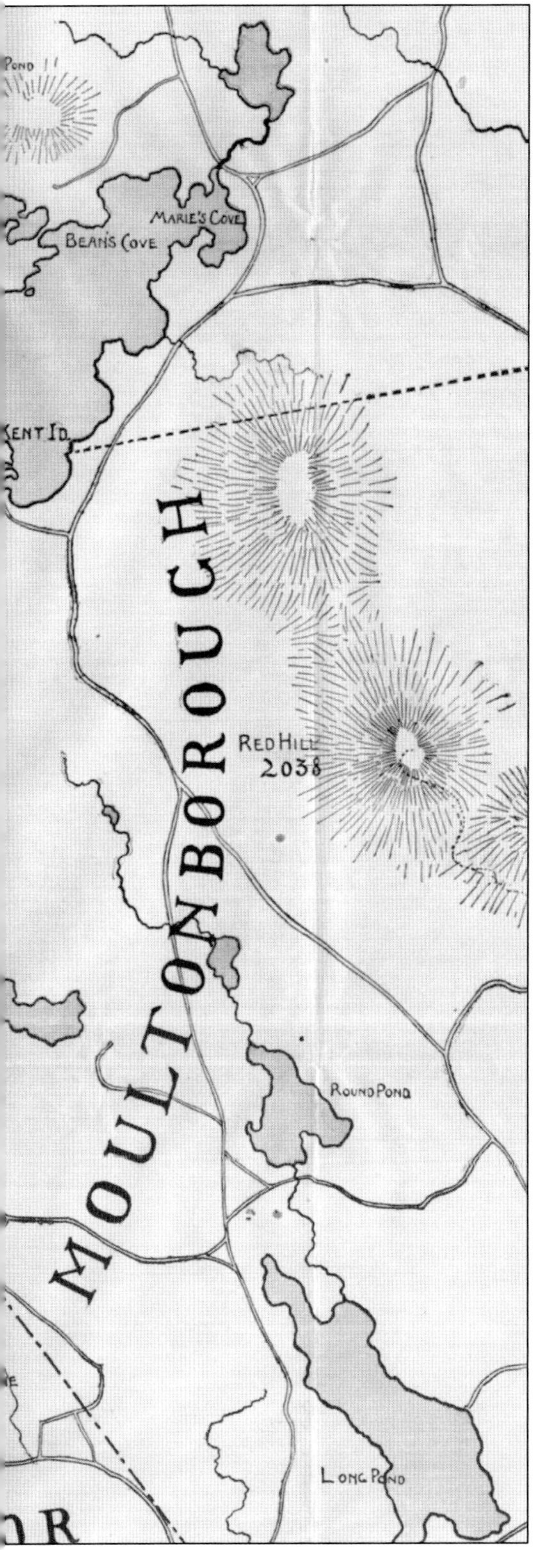

A Map of Squam Lake. This lake is divided into two sections, between which are several long islands parallel with each other. There are 16 islands in the lake, several of which were originally used for pasturing horses and sheep, but are now are habitable.

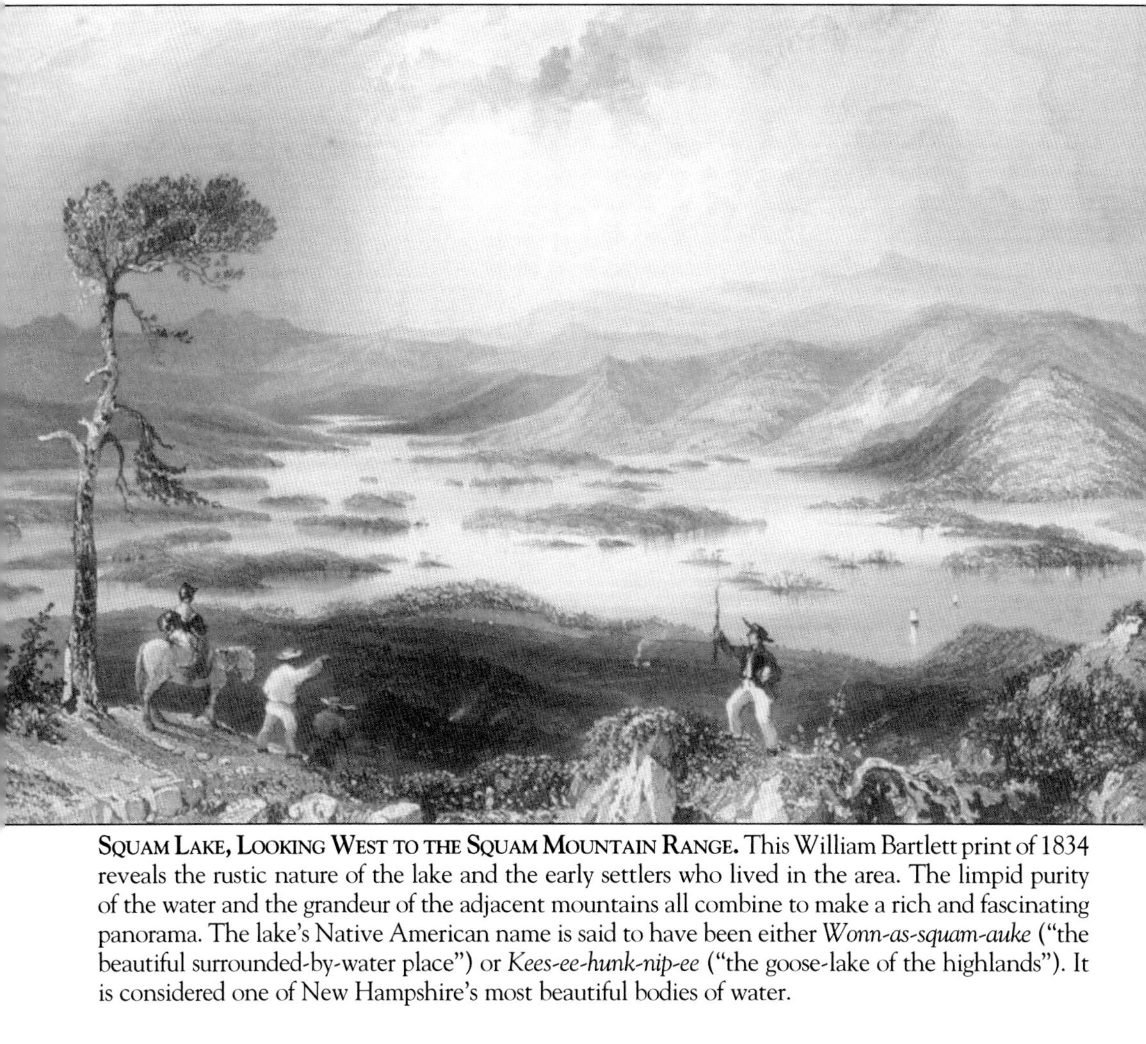

Squam Lake, Looking West to the Squam Mountain Range. This William Bartlett print of 1834 reveals the rustic nature of the lake and the early settlers who lived in the area. The limpid purity of the water and the grandeur of the adjacent mountains all combine to make a rich and fascinating panorama. The lake's Native American name is said to have been either *Wonn-as-squam-auke* ("the beautiful surrounded-by-water place") or *Kees-ee-hunk-nip-ee* ("the goose-lake of the highlands"). It is considered one of New Hampshire's most beautiful bodies of water.

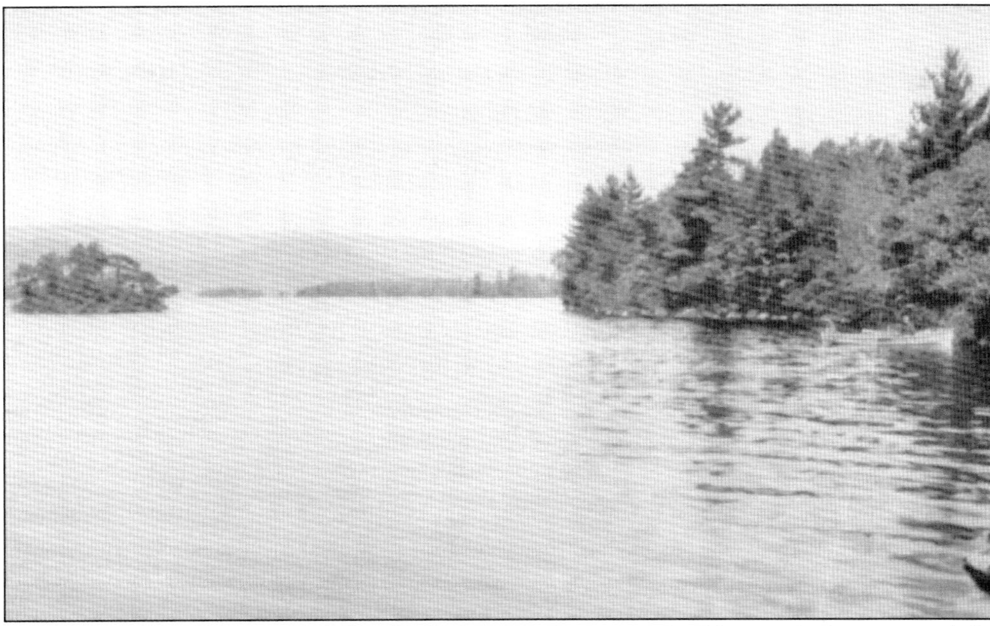

SQUAM LAKE, HOLDERNESS. Officially known as Asquam, the Native American word for "water," and popularly known as Big Squam, the lake is surrounded by high green hills and heavily forested shores. Its waters flow not into its neighboring Lake Winnipesaukee, but into the Pemigewasset River, which eventually unites with the Winnipesaukee River at Franklin Falls to become the Merrimack River.

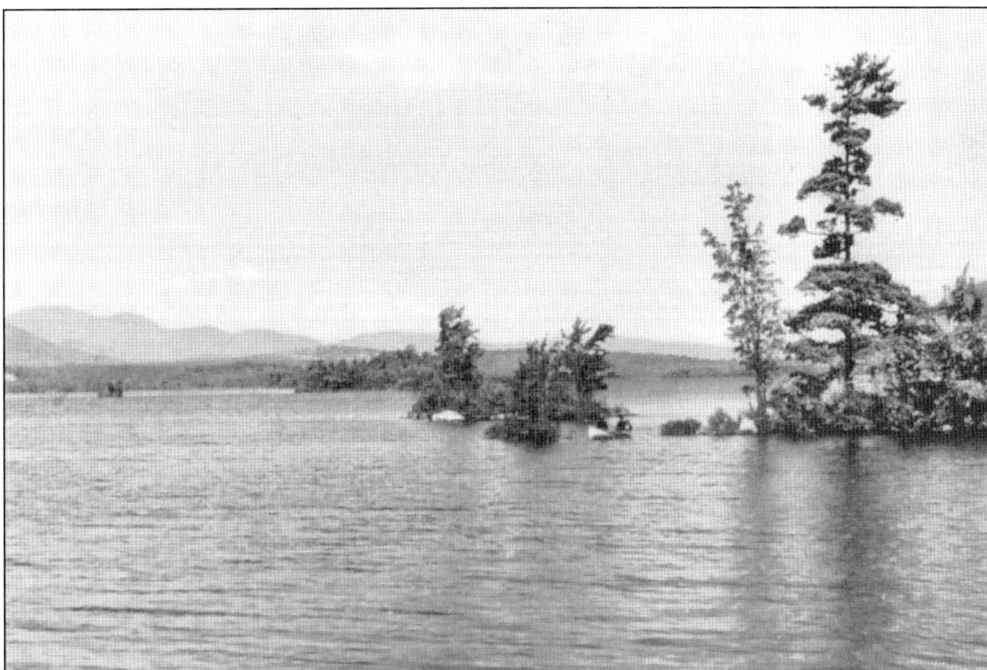

SQUAM LAKE, HOLDERNESS, ANOTHER VIEW. This lake was referred to by Capt. John Lovewell in his 1724 journal: "We travelled 16 miles and camped at the north side of Cusumpy Pond." Shown is a brief glimpse at the many islands that dot the surface of Squam Lake.

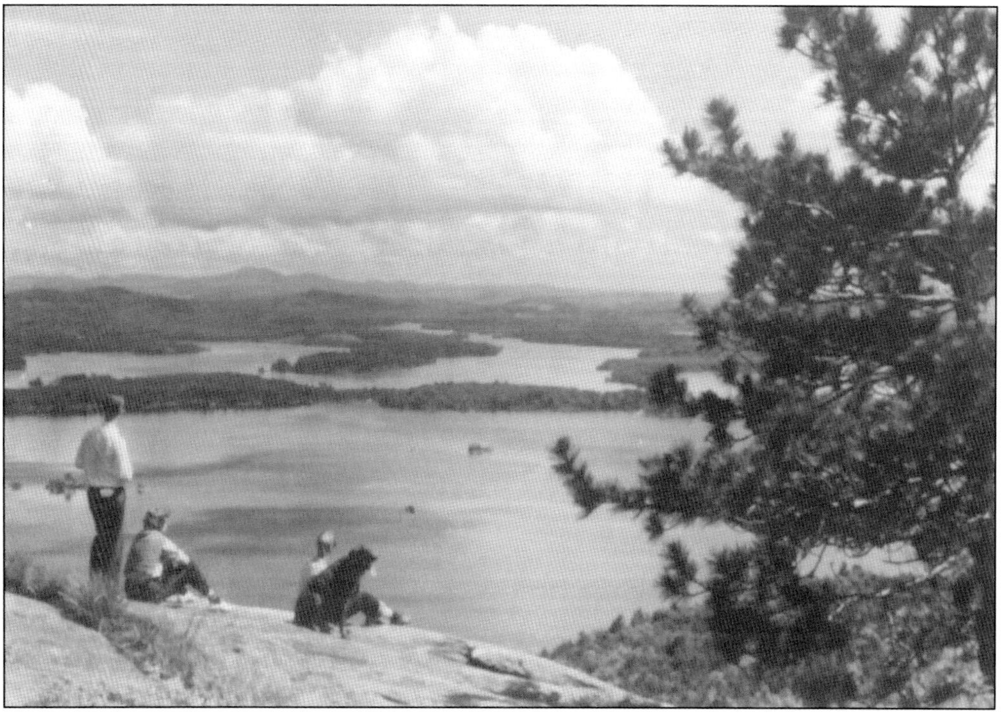

SQUAM LAKE, FROM RATTLESNAKE MOUNTAIN, ROCKYWOLD, DEEPHAVEN CAMPS, HOLDERNESS. One of the best views of the vastness of this lake and its many islands and surrounding mountains is seen from this mountain.

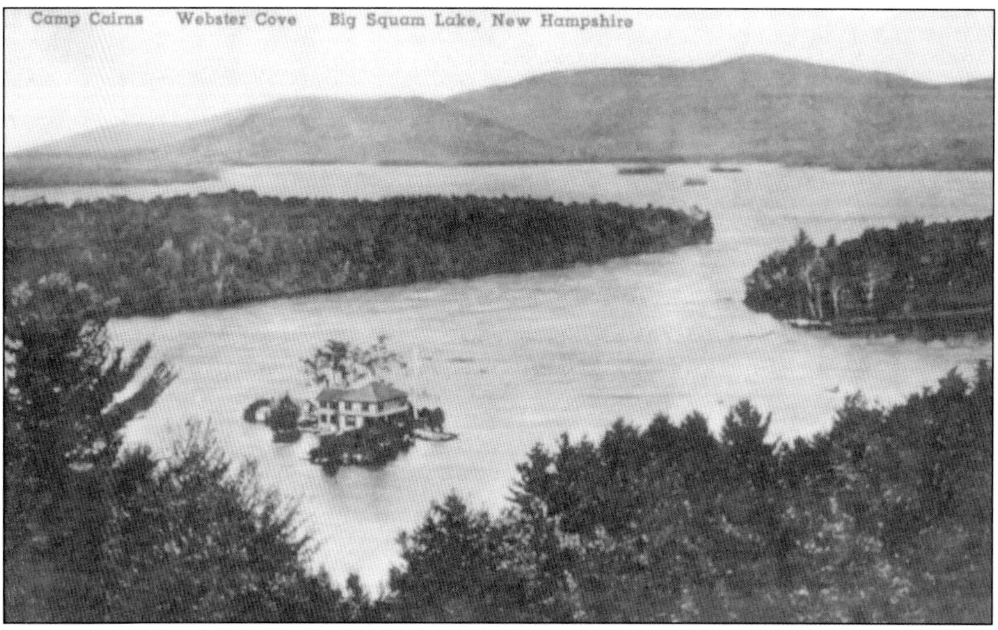

SQUAM LAKE, WEBSTER COVE. For many years, Squam Lake has attracted summer residents to its shores and has always had a conservative air about it, revealed in the large estates on the northern and eastern shores. Fishing is very good in this lake, with lake trout, salmon, pickerel, yellow perch, bass, and horned pout all being taken in their proper season.

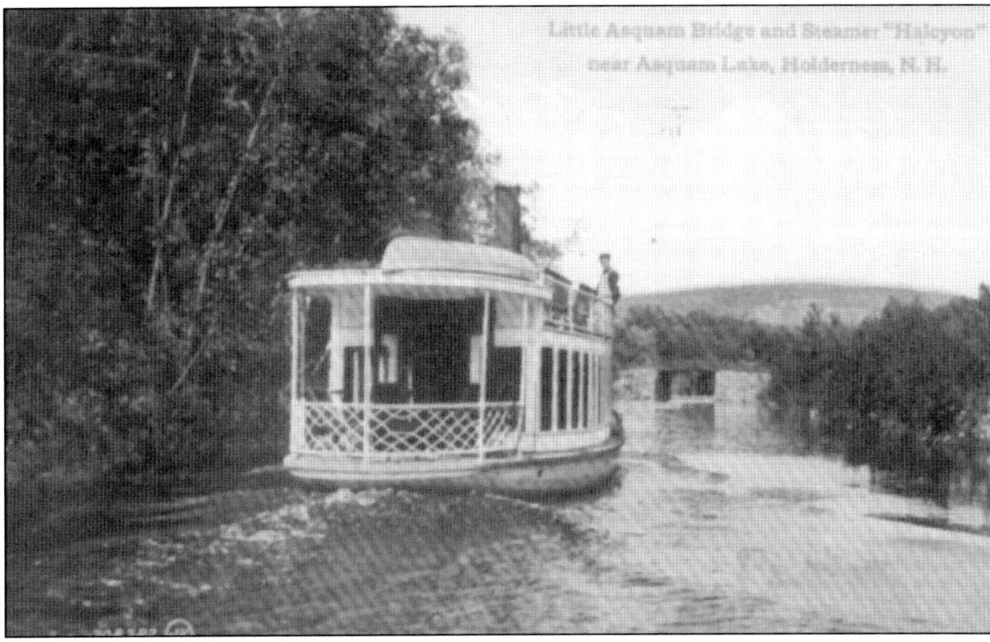

LITTLE ASQUAM BRIDGE, HOLDERNESS, 1912. The steamer *Halcyon* quietly sails near the bridge separating Big Squam from Little Squam Lake.

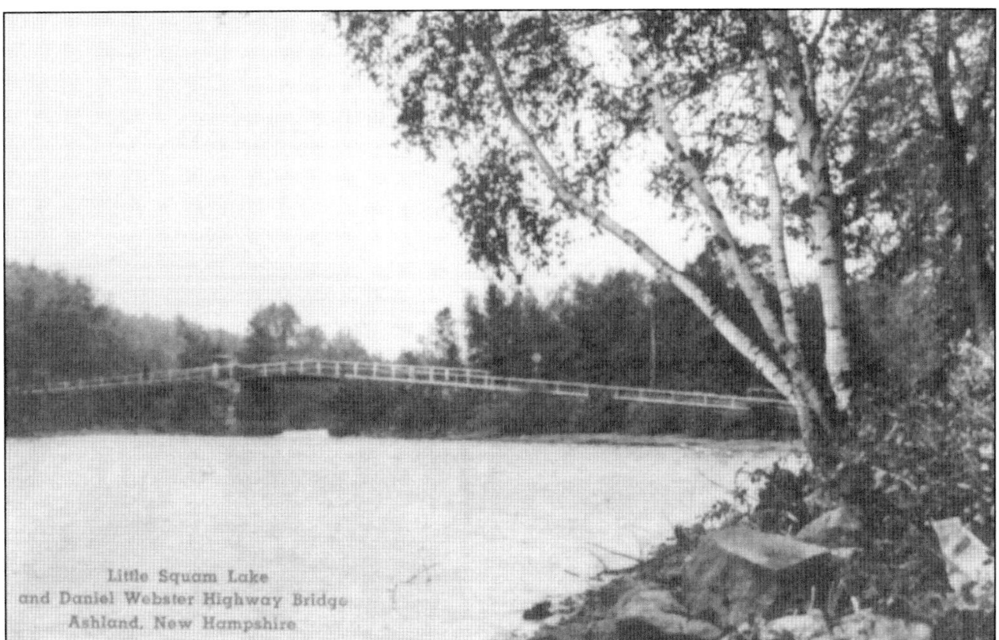

LITTLE SQUAM LAKE (408 ACRES), ASHLAND AND HOLDERNESS. This body of water appears to be an extension of Big Squam Lake, which enters in the town of Ashland. The area that divided Big and Little Squam Lakes was once referred to as the "Great Waste." Native Americans used to pass through it on a pathway that they used for transporting captives between St. Francis in Canada and the mouth of the Androscoggin River near Portland, Maine.

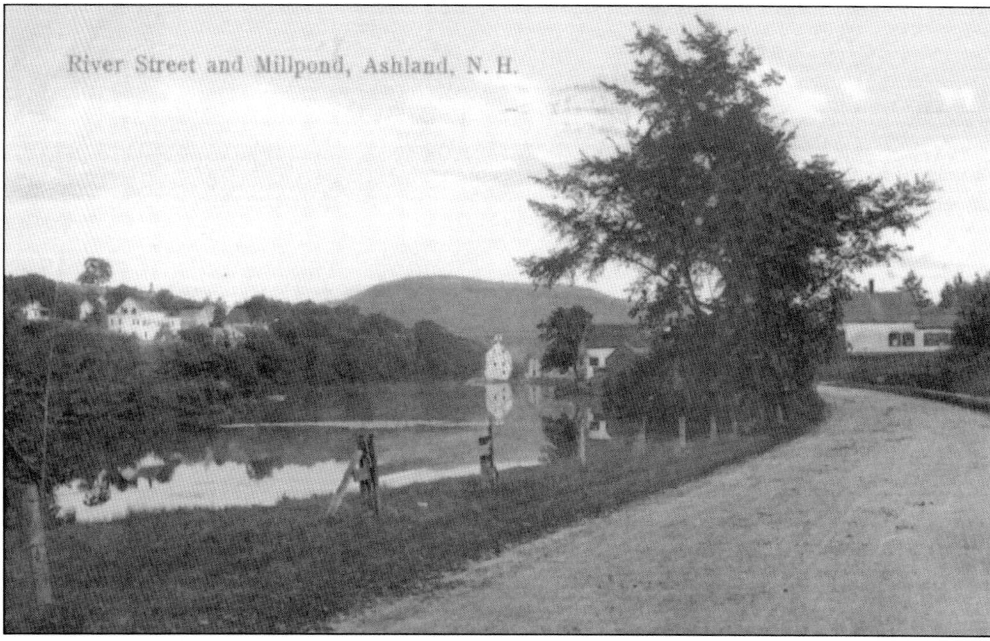

LITTLE SQUAM LAKE, ASHLAND. This town (above), situated on the Squam River, was originally a part of Holderness. Due to its excellence as a site for mills (the Squam River drops about 112 feet from Little Squam Lake to the Pemigewasset), a thriving town grew in the area. Because of the navigable river that opened the Ashland-Holderness area to the Squam Lakes, Ashland was for a long time an important manufacturing and commercial town (below).

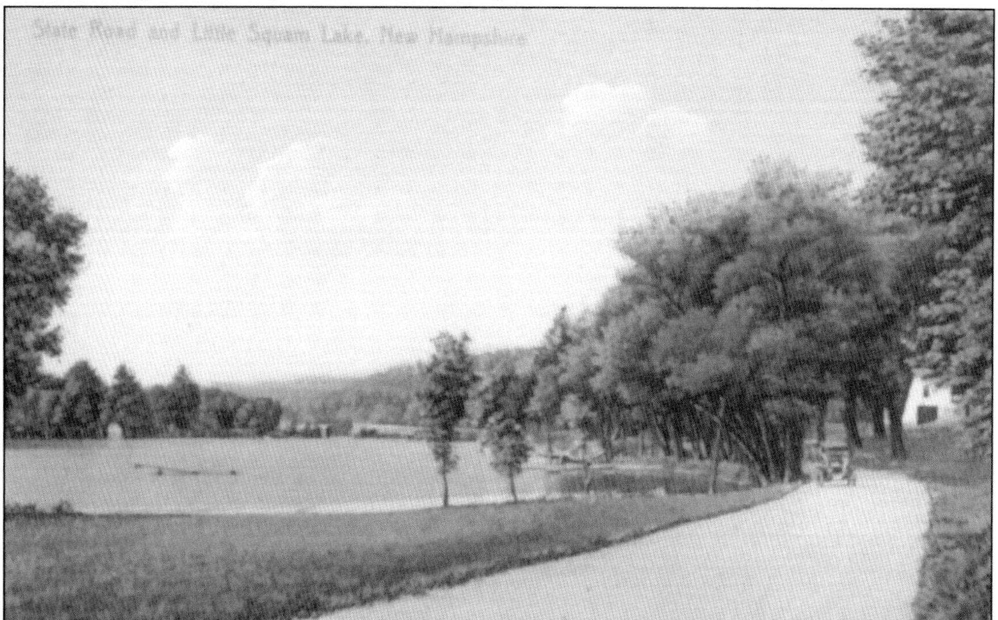

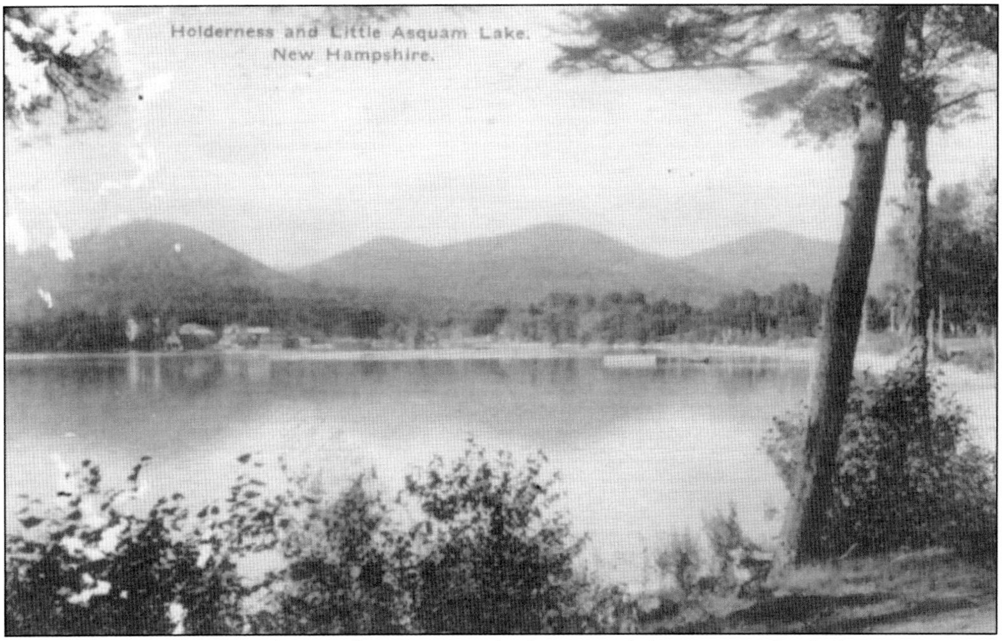

LITTLE SQUAM LAKE. Until recently, water was the fastest and cheapest method of transportation, and goods were shipped from Thornton through Sandwich Notch to the head of Squam Lake and then ferried on barges to Ashland and the Pemigewasset and down to the seaports. Today, many camps and year-round homes have developed along its shores, with excellent beaches and boating facilities. Fishing is very good here, with brook and rainbow trout, whitefish, bass, pickerel, and horned pout being readily available.

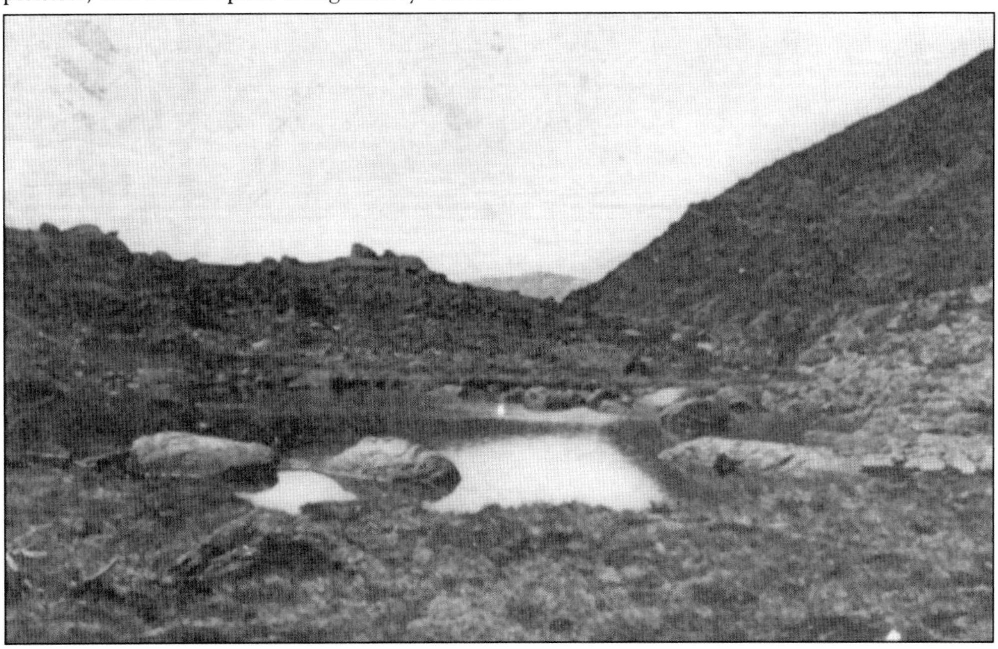

STAR LAKE, MOUNT MADISON. Here, in this alpine world, this tiny lake maintains a mysterious existence. Clear-watered Star Lake (altitude 4,900), located between Mount Adams and Mount Madison, has no visible outlet.

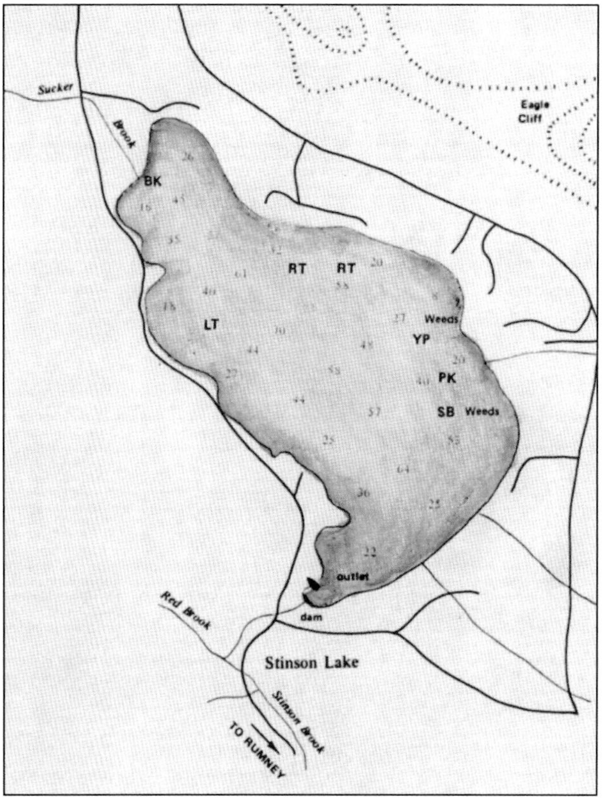

A Map of Stinson Lake (346 Acres), Rumney. This lake is considered to be the largest body of water within the New Hampshire National Forest boundary, covering an area of 346 acres. However, its shore is privately owned and quite heavily developed. This lake is nicely shadowed by Stinson Mount. The waters offer good fishing for lake trout, pickerel, and horned pout.

Sunapee Lake (4,090 Acres), New London, Newbury, and Sunapee. This lake, measuring 9 miles long and three 3 miles wide, is delightfully situated in a hollow between hills, with Mount Sunapee rising above its southern end. It is an open body of water with only one large island, Great Island, which is so situated as to divide the lake into two parts. In the distance, the rolling hills that surround the lake give it a quiet atmosphere.

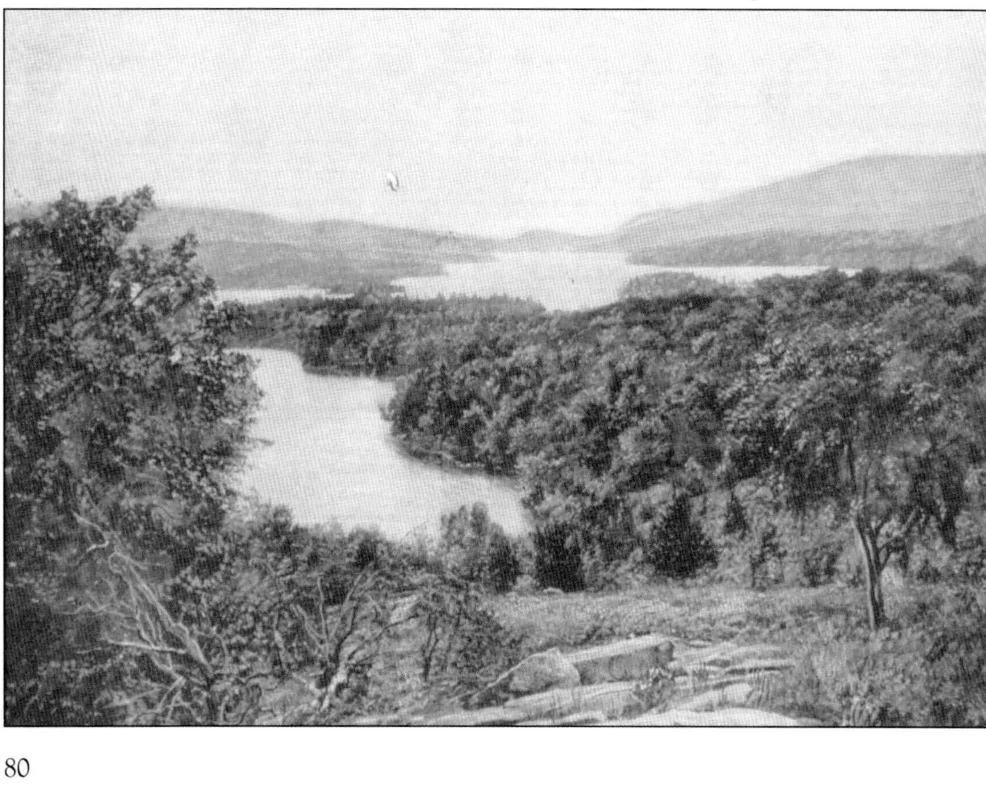

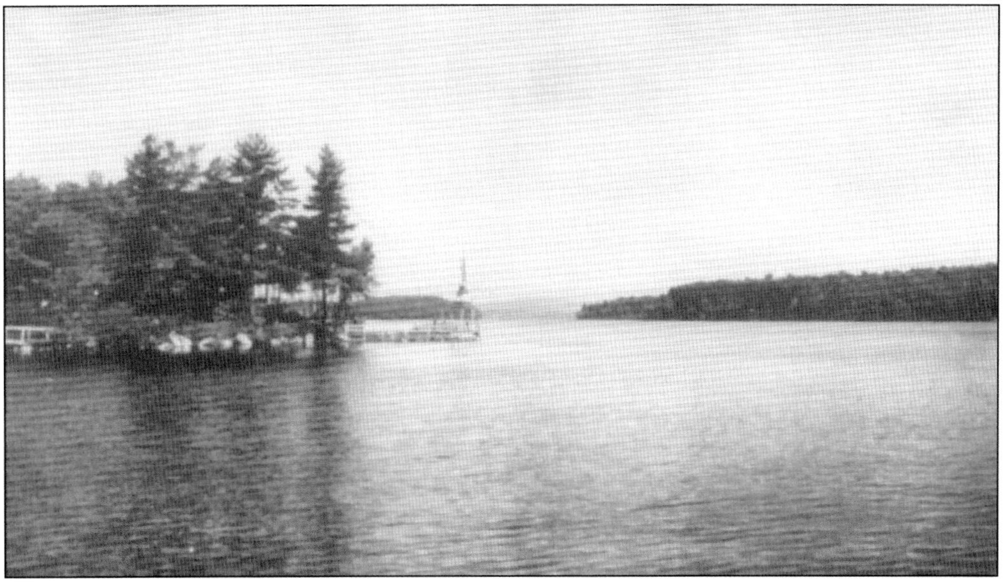

Sunapee Lake, from Bay Point, Sunapee. Native Americans called the lake *Soo-ni-pi*, "wild goose water," probably because of the presence of wild geese during seasonal migrations. The Penacook Indians had a hunting ground here, and during the French and Indian War (1756–63), they brought Timothy Corliss from the Weare Meadows to it as a captive. They are said to have shown him a vein of lead on the eastern slopes of Mount Sunapee from which they took ore and made bullets. Corliss was kept a prisoner until the fall of Quebec, but he could never find the mine again, and it is still unidentified. The location pictured is a reef where the golden trout spawn.

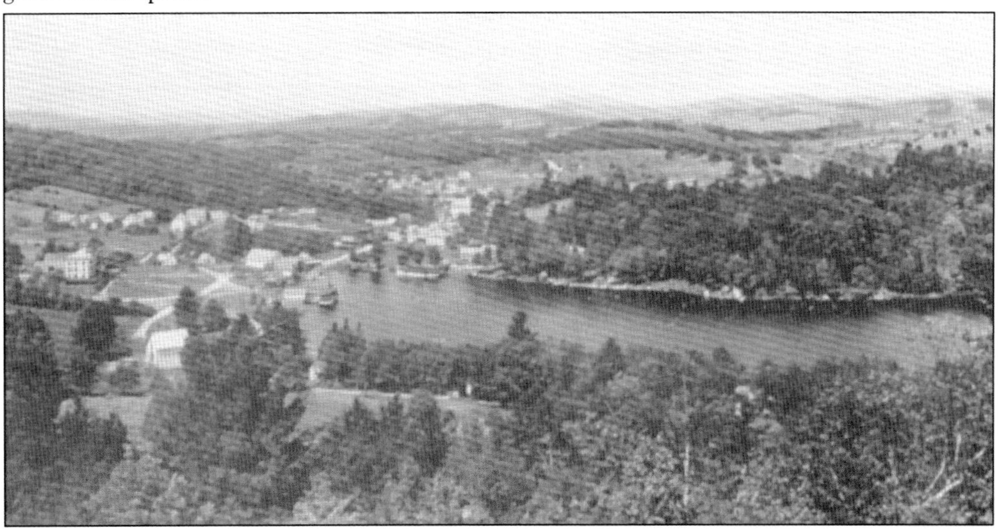

Sunapee Harbor, Sunapee. The first European settler to have looked on the lake is believed to have been a scout in advance of an exploring party from Boston in 1630. Sunapee was called Corey's Town in honor of Oliver Corey, one of the grantees. Later it was called Seville. At its incorporation, it took the name of Wendell from John Wendell, another grantee. By 1850, however, sentiment for the old Indian title of the lake became so strong that the present name was adopted. Much of Sunapee's early activity centered around the Sugar River, which has its egress from the lake here.

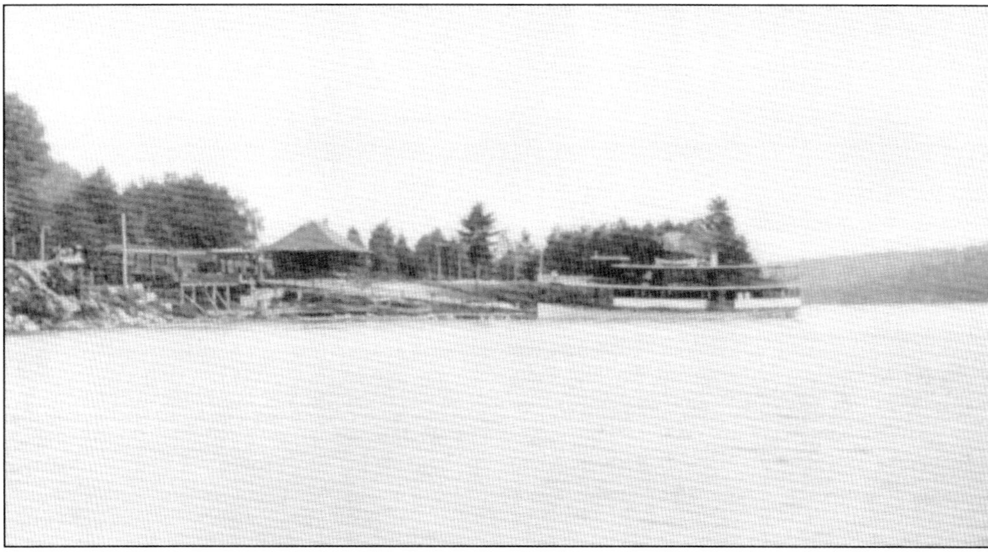

SUNAPEE LAKE, WITH RAILROAD STATION. Since the name of the lake, spelled as Sunope and Sunipee, appears on maps published in London and Paris in 1750, it is evident that the king's surveyors knew of its existence. In 1816, a proposal was made to use the lake as a part of a canal between the Connecticut and Merrimack Rivers. It was during the first half of the 19th century that rail transportation began and soon flourished in the area, bringing many visitors to the lake and lake steamer.

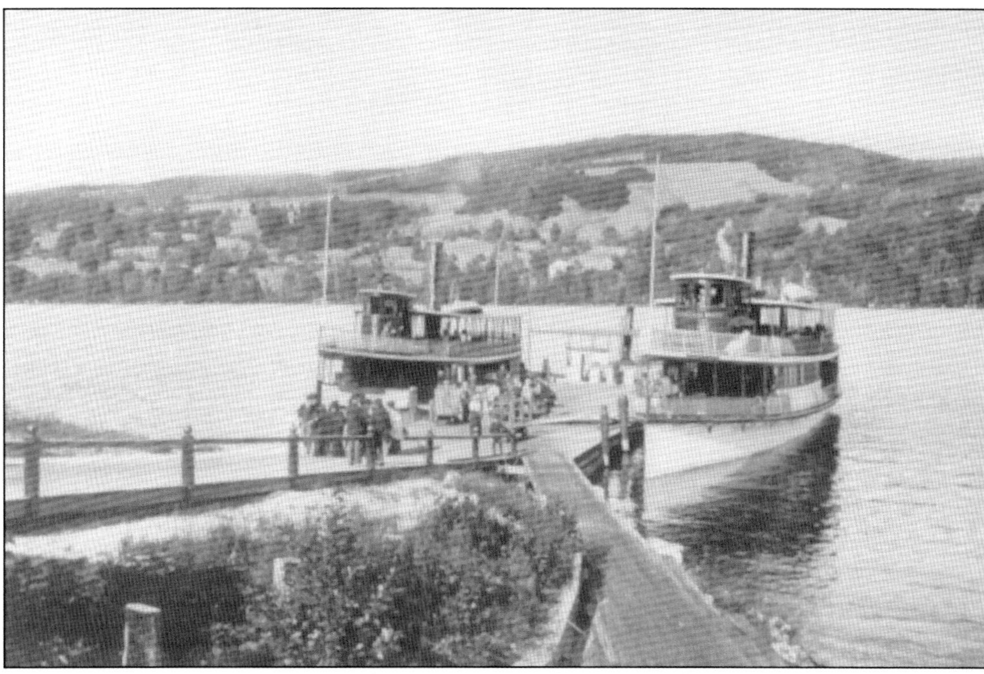

SUNAPEE LAKE, WITH STEAMERS. Lake transportation began as early as 1876. That year, Nathan Young's the *Mountain Maid*, remodeled with a screw propeller from the *Penacook*, was running. In the same year, the Woodsum era began: brothers Frank and Daniel Woodsum came from Maine and built the *Lady Woodsum*. These were the first of many powered vessels to sail on this beautiful lake.

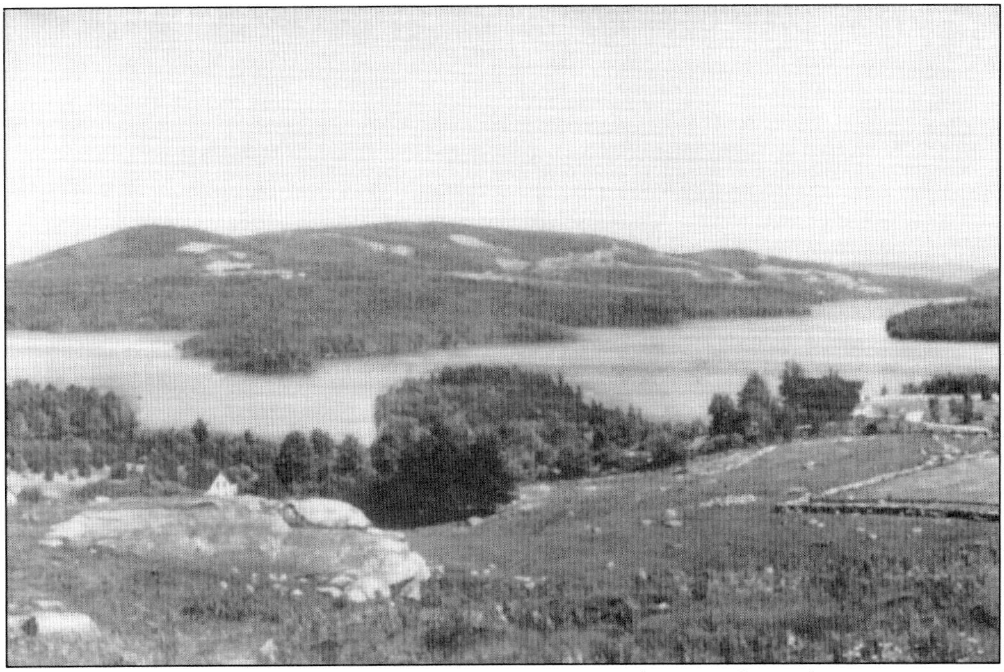

SUNAPEE LAKE, LOOKING DOWN FROM BURKEHAVEN HILL. This view shows the vast expanse of this beautiful lake with the rolling hills in the distance.

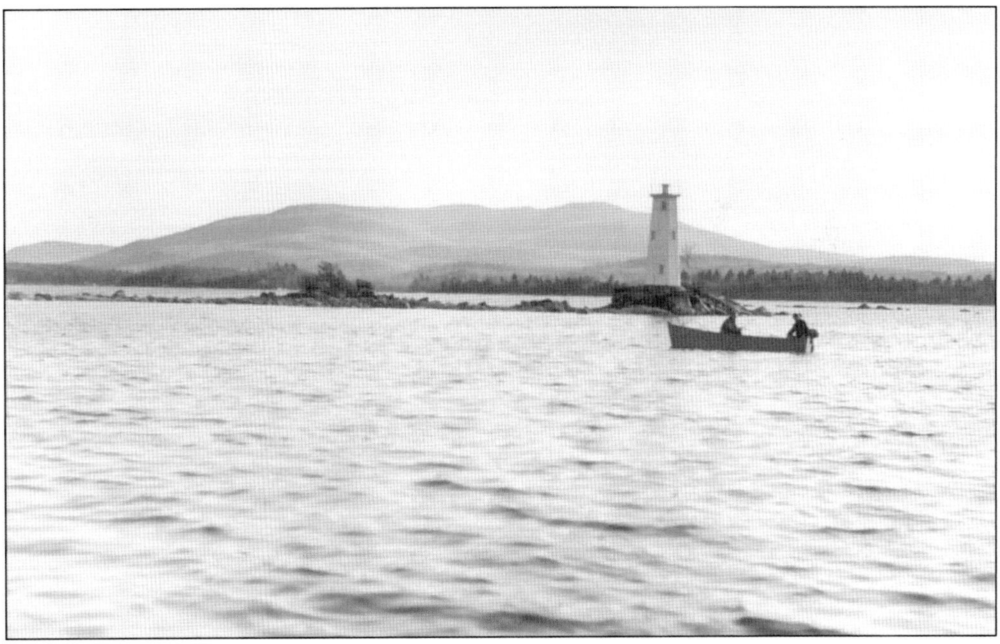

SUNAPEE LAKE. According the New Hampshire Fish and Game Department, "This reef is where golden spawn." The superior fishing and attractive surroundings have brought this lake into great prominence. The lake is stocked with a large variety of freshwater fish—trout, pickerel, and perch. Two prizewinning fish caught in this lake were a Sunapee trout weighing 11 pounds 8 ounces and measuring 33 inches long, and a cusk weighing 11 pounds 2.2 ounces and measuring 34.25 inches.

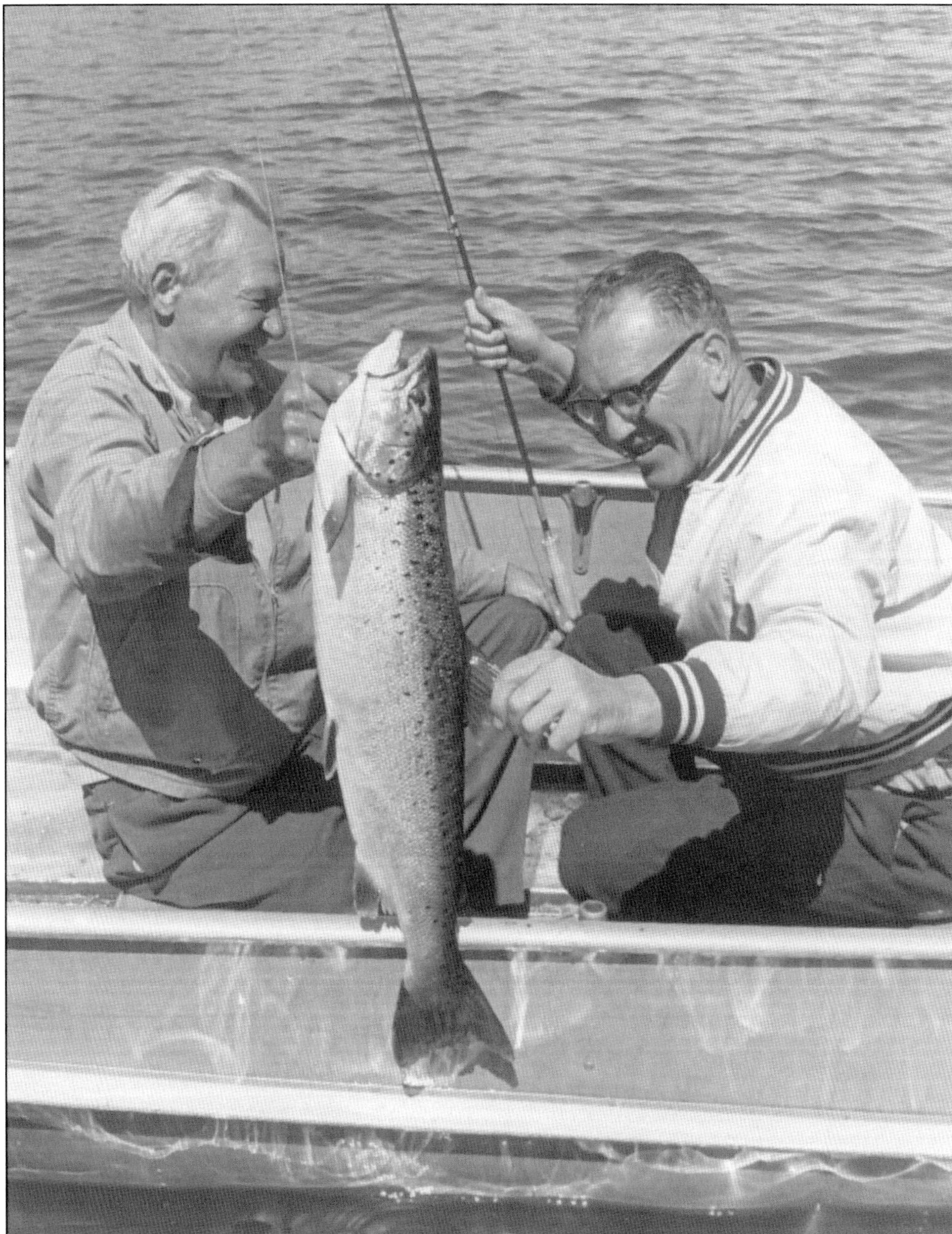

SUNAPEE LAKE, APRIL 17, 1968. Larry Bonner, an angler, displays his salmon—the trophy of the day.

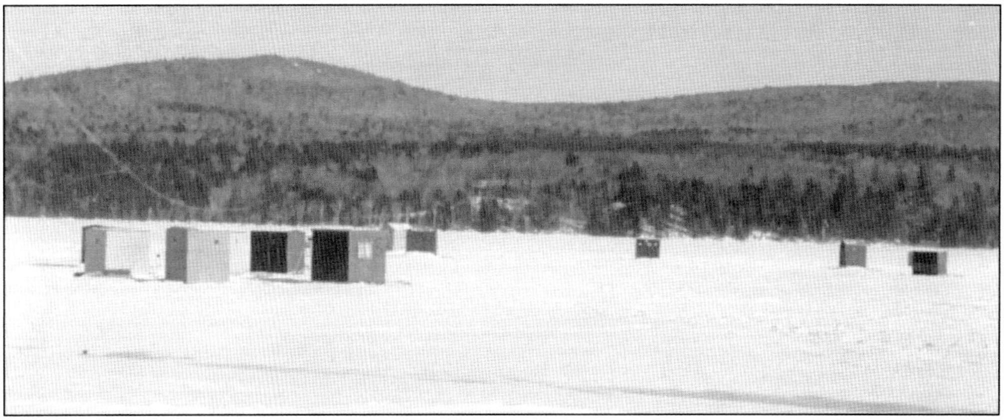

Sunapee Lake, in Winter. During the winter, Lake Sunapee becomes very cluttered with fishing shacks (bob houses) for the ice fishermen.

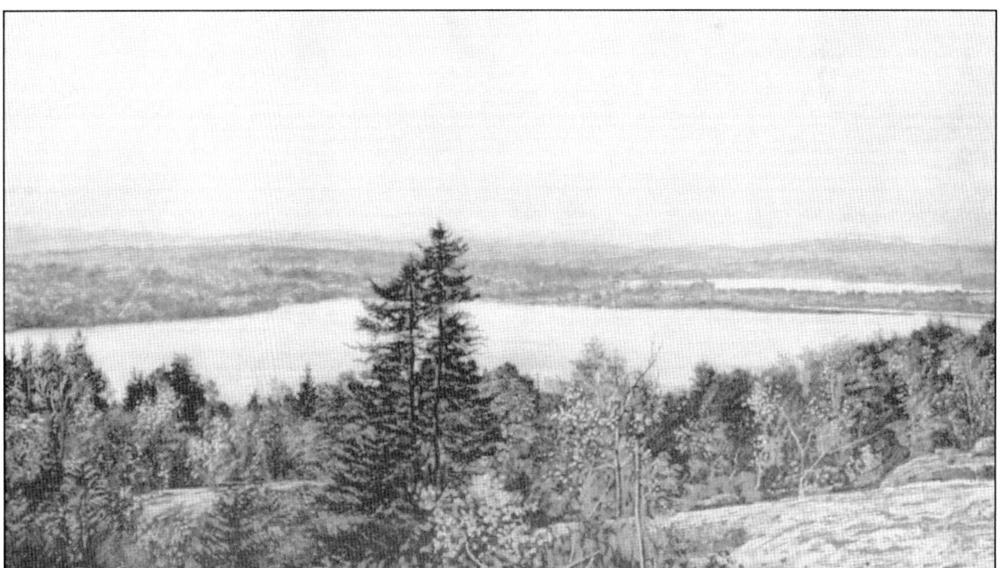

Little Sunapee Lake, (471 Acres), New London. Like Big Sunapee Lake, Little Sunapee is well supplied with a large variety of fish.

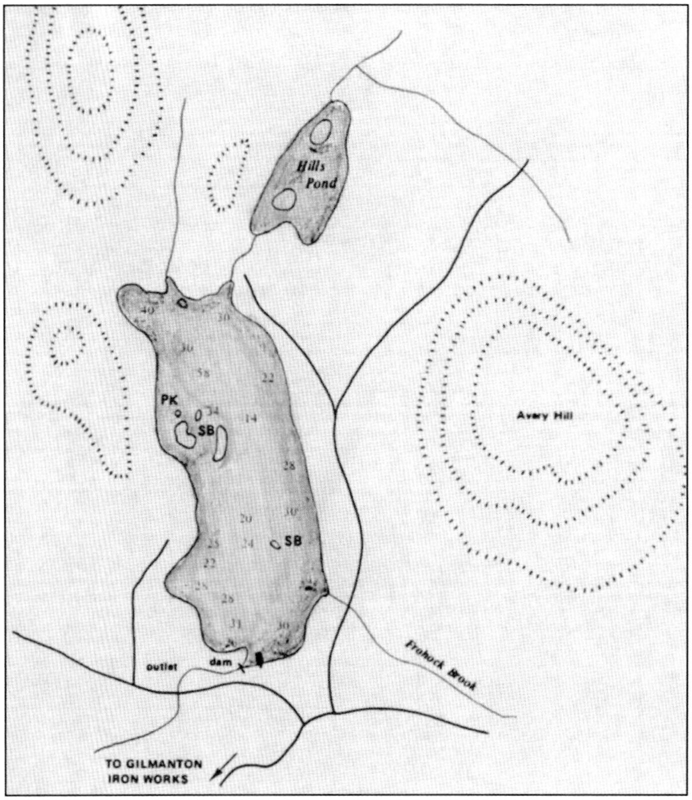

A Map of Sunset Lake (205 Acres), Gilmanton. This lake, also known as Places Pond, is a natural body of water raised by a dam and is the headwaters of Suncook River. This small lake is very popular with the fishermen. The best fishing being smallmouth bass, but the usual warm-water fish are also available.

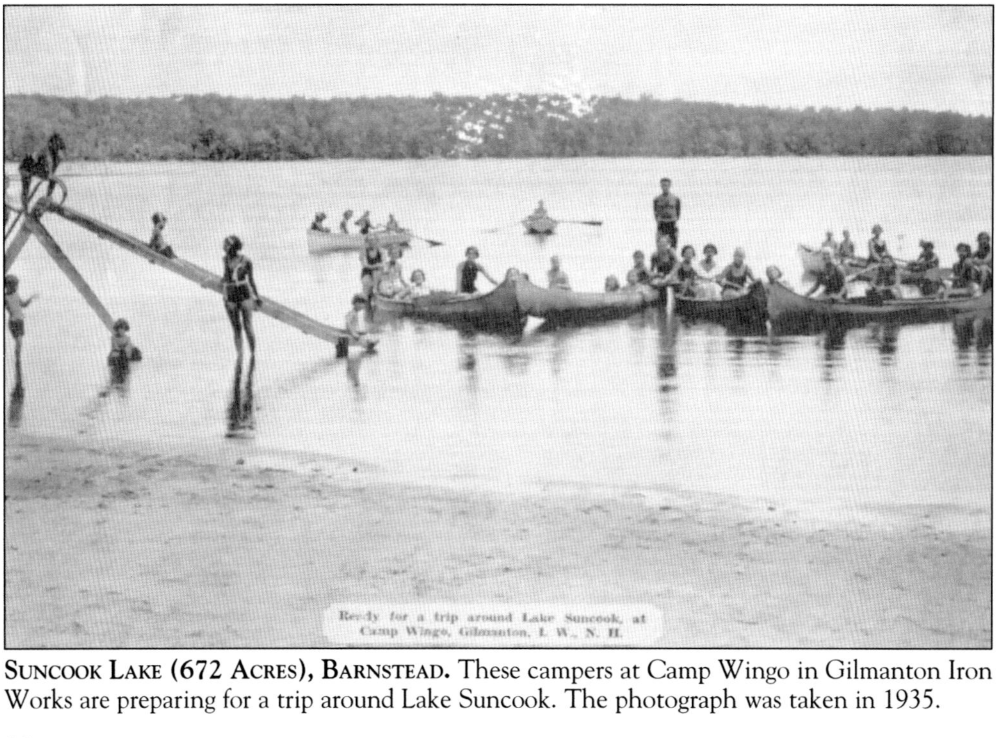

Suncook Lake (672 Acres), Barnstead. These campers at Camp Wingo in Gilmanton Iron Works are preparing for a trip around Lake Suncook. The photograph was taken in 1935.

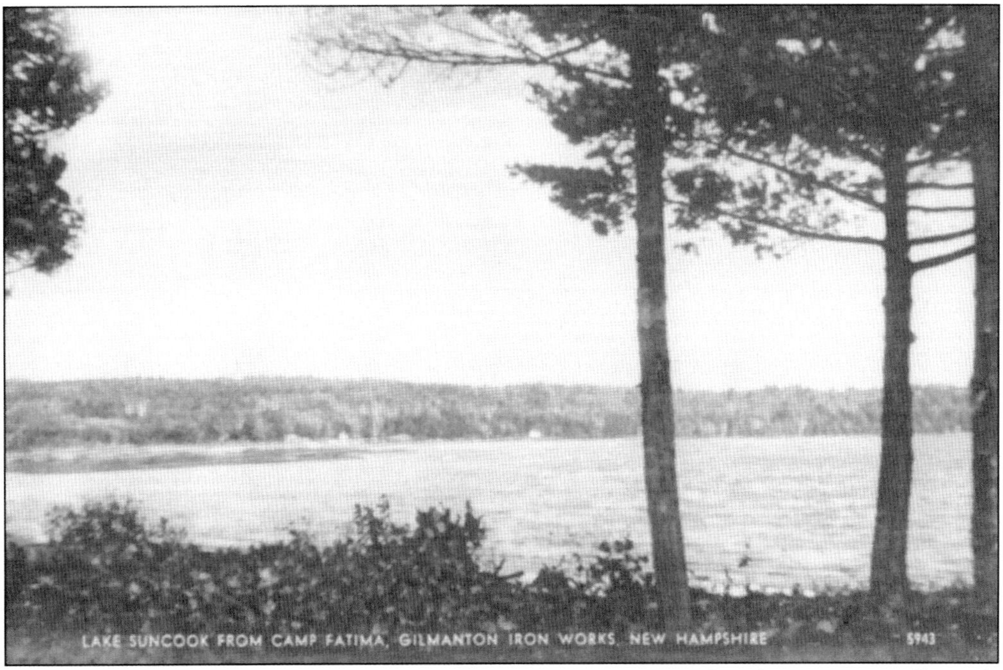

SUNCOOK LAKE, FROM CAMP FATIMA, GILMANTON IRON WORKS. Rainbow trout, smallmouth and largemouth bass, pickerel, horned pout, and white perch are plentiful here.

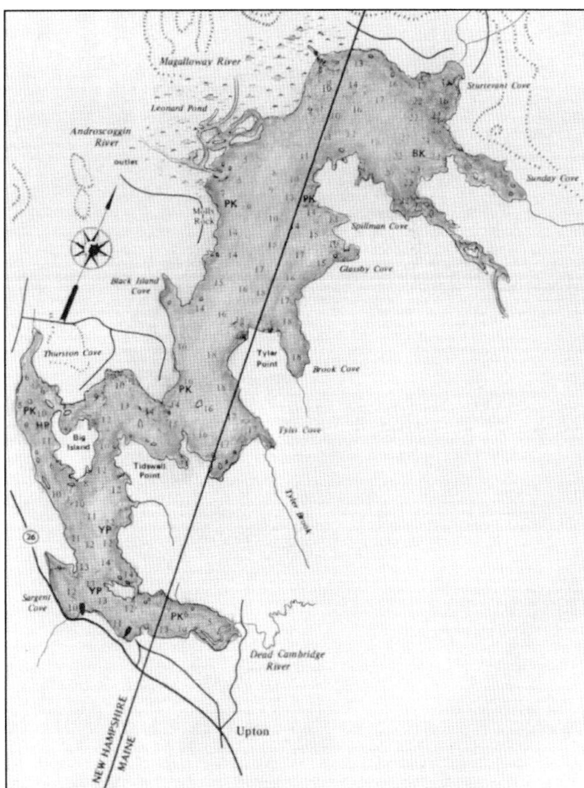

A MAP OF UMBAGOG LAKE (7,850 ACRES), ERROL AND CAMBRIDGE. As indicated by the map, this lake is located in both New Hampshire and Maine. Although Umbagog is the Native American word for "muddy water," the 12-mile-long, 1- to 2-mile-wide Lake Umbagog is a sparkling body of water surrounded by blue mountains. The lake is fed by two major streams, the Cambridge River and the Rapid River—the latter coming from the Rangeley Lakes Region of Maine. These streams teem with brook trout and salmon. The lake's outlet on the western shore joins with the Magalloway River to form the Androscoggin River. The lake is secluded and abounds with wildlife and fish—bass, pickerel, pike, yellow perch, horn pout, and smelt—making it a perfect getaway for sportsmen.

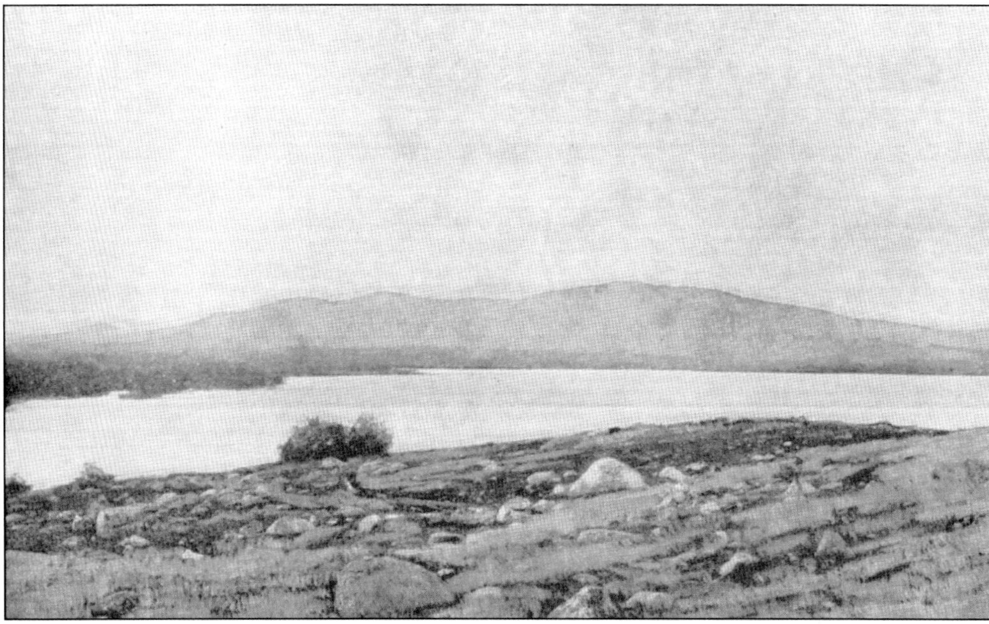

Walker's Pond, Conway. This small pond nestles quietly in the resort town of Conway. Shadowed by the majestic White Hills, it invites solitude for those requiring a restful moment.

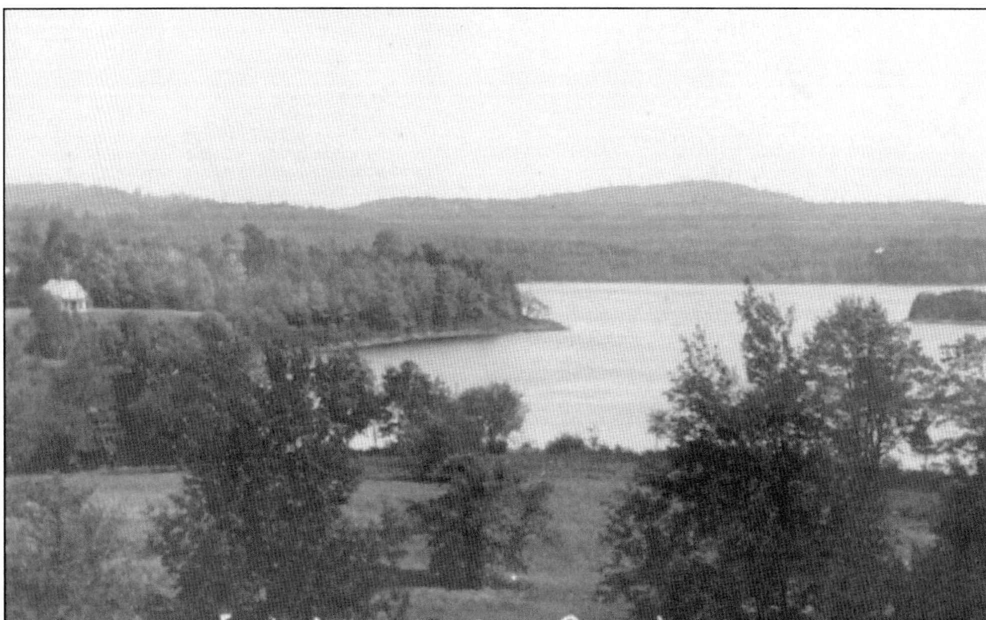

Warren Lake (185.5 Acres), Alstead. This lake offers a variety of fish for the angler. Rainbow trout, smallmouth and largemouth bass, pickerel, and horned pout are standard fish for this beautiful body of water.

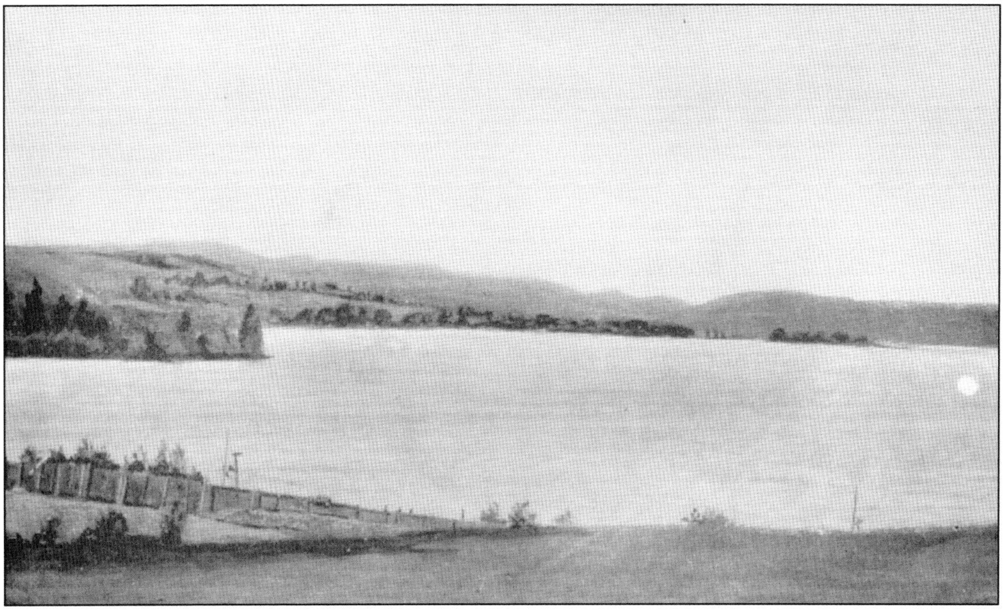

WAUKEWAN LAKE (912 ACRES), (MEASLEY POND), MEREDITH, NEW HAMPTON. The shoreline of this natural lake is dotted with summer homes and beaches, and the lake is considered to be a fine place for fishing. It is well stocked with smallmouth bass, landlocked salmon, chain pickerel, lake trout, and yellow perch.

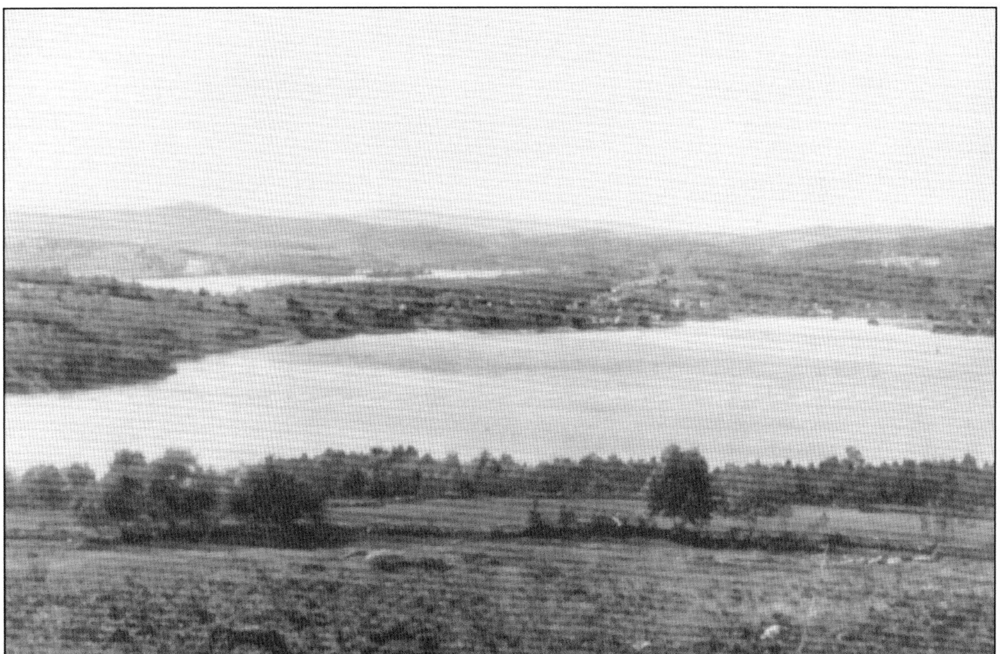

WAUKEWAN LAKE, MEREDITH. A very nice town beach is located on the south shore of Lake Waukewan. Framing the rest of the lake are rolling, wooded hills and many attractive summer and year-round homes.

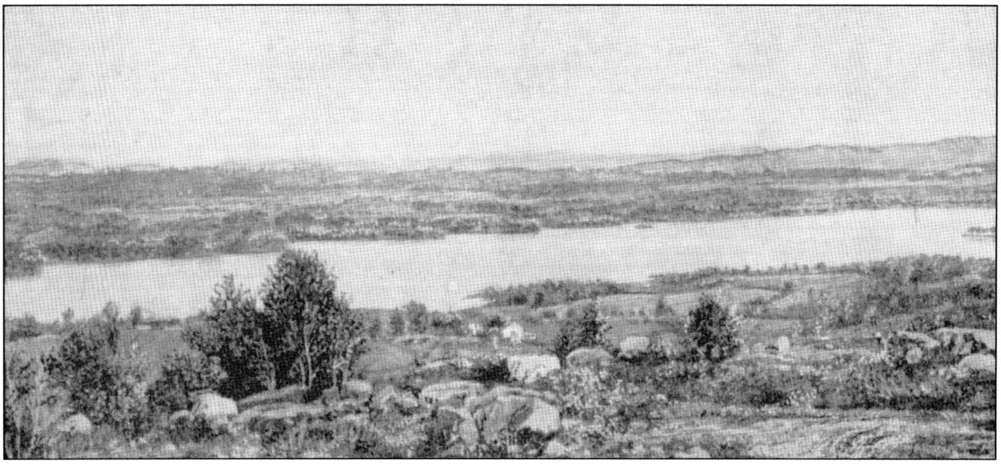

WEBSTER LAKE (612 ACRES), FRANKLIN. This attractive body of water has numerous cottages dotting its shore. There is a bathing beach with all facilities near Route 11. Webster Lake is a natural lake that is stocked with mixed sizes of smallmouth bass and horned pout. It also contains suckers, sunfish, white and yellow perch, and pickerel. This is a tributary to Chance Pond Brook (Sucker Brook), which eventually flows into the Pemigewasset River.

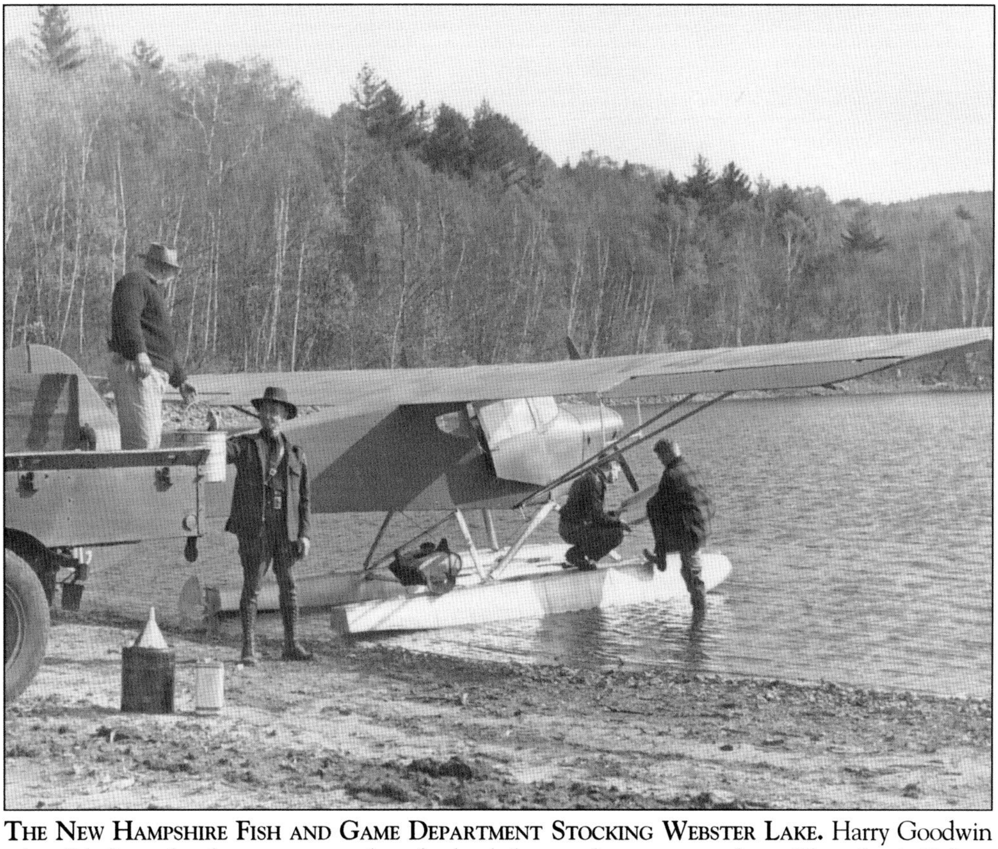

THE NEW HAMPSHIRE FISH AND GAME DEPARTMENT STOCKING WEBSTER LAKE. Harry Goodwin takes fish from the department truck to be loaded onto the pontoon plane. The pilot is Robert Knowlton. The photograph dates from 1952. Popular fish in Webster Lake include rainbow trout, brown trout, smallmouth and largemouth bass, pickerel, horned pout, and white perch.

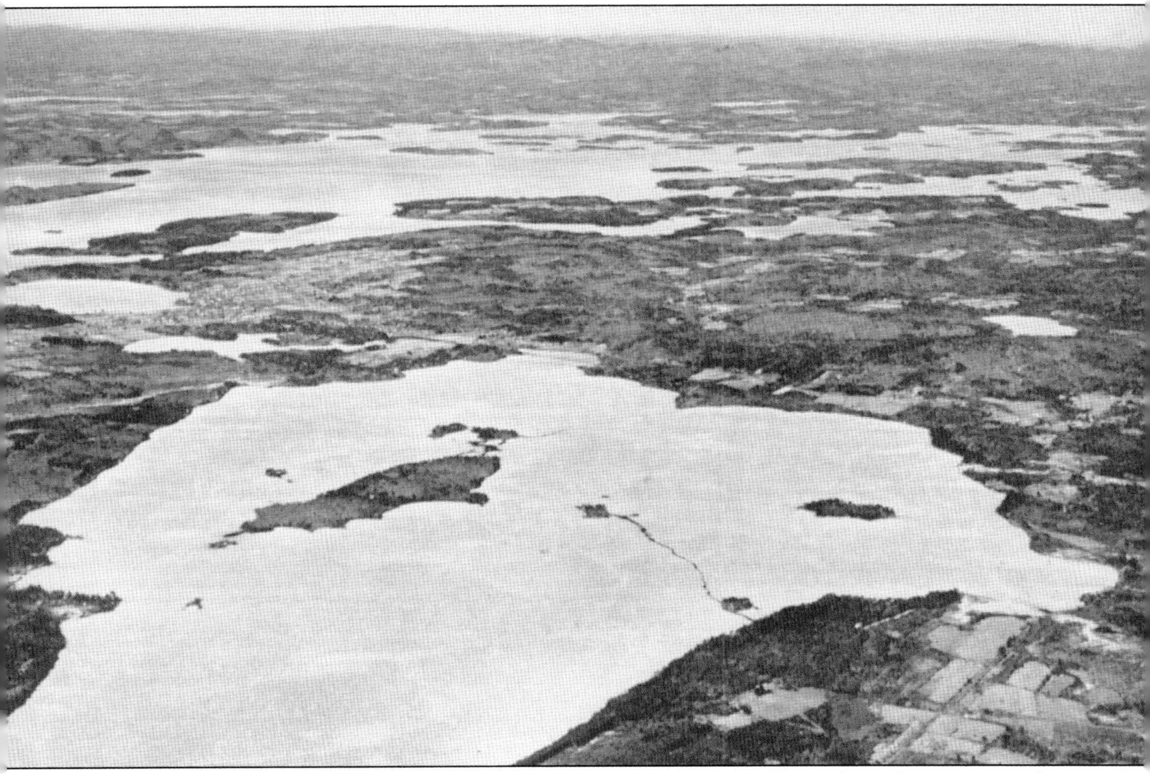

WENTWORTH LAKE (3,015 ACRES), WOLFEBORO. This aerial view shows the Lake Wentworth and Lake Winnipesaukee quadrangle. Looking to the west, Lake Wentworth and Wolfeboro village may be seen in the center and foreground.

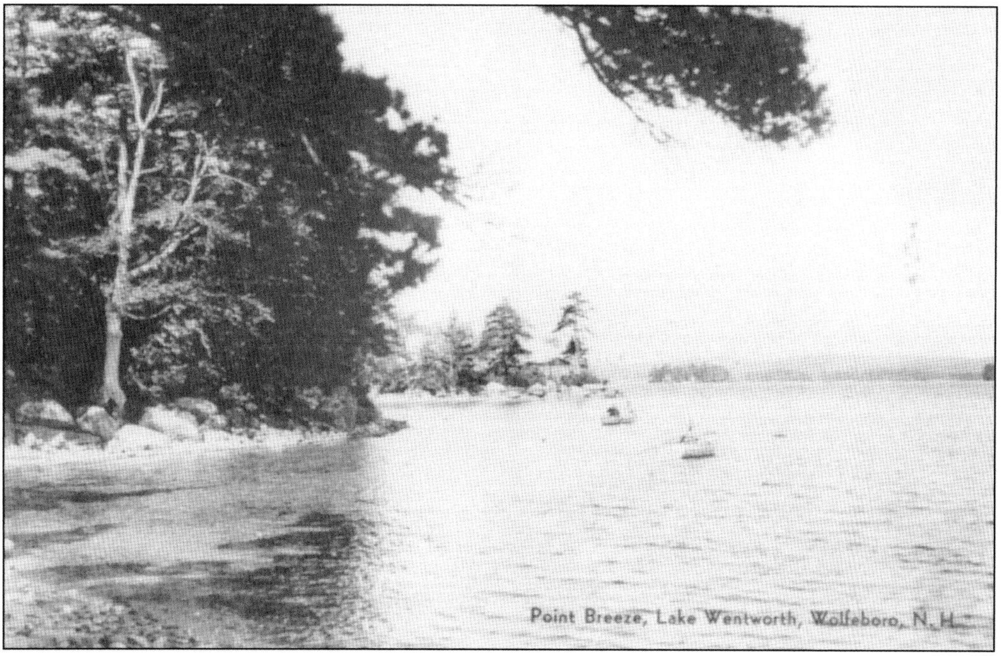

WENTWORTH LAKE, POINT BREEZE, WOLFEBORO. This lake is a wonderful inland sea; clustered around its shores and on the islands, which diversify its surface, are some of the most charming of all New England's summer resorts. The lake's most impressive role, however, is the part it plays in the great panorama that stretches away from the lake, with its islands in the foreground, to all the peaks and groups of three mountain ranges at the foothills of the White Mountains.

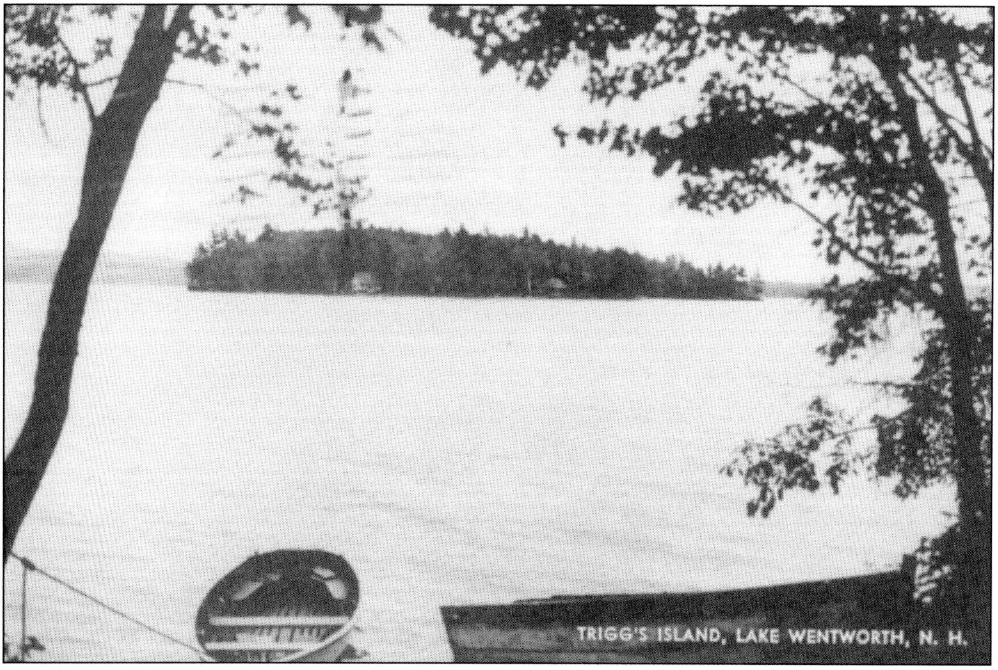

WENTWORTH LAKE, WOLFEBORO. Centered in this view is Trigg's Island.

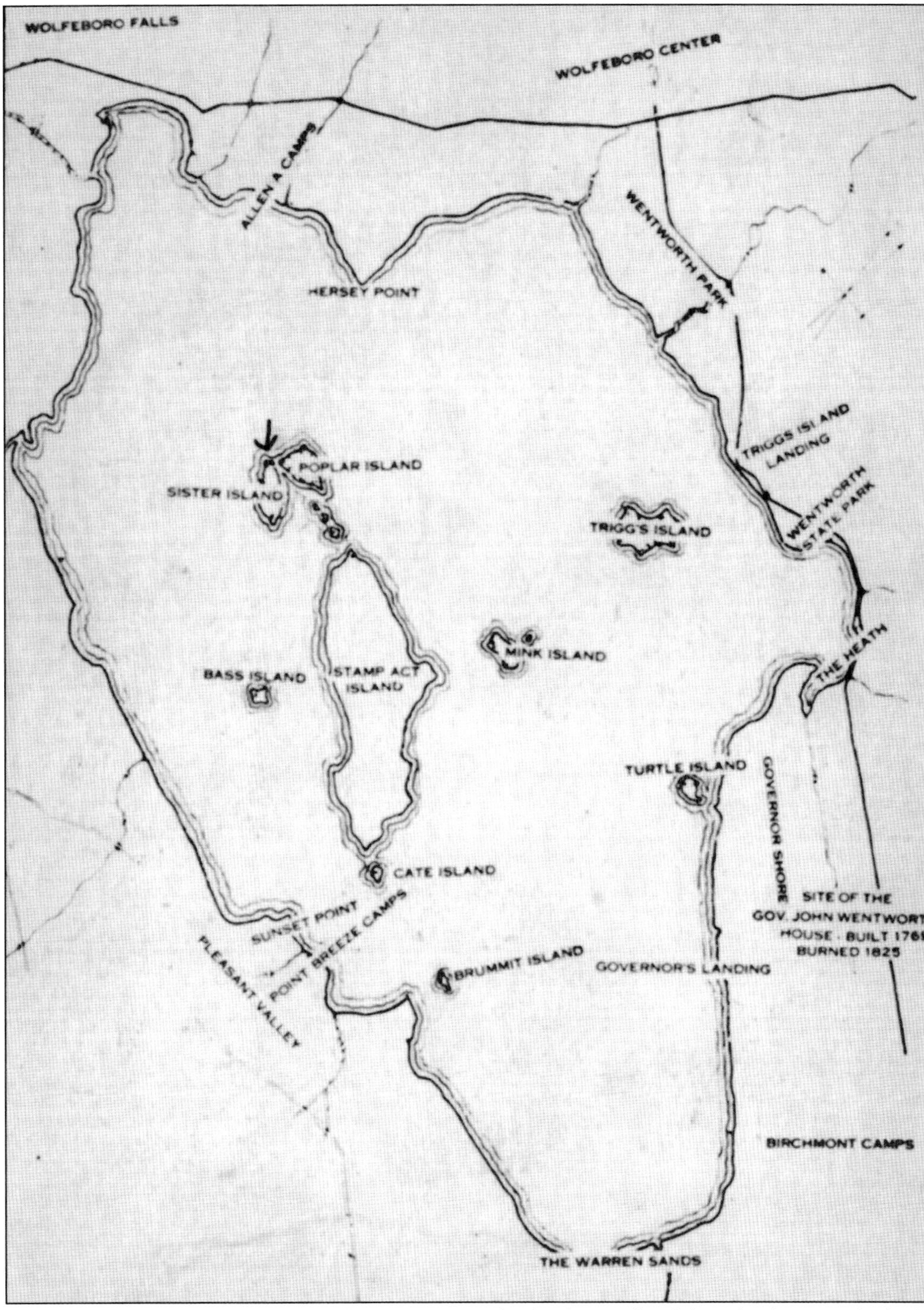

A Map of Wentworth Lake. There are several islands on this lake, the largest of which is Stamp Act Island, nearly three-quarters of a mile long. This attractive sheet of water is surrounded by low hills and numerous summer homes. Here, in 1768, Colonial Gov. John Wentworth began building an imposing summer home 500 feet from the lake. The home was only partly completed and, in the early part of the 19th century, it burned.

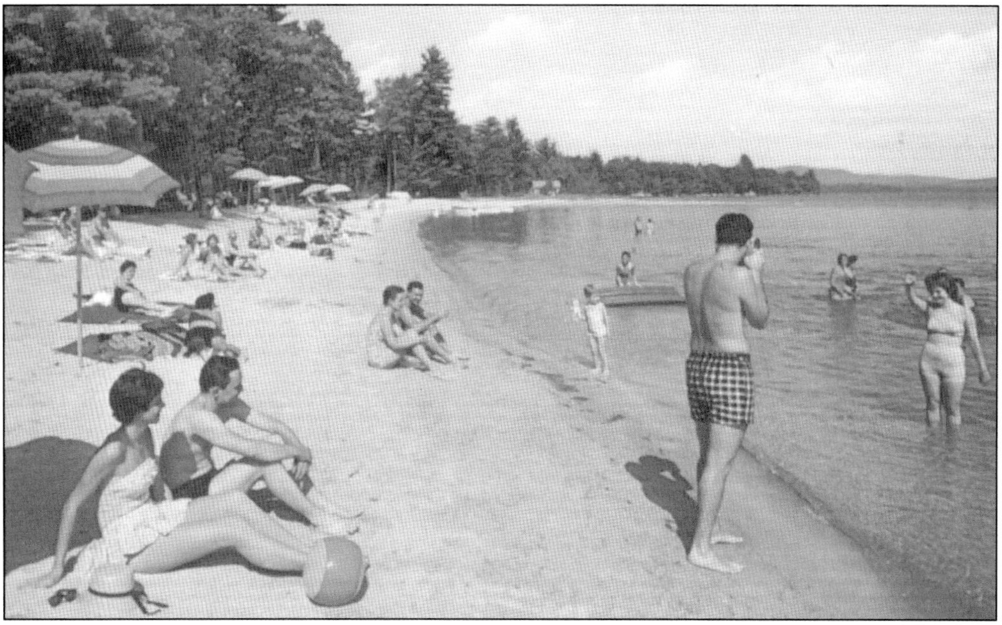

WENTWORTH LAKE. In the mid-20th century, the popular Allen A Resort made its home on the shore of Lake Wentworth. This square-mile resort offered every attraction possible to the vacationer. Today, this location has become the home of the New Hampshire Antique & Classic Boat Museum.

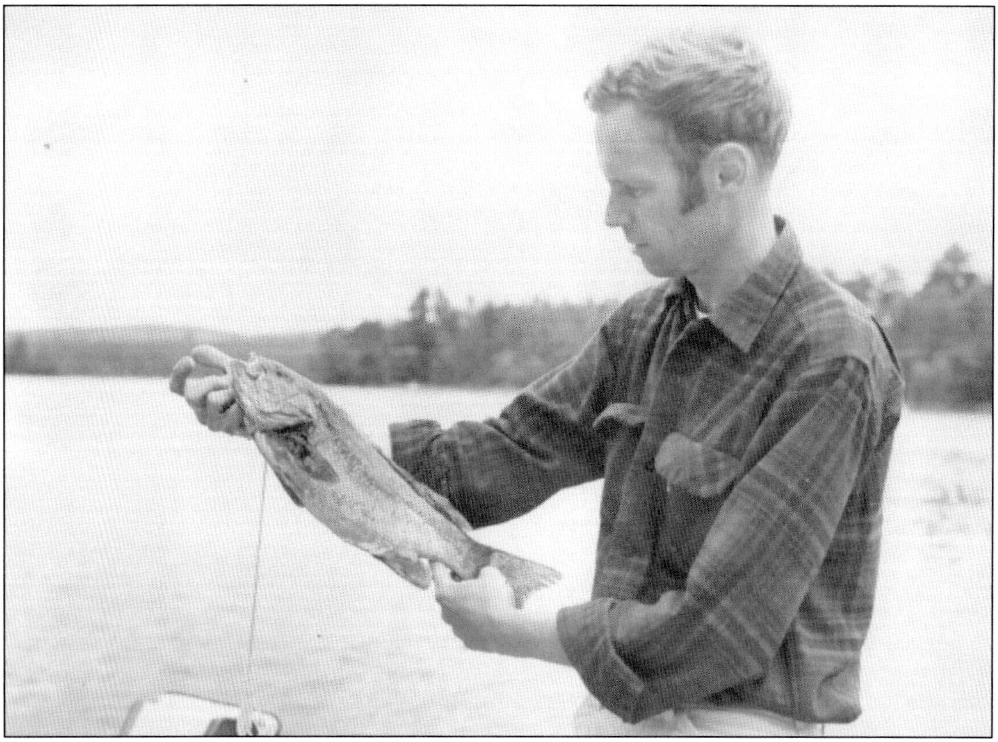

FISHING AT WENTWORTH LAKE. One of the better bass caught at this lake was this 2.5-pounder taken by Tom Shorter, writer and editor for the Maine Fish and Game Department magazine.

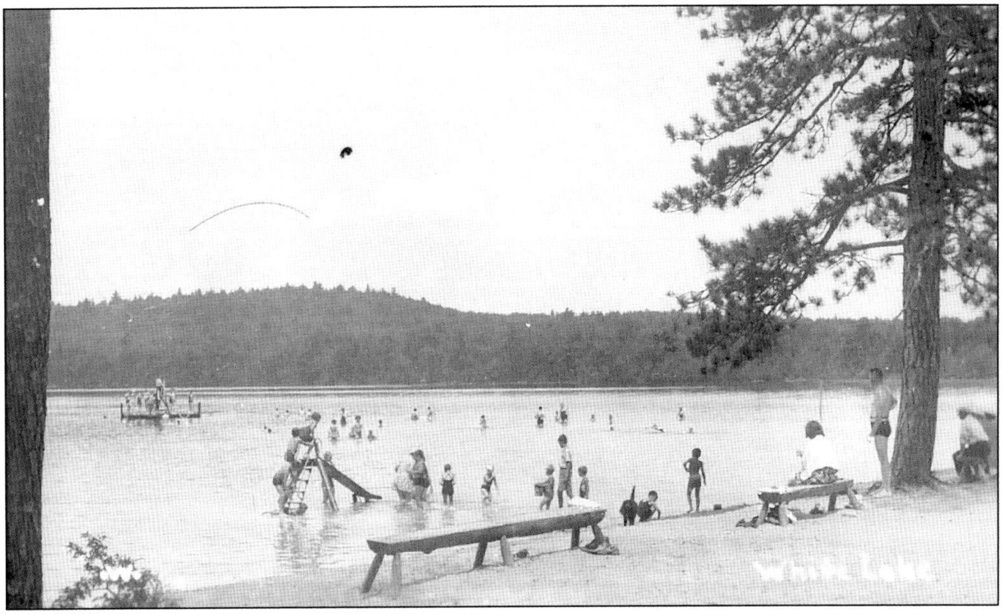

White Lake (124 Acres), Tamworth. This lake is very popular for bathing, picnicking, and fishing. Brook and lake trout, pickerel, yellow perch, and horned pout are popular catches in the lake.

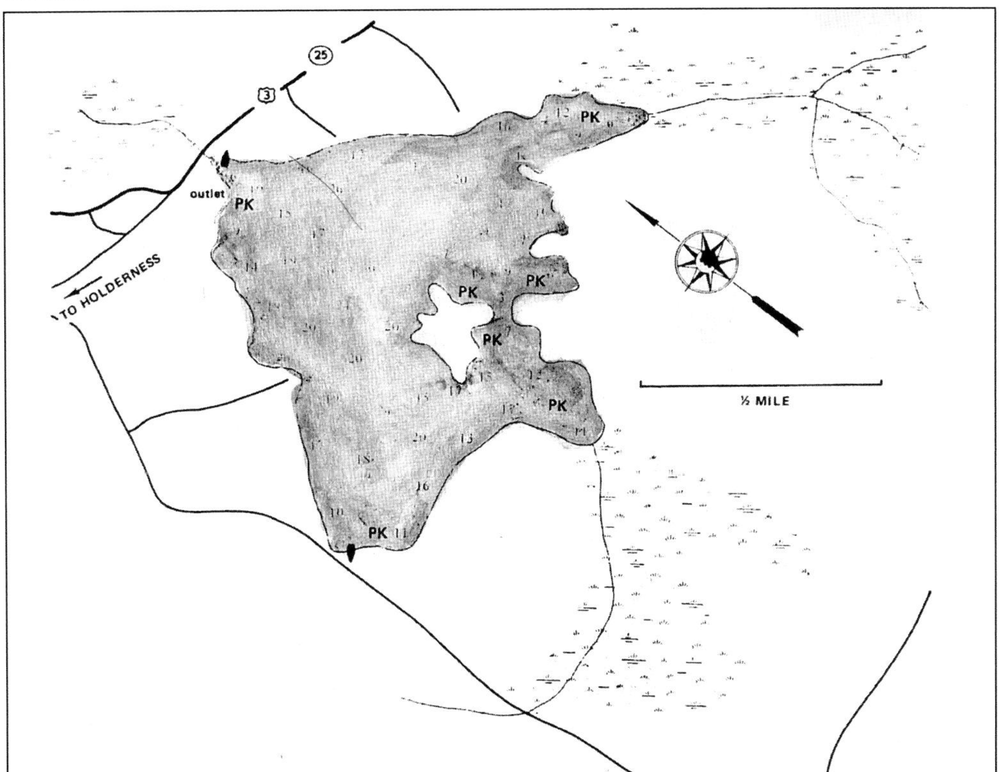

A Map of White Oak Pond (291 Acres), Holderness. This charming body of water, a stone's throw from Squam Lake, is an excellent spot for pickerel fishing.

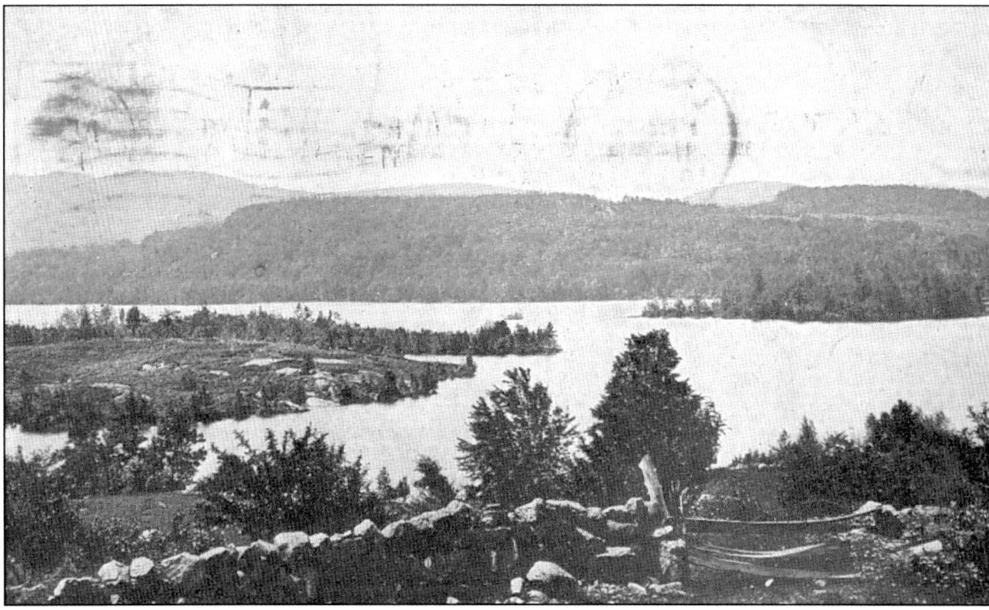

Wicwas Lake (328 Acres), from Smith's Corner, Meredith Center, 1916. This natural lake is well stocked with pickerel, yellow perch, bass, and horned pout.

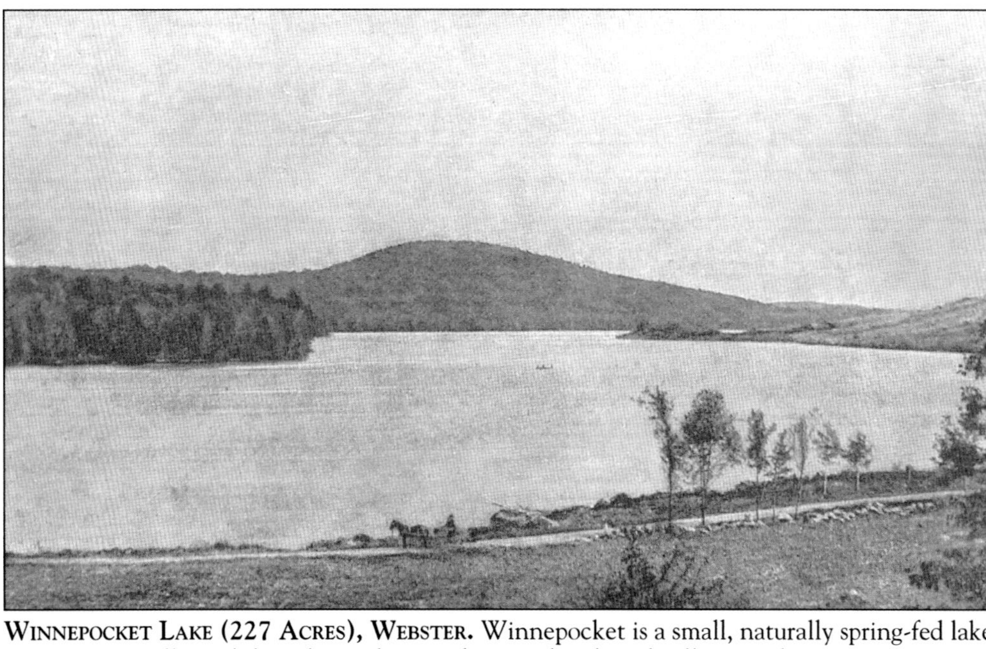

Winnepocket Lake (227 Acres), Webster. Winnepocket is a small, naturally spring-fed lake containing smallmouth bass, horned pout, chain pickerel, and yellow perch.

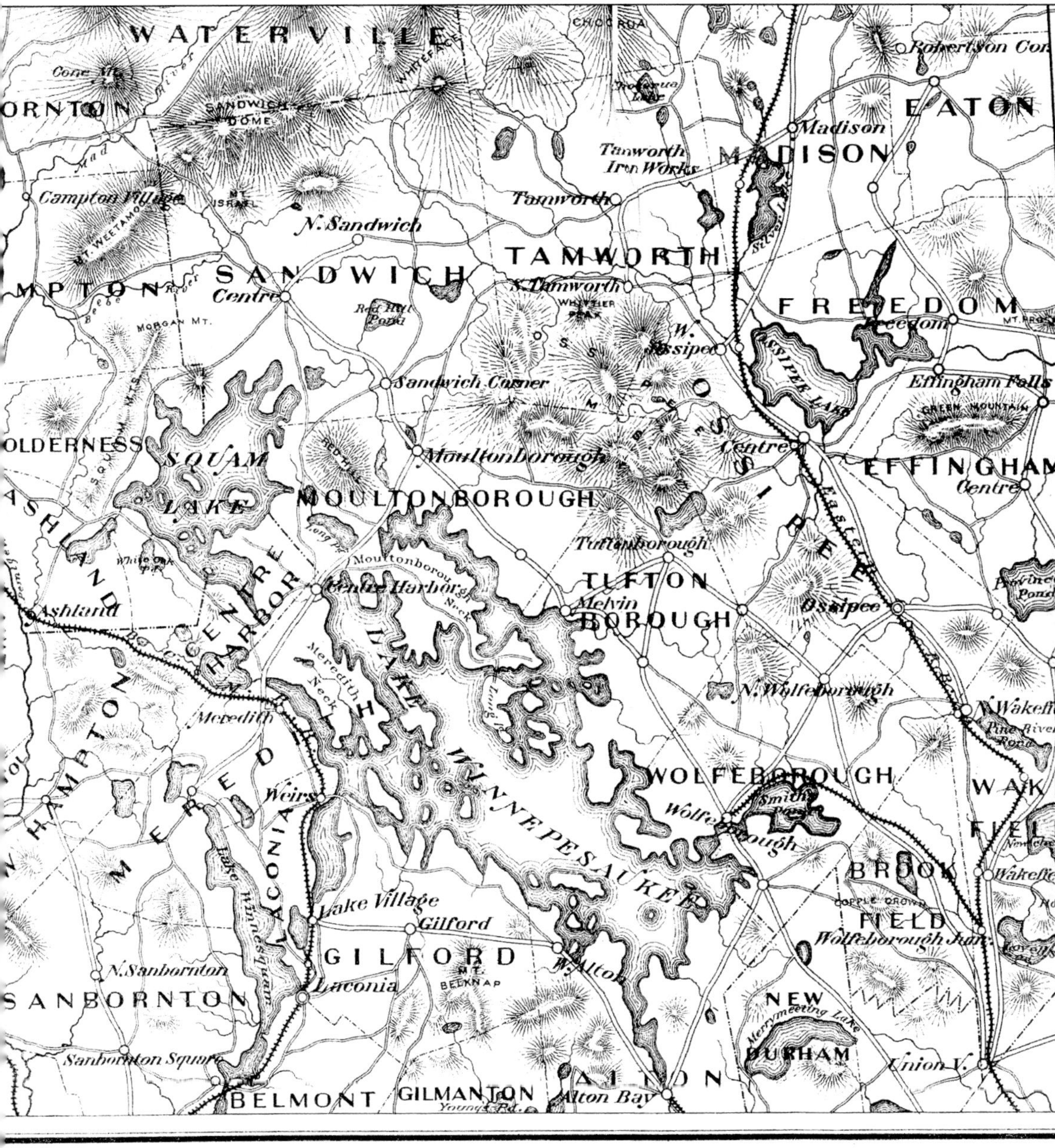

The Lake Country of New Hampshire

A Map of the Lakes Country of New Hampshire, 1876. More than 1,300 ponds, lakes, river systems, and brooks adorn our state's 9,341 square acres, all of which have their allure, whether it be the gleaming expanse of Winnipesaukee or the reflection of Squam Lake in Sandwich and Holderness. Many of New Hampshire's lakes, as seen on this map, are clustered in central New Hampshire and form what is known as the Lakes Region. This region is bounded on the south by Rochester and Pittsfield; on the west by Franklin and Bristol; on the north by Plymouth, Sandwich, Tamworth, and Madison; and on the east by Ossipee, Wakefield, and Milton.

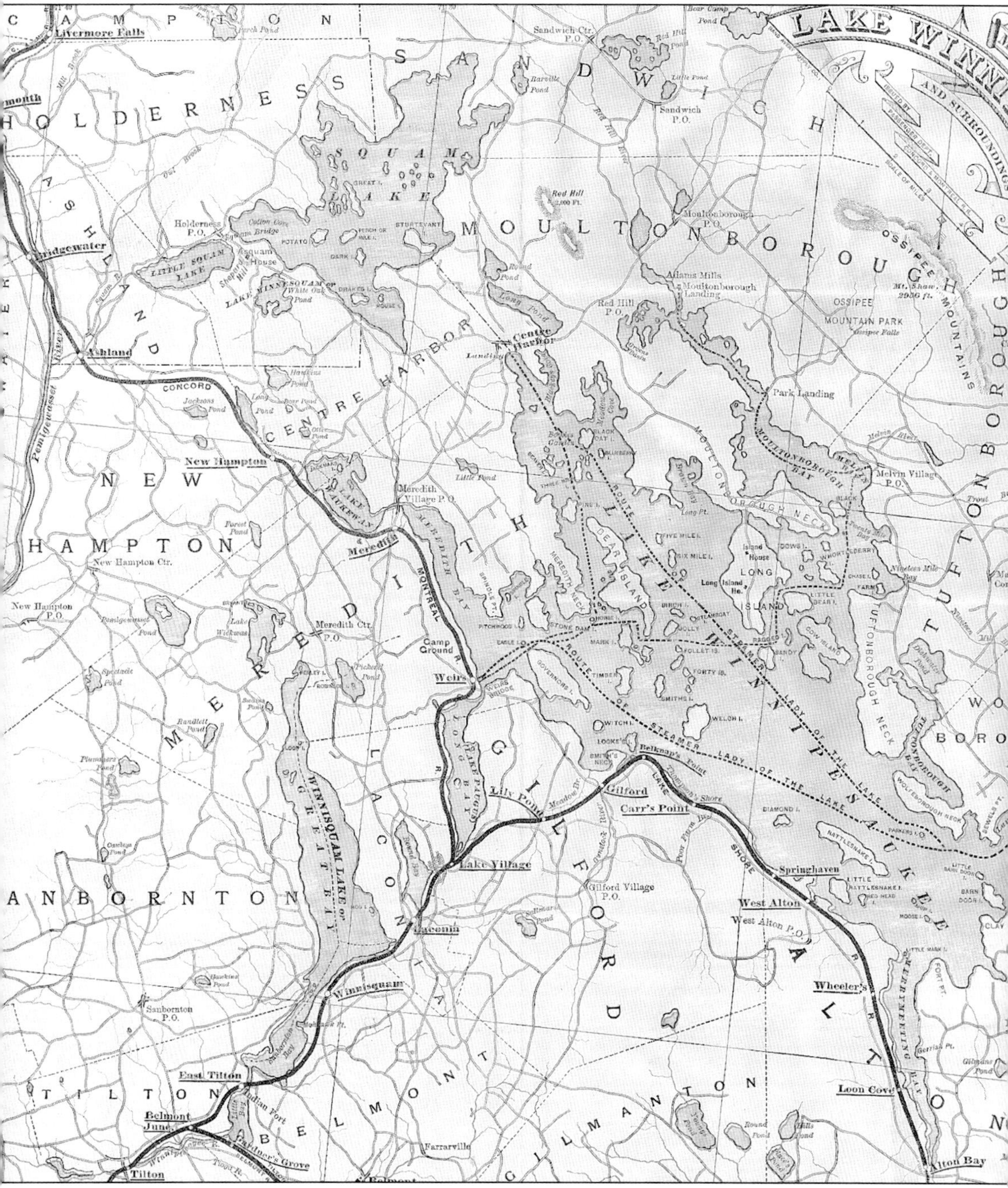

A MAP OF LAKE WINNIPESAUKEE AND SURROUNDINGS, 1890, (BOSTON: RAND AVERY). This map was issued by the Passenger Department of the Boston, Concord, & Montreal Railroad. People say that the best-known lakes are Winnipesaukee, Winnisquam, Squam, Newfound, Ossipee, Wentworth, Silver, Great East, Lovell, Crystal, Loon, Paugus, Webster, and Merrymeeting. For generations people have come to these lakes and ponds to spend their vacation in cottages beside the waters of their choice. The pictures that follow elaborate on Lake Winnipesaukee's many charms, which have made it the magnetic center of the state.

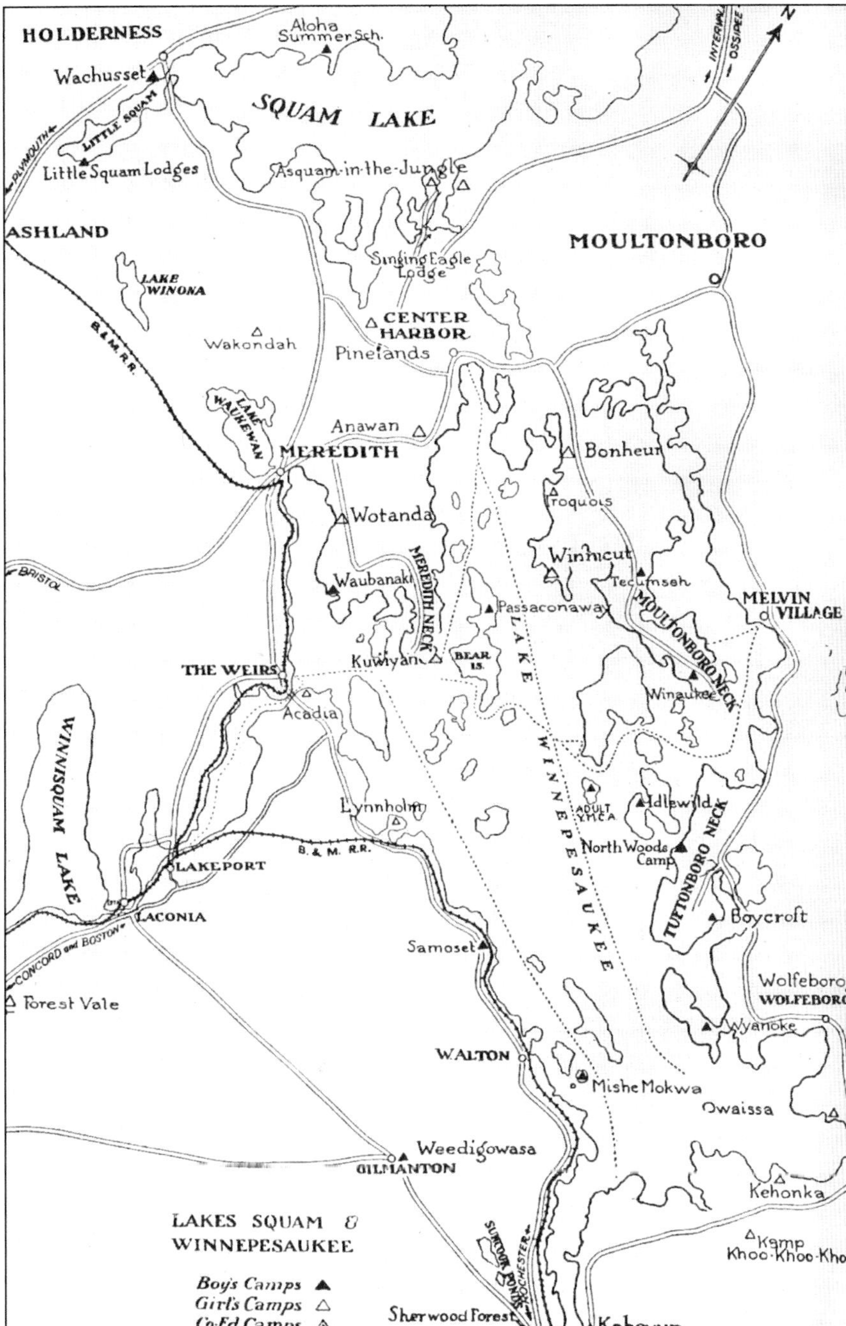

A Map of the Lakes Region, 1931. This map indicates the locations of the organized and summer camps on Lakes Squam and Winnipesaukee. During the 1930s, there were more than 72 camps in the Lakes Region, and by 1950 there were 218 camps in the entire state, housing 23,000 young people and 3,000 counselors. It is interesting to note that Camp Chocorua, the first boys' camp, was organized on Squam Lake in 1881. The first girls' camp was organized on Newfound Lake in 1900. The first boys' camp on Lake Winnipesaukee was Camp Idlewild on Cow Island. New Hampshire was the birthplace of the organized camp movement.

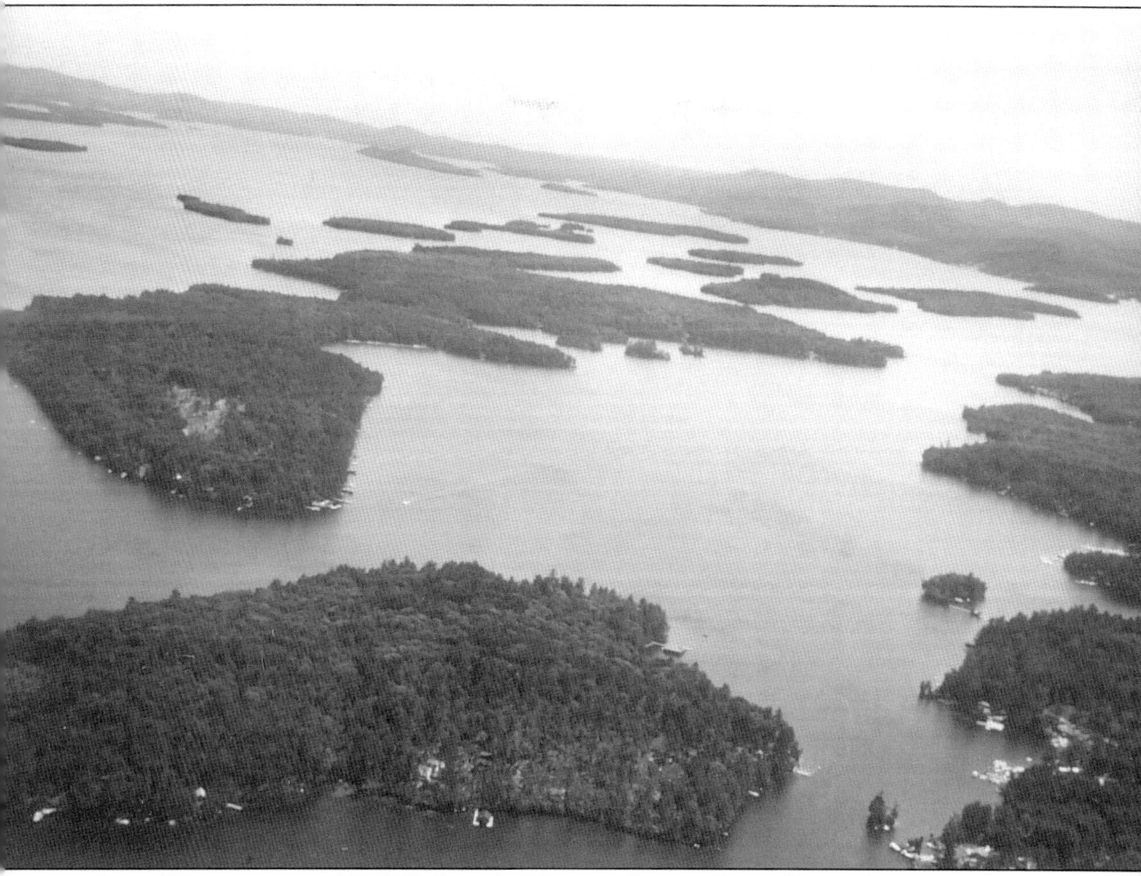

LAKE WINNIPESAUKEE (44,586 ACRES). This aerial view shows the southern exposure of the massive lake, featuring Bear Island in the center. This glacially formed lake is bounded by the towns of Alton, Center Harbor, Gilford, Laconia, Meredith, Moultonboro, Tuftonboro, and Wolfeboro. It is a natural spring-fed lake with an area of 72 square miles. Winnipesaukee, New Hampshire's largest lake, has a mainland shoreline of 186 miles with a length of approximately 23 miles and a width ranging from 1 to 9 miles. It is a large freshwater lake that is very irregular in form, with three bays on the western side, one on the northern side, and three on the eastern side.

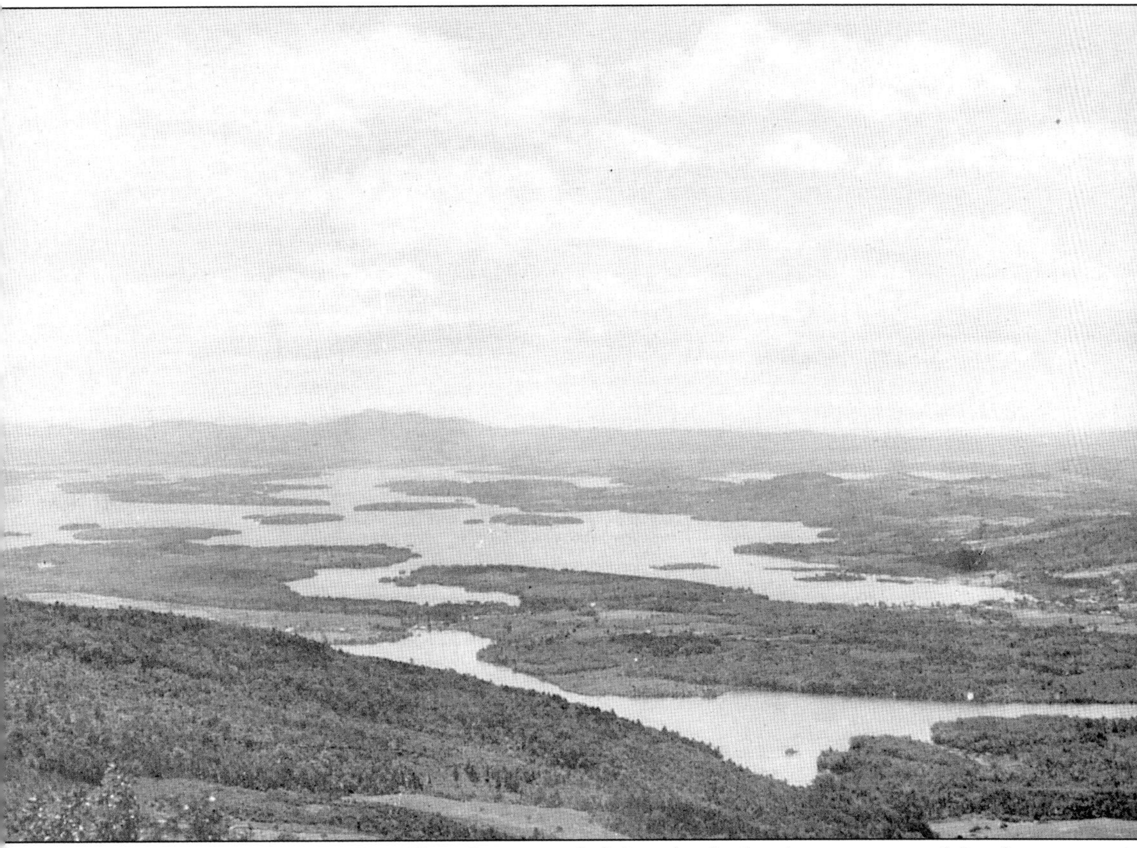

Lake Winnipesaukee from Red Hill. It is recorded that this body of water is one of the three largest freshwater lakes in the continental United States that lies wholly within the borders of one state. This lake, one of the most scenic areas in the world, is dotted with 274 habitable islands and surrounded by the foothills of the White Mountains. Islands in the lake range in size from those of more than 1,000 acres to tiny dots of rock and turf that are scarcely large enough to hold a small summer camp.

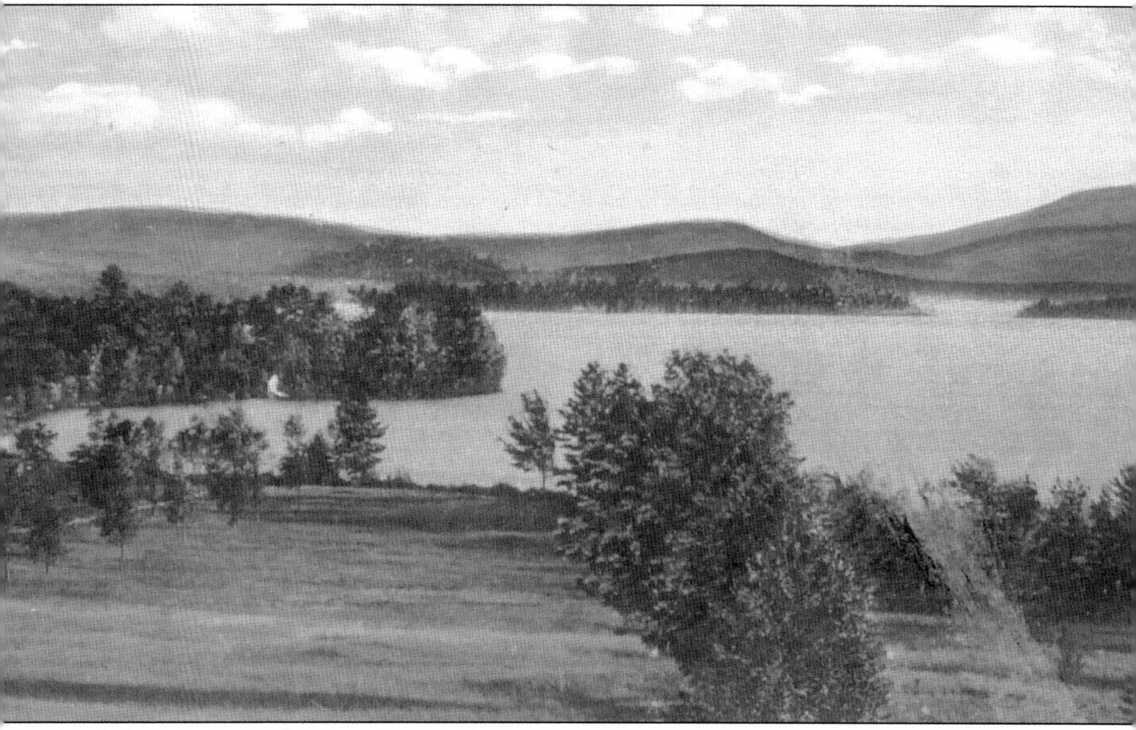

A Panoramic View of Lake Winnipesaukee, Looking Northeast from Gilford. Rattlesnake Island is on the right, with the Ossipee Mountain Range in the background. Nothing can exceed the beauty of the mountains on the north shore: they are the Ossipee,

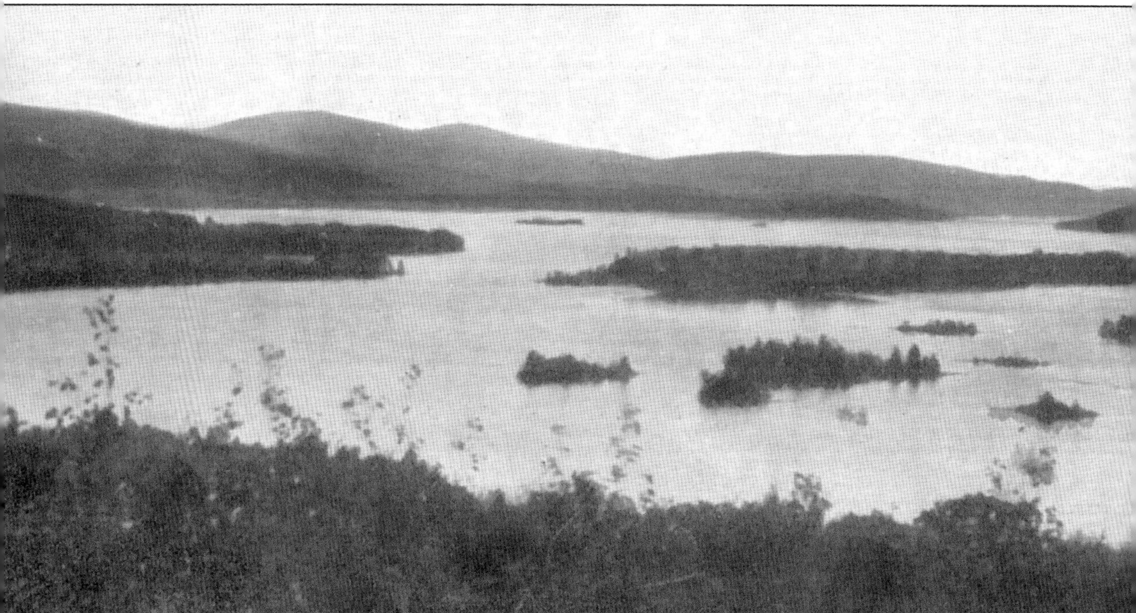

A Panoramic View of Lake Winnipesaukee, Looking Northeast from Wolfeboro. In the background is Rattlesnake Island, with the Belknap Mountain Range on the far left. An examination of a topographical map indicates that, at one time, the Belknap and Ossipee

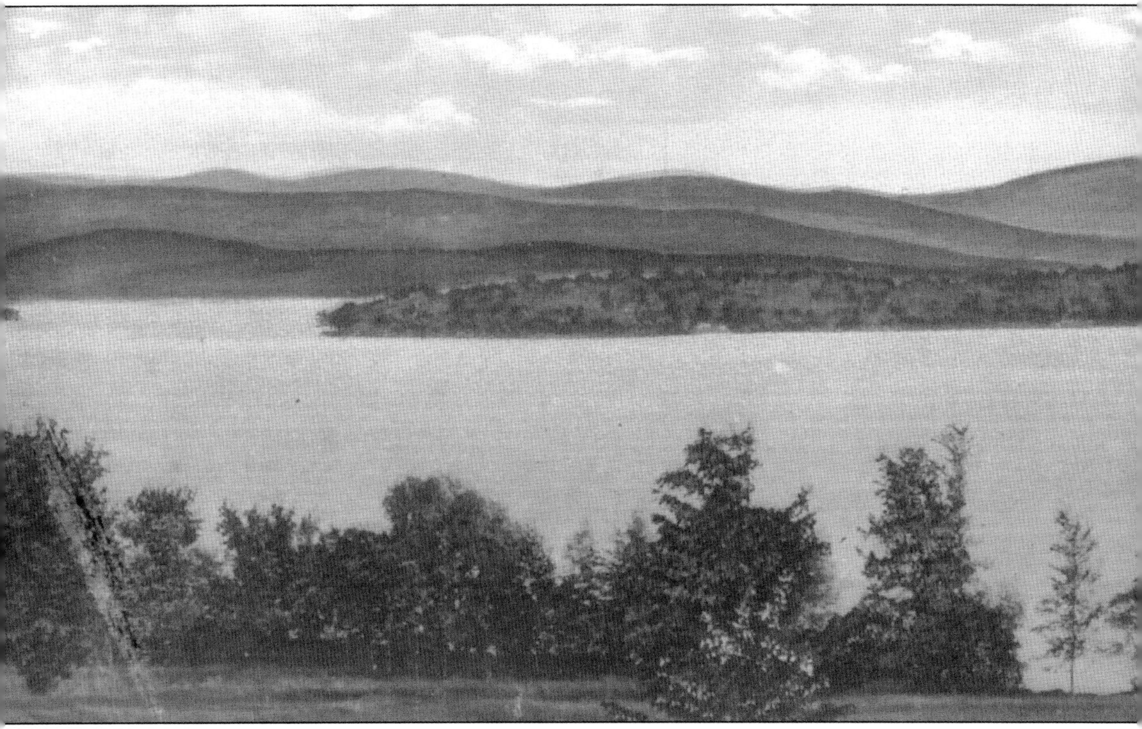

Sandwich, and Presidential Ranges in the White Mountains, framing the water's edge. The waters of Winnipesaukee empty into the Winnipesaukee River, which joins the Pemigewasset River. These two rivers unite to form the Merrimack River at Franklin Falls.

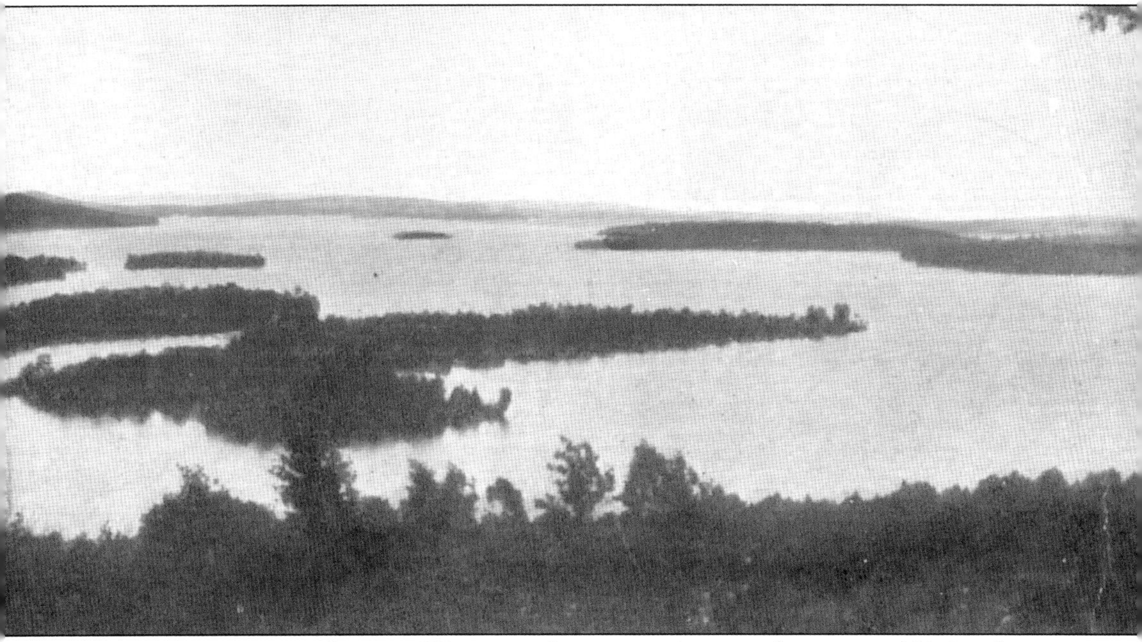

Mountains were active volcanoes. Winnipesaukee is very deep, in places up to 200 feet deep, and is mostly spring fed. Many of the cottages around its shores take their water directly from the lake without any treatment.

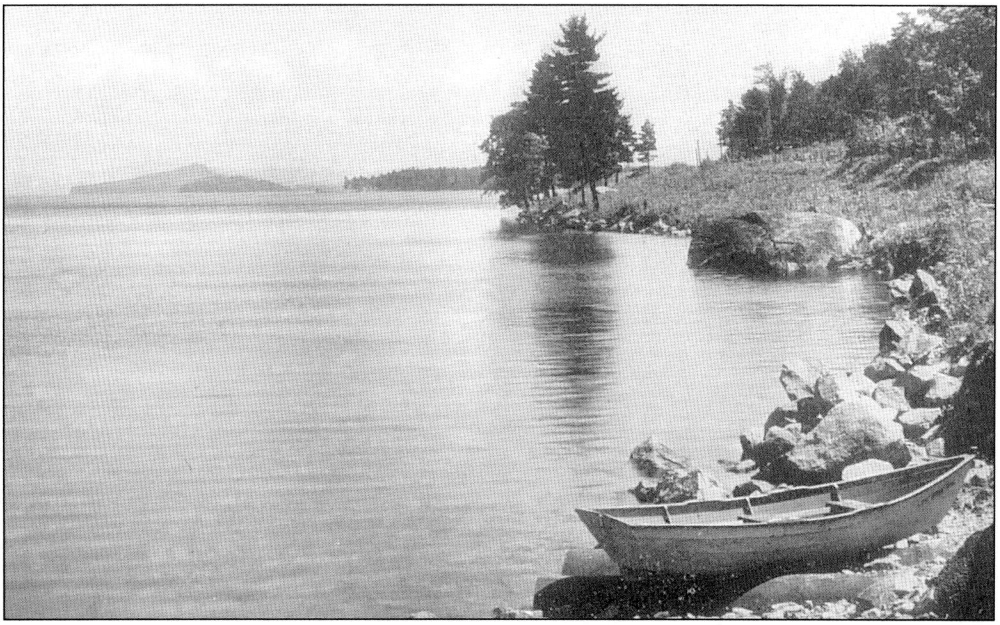

LAKE WINNIPESAUKEE AT BELKNAP POINT, LOOKING SOUTHEAST TOWARD RATTLESNAKE ISLAND. Along the shores of this beautiful lake, countless summers cottages and camps cluster themselves in the pines to take advantage of the lake's cool breezes and the mountain vistas.

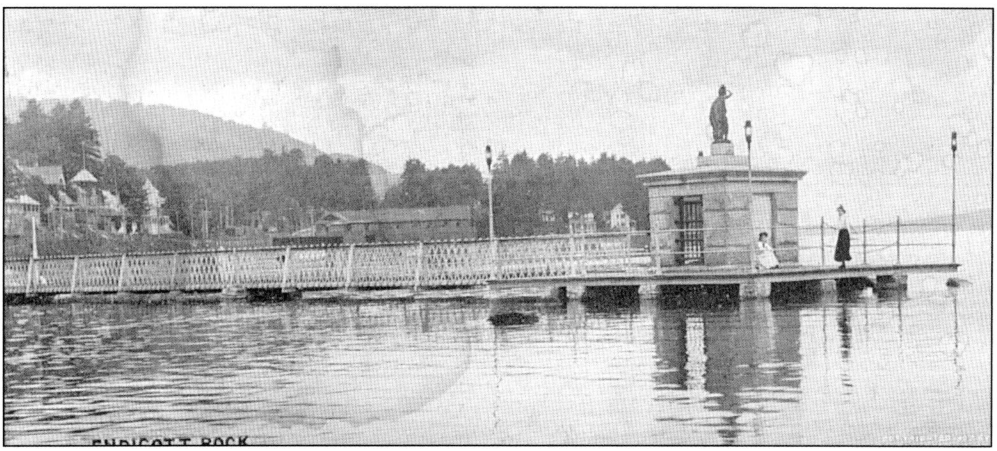

LAKE WINNIPESAUKEE (ALTITUDE 504 FEET), ENDICOTT ROCK MONUMENT. Winnipesaukee was known to the Native Americans, who first inhabited its shore, as the "smile of the Great Spirit." A proper translation of the name, however, means "beautiful water in a high place." Still another translation is derived from *Wiwininebesaki*, meaning "the lake in the vicinity of which there are other lakes and ponds," or perhaps "the Lakes Region." This particular location was called the Weirs. The Weirs derived its name from an Indian fishing weir located near Endicott Rock. The Indian village Aquadoctan was located on the hills to the north, and west and was the largest Indian village in this region. The ruins of the Weirs, which was a triangular enclosure of rocks and logs used for trapping fish, could at one time be seen in the waters just north of Endicott Rock Monument. These stones, which once held the uprights of the wooden fish weirs in place, showed the first settlers where the original Indian fish weirs were located. The stones were used in 1766 to make a wing dam for Ebenezer Smith's sawmill, which had been constructed on the Gilmanton side of the channel the preceding autumn.

LAKE WINNIPESAUKEE. The lake was discovered by white men in 1652—a party of surveyors seeking the source of the Merrimack River to mark the northern boundary of the Massachusetts Bay Colony. The men placed the boundary at the Indian village of Aquadoctan, which is now the Weirs, and marked it on the boulder now enshrined there as Endicott Rock. Although there are 144 different spellings of Winnipesaukee on record, the present spelling was established by an act of the New Hampshire legislature in 1931 and approved by the U.S. Geographical Board in 1933.

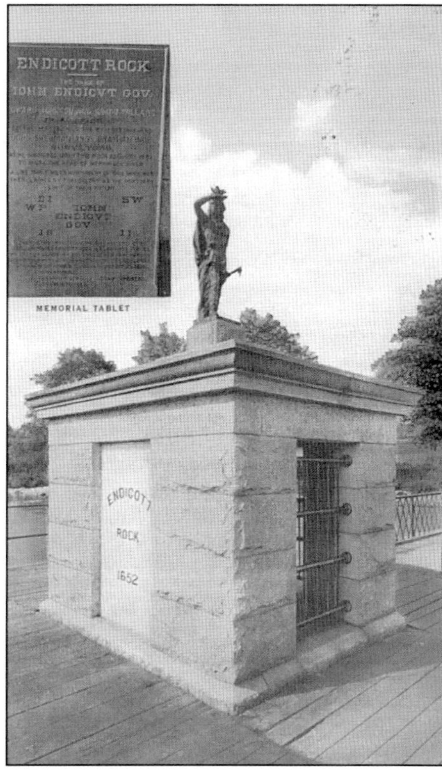

LAKE WINNIPESAUKEE, ROBERTS COVE, MEREDITH. The lake freezes over during the winter months. Ice begins to form between Christmas and New Year's and breaks up about mid-April. During a very cold winter, ice as deep as 30 inches can cover the lake.

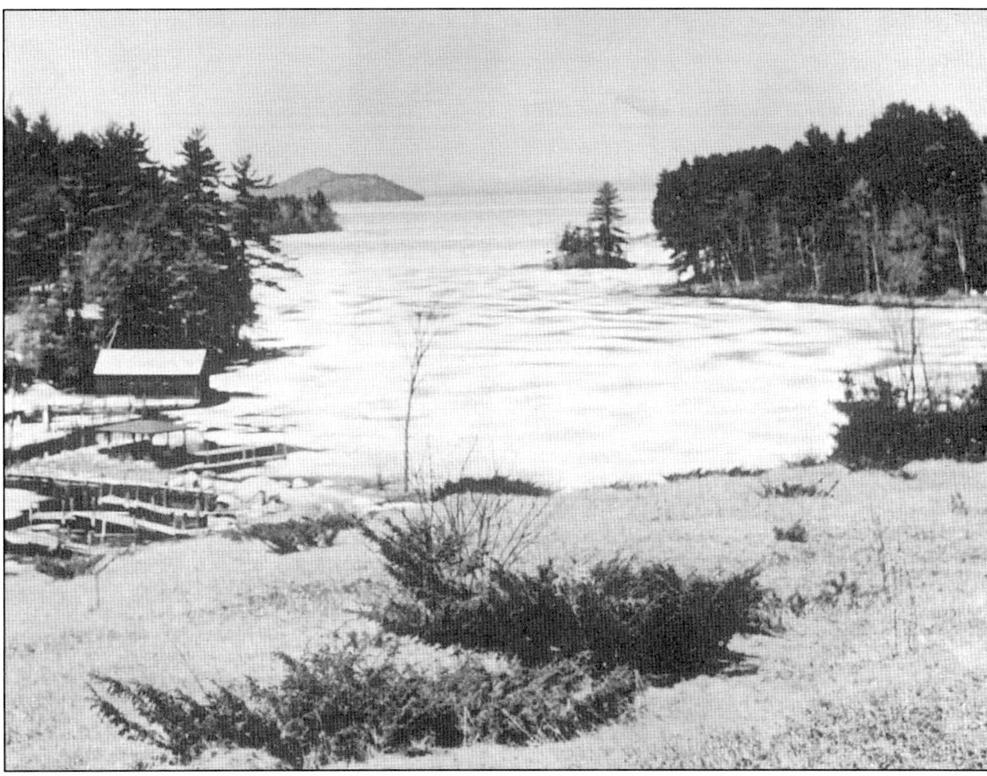

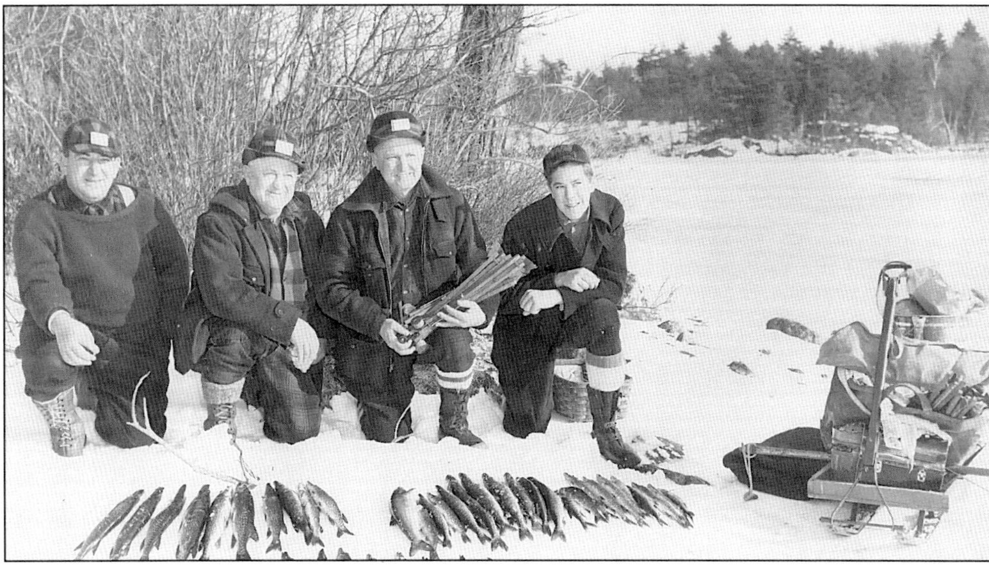

ICE FISHING, LAKE WINNIPESAUKEE. One of the favorite winter sports is ice fishing. The lake is stocked with salmon, which are taken from early spring through the summer months. Lake trout, native to the lake, are caught from January 1 through September 30. Smelt, whitefish, smallmouth bass, yellow perch, horned pout, suckers, and chain pickerel are all taken in season. Four proud fishermen display their prize fish caught in Lake Winnipesaukee at Greene's Basin, Moultonboro in 1950. From left to right, they are William Luffenberger, Alfred Nicol, Wilfred Nicol, and Maurice Nicol of Manchester.

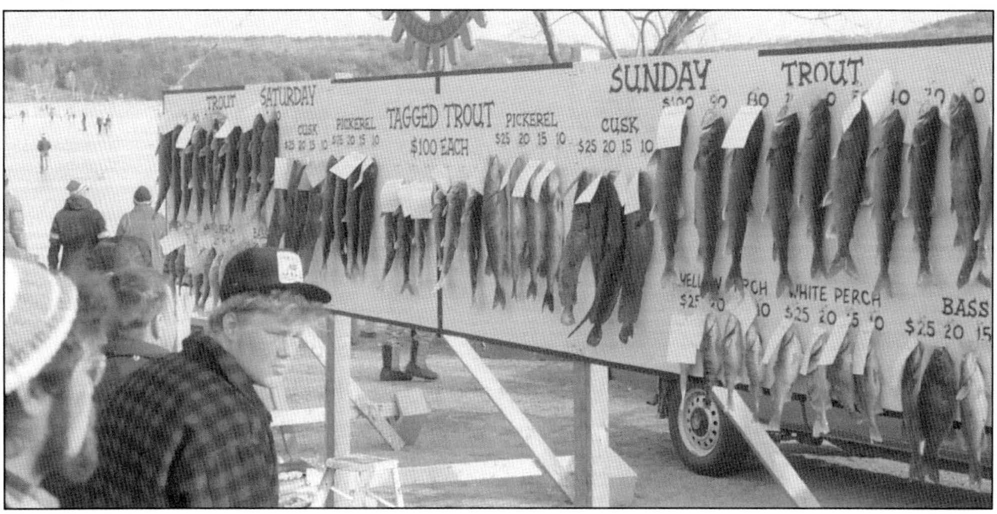

THE BIG FISH. For the past 21 years, the Meredith Rotary Club has sponsored the Great Rotary Club Fishing Derby as an annual fundraiser for the many projects of the club. This derby is usually conducted during the first half of February each year and attracts thousands of participants from all over the east coast of the United States and Canada. Pictured is the display board of caught fish by weight and size. The person who catches the big fish get the big money. Among the prizewinning fish that have been caught in Lake Winnipesaukee over the years are a lake whitefish weighing 5 pounds and 1 ounce and measuring 21.75 inches, in 1974; a white perch weighing 3 pounds 11.5 ounces and measuring 17.2 inches, in 1986; and a fall fish weighing 3 pounds 8.96 ounces and measuring 20.75 inches.

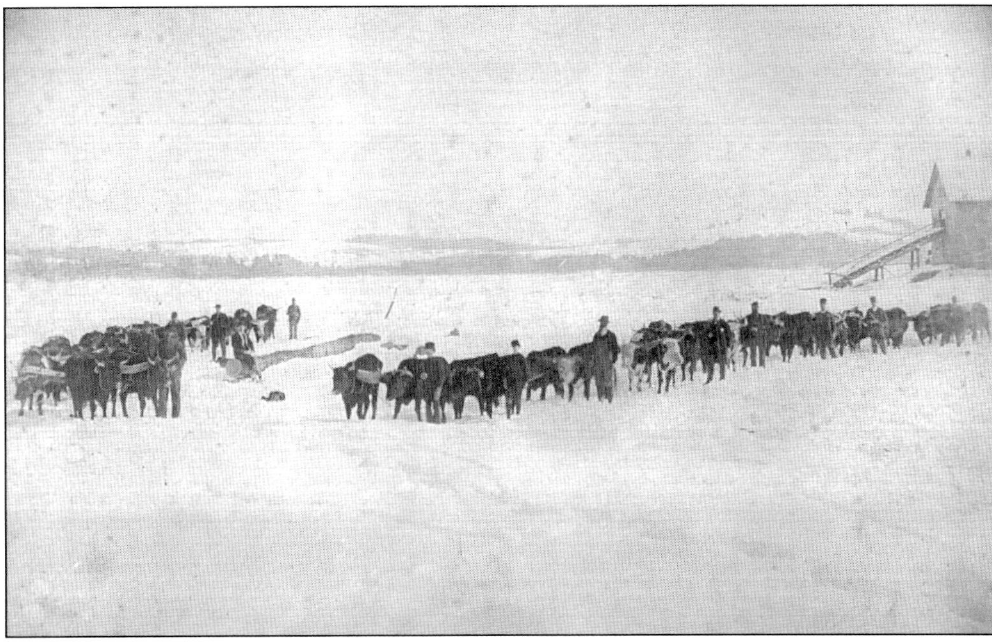

THE OLD TOWN TEAM ON MEREDITH BAY, 1880S. The Shook Lumber Company can be seen on the right. The team was used to break roads throughout the town. Today, the site of the lumber company is the location of St. Charles Catholic Church.

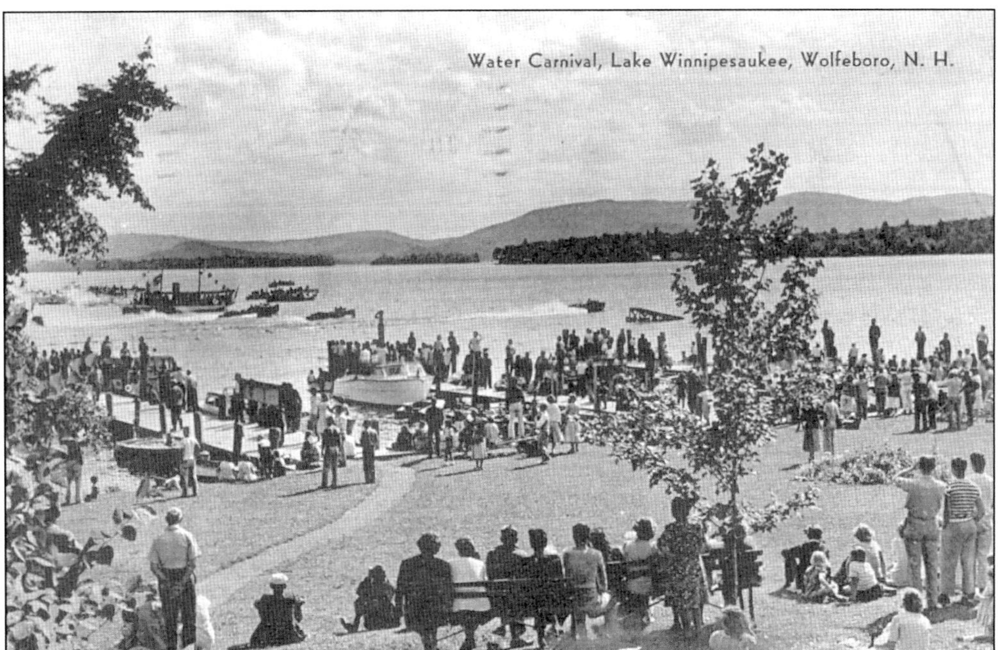

A 1951 WINTER CARNIVAL, WOLFEBORO BAY. Skiing, iceboating, skating, and ice fishing combine to make the Lakes Region more than just a summer vacation destination.

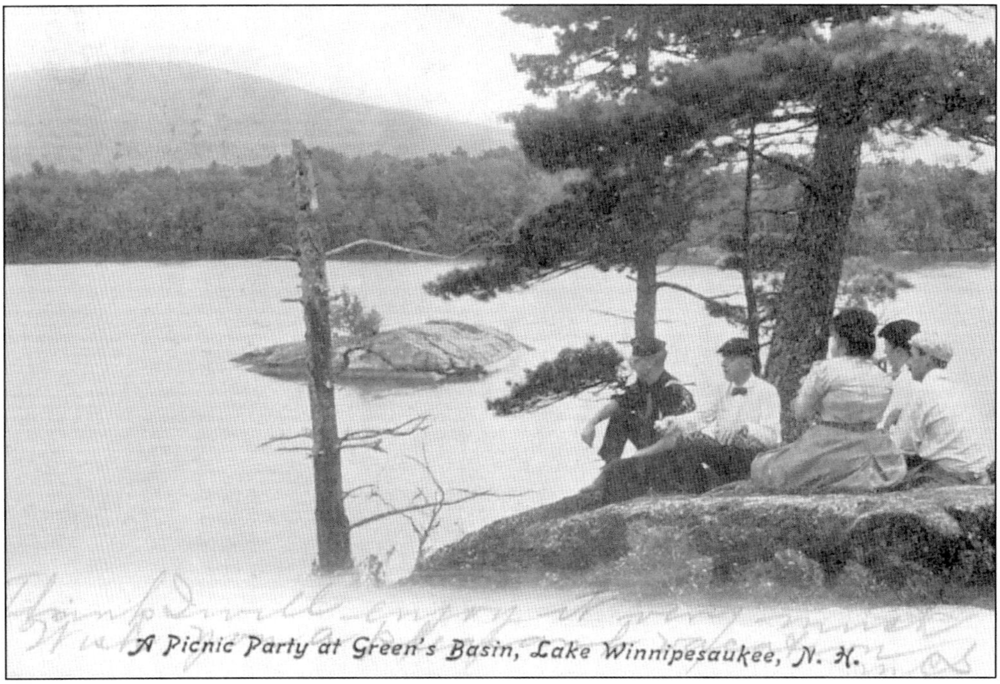

A PICNIC AT GREEN'S BASIN, LAKE WINNIPESAUKEE, MOULTONBORO, 1910. In the Lakes Region, visitors can find the exact vacation spot suited to their temperament. This view shows quiet seclusion on the shores of Winnipesaukee.

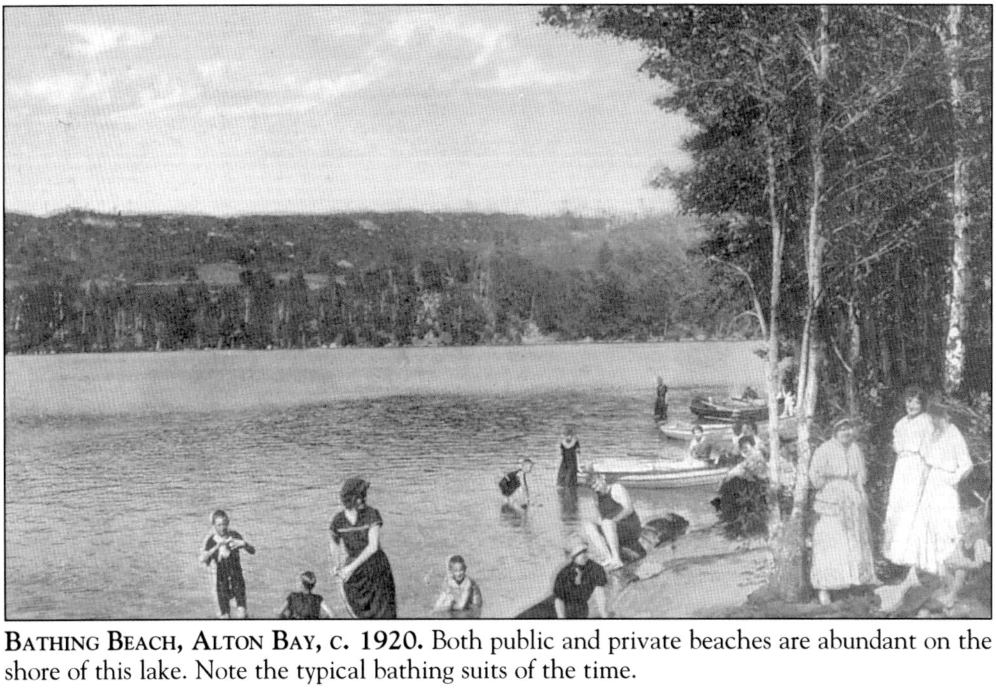

BATHING BEACH, ALTON BAY, C. 1920. Both public and private beaches are abundant on the shore of this lake. Note the typical bathing suits of the time.

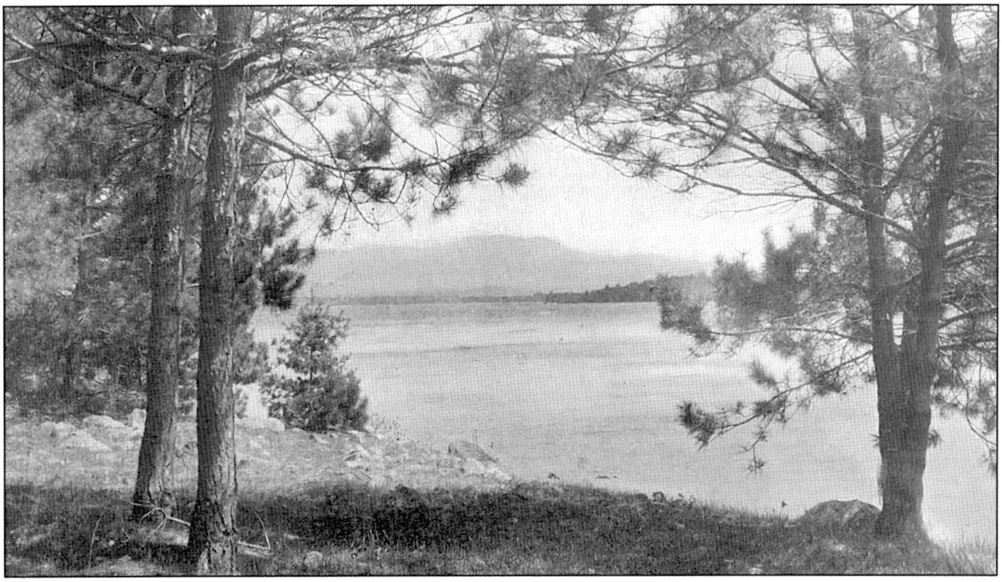

Mountain View, from Bear Island. When fall comes to the Lakes Region, the beauty of the area takes on new splendor. The hillsides, startling in their autumn colors, are set off splendidly by the deep blue waters of the lakes that bathe their feet.

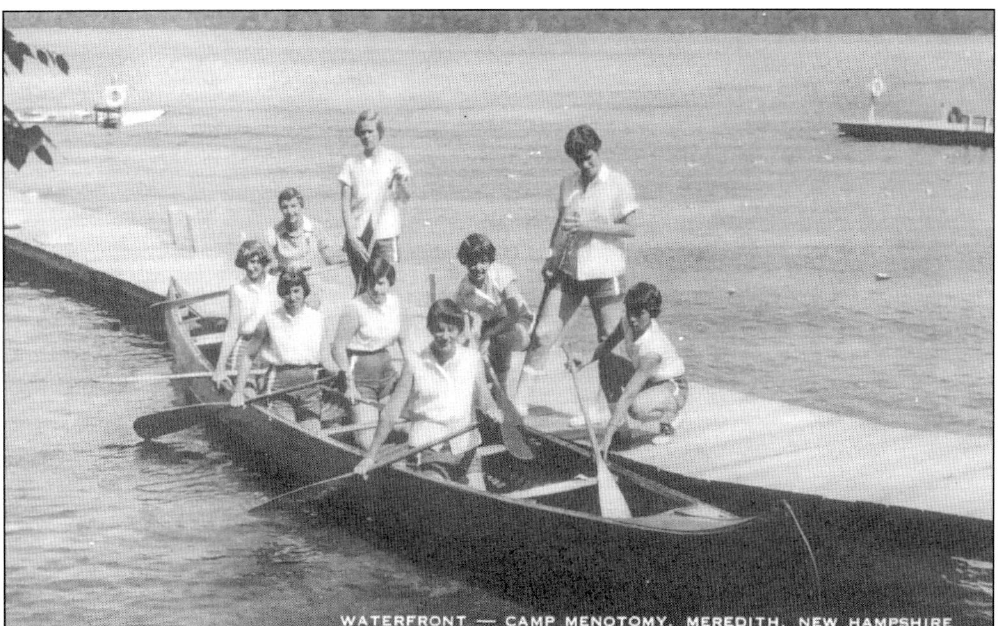

Camp Menotomy, Lake Winnipesaukee, Meredith. Campers prepare to make a canoe trip across the lake.

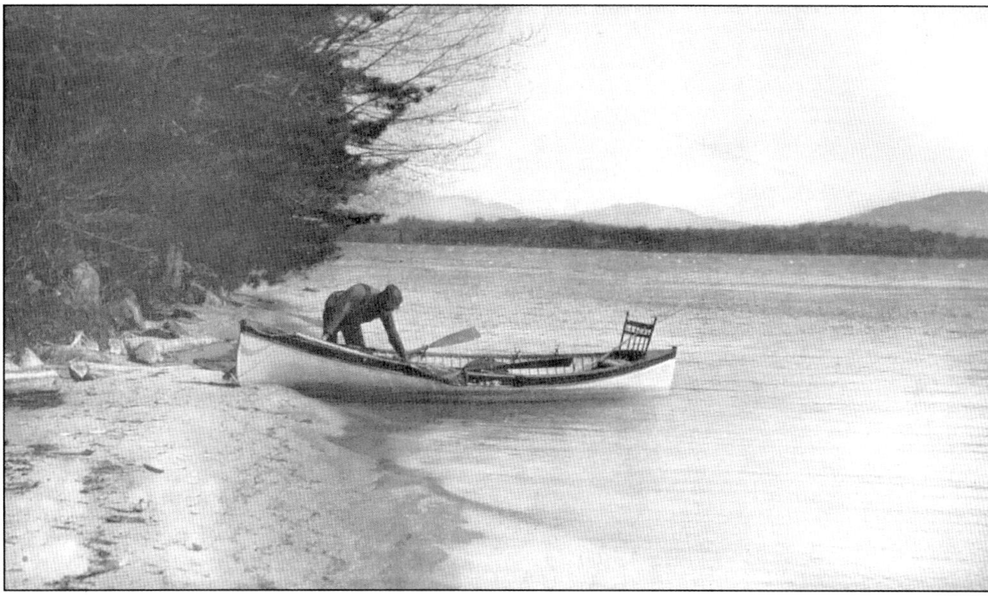

Bear Island, Ready for Fishing. New Hampshire's lakes and ponds offer excellent fishing of almost every type. In Winnipesaukee, lake trout is the most popular type of fishing.

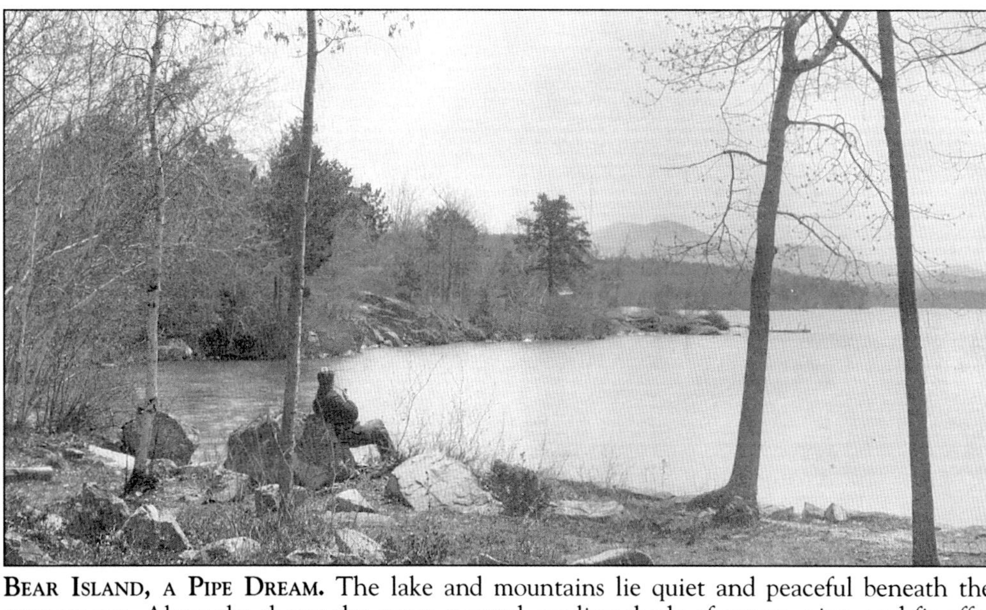

Bear Island, a Pipe Dream. The lake and mountains lie quiet and peaceful beneath the summer sun. Along the shores the sweet-scented, cooling shade of spruce, pine, and fir offer rest and contentment for all.

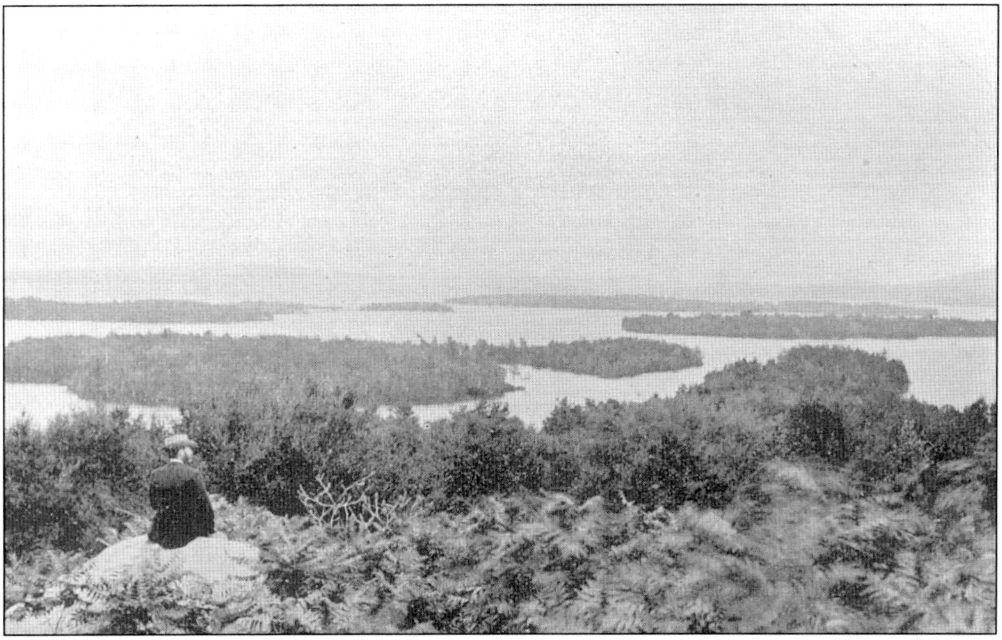

LAKE WINNIPESAUKEE, FROM MARK ISLAND. Here is perfect harmony in nature; there is no room for disturbing thoughts, no place for worry or care—just rest, and peace.

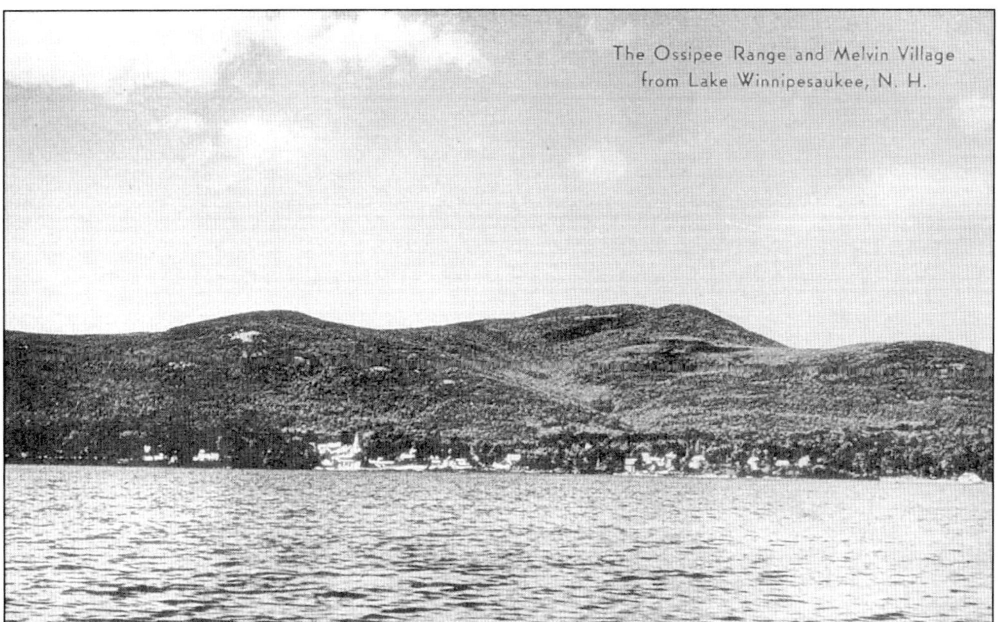

THE OSSIPEE RANGE AND MELVIN VILLAGE, FROM LAKE WINNIPESAUKEE, 1945. For peace and contentment, New Hampshire is unequaled, with its broad and fertile valleys, its mountain sanctuaries, and its people's hospitality.

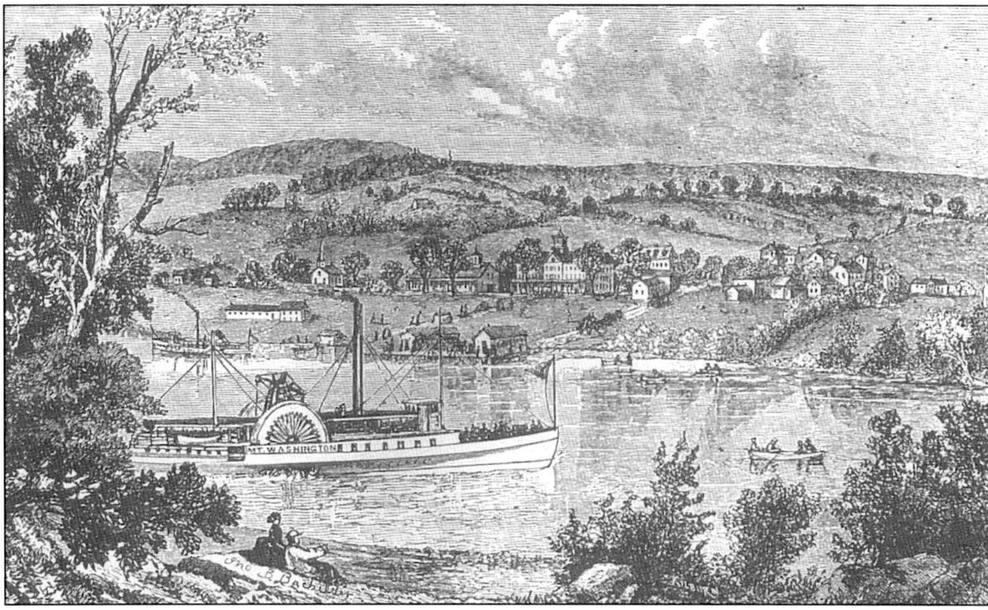

Wolfeboro Bay. The Lakes Region is recognized as the oldest summer resort in America, for it was to the heart of this region that Gov. John Wentworth came from Portsmouth before the Revolution to build a summer home overlooking the waters of the lake in Wolfeboro that is now named for him.

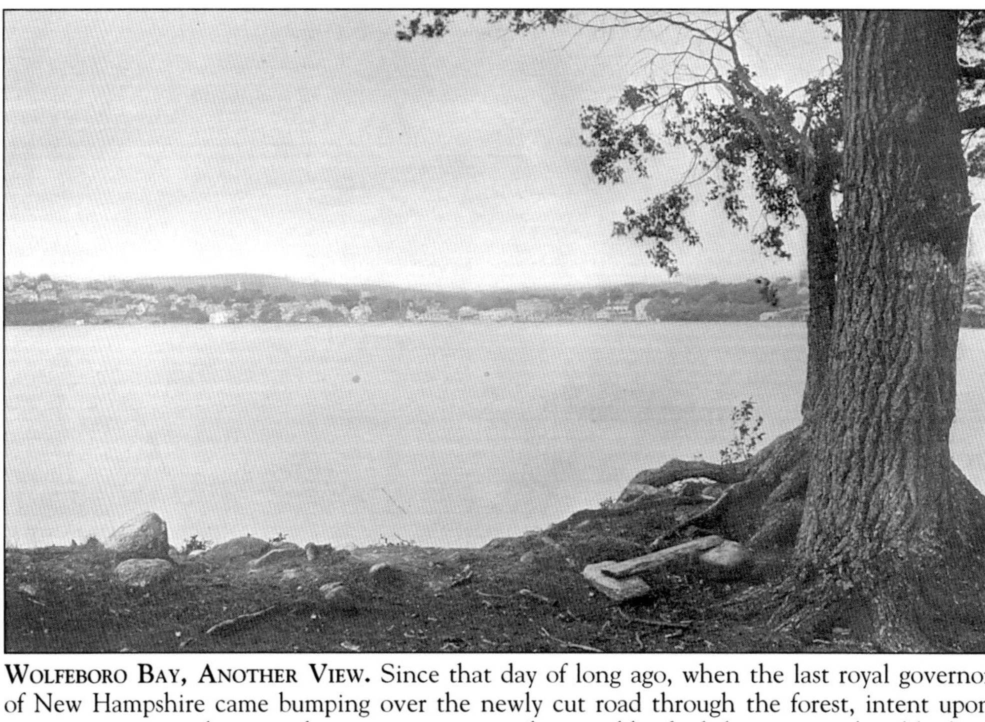

Wolfeboro Bay, Another View. Since that day of long ago, when the last royal governor of New Hampshire came bumping over the newly cut road through the forest, intent upon creating a summer home and passing a vacation that would refresh him in mind and body, a steadily increasing number of people, with similar intent, have journeyed into this area. Now, the Lakes Region is a year-round vacation area.

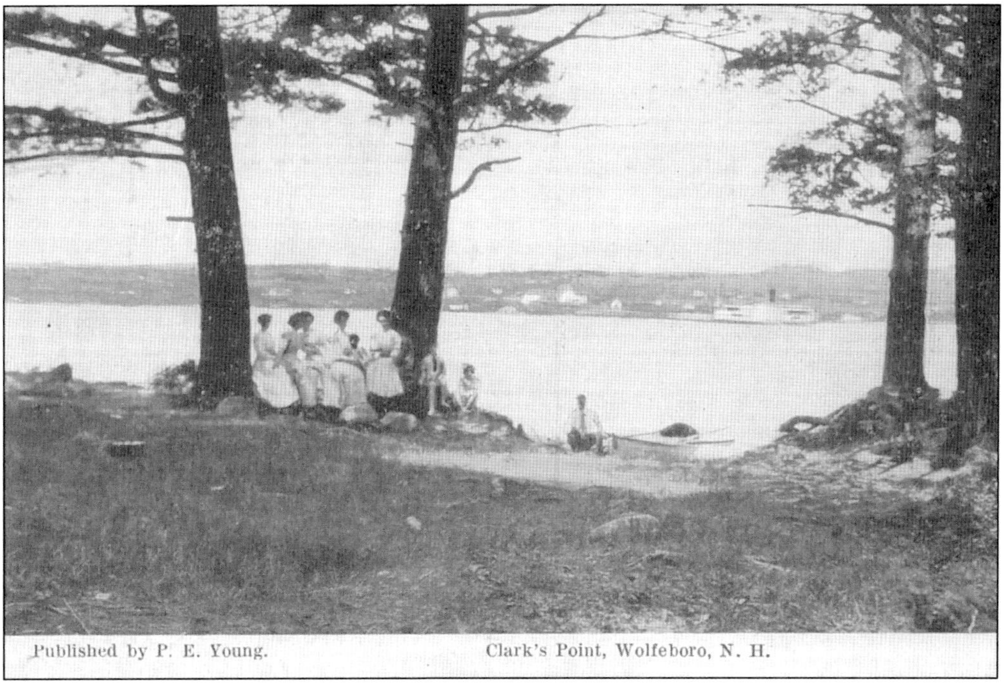

CLARK'S POINT, WOLFEBORO BAY. The steamer *Mount Washington* is seen at the public docks in the early 1900s. From 1872 to the present, the *Mount Washington* has made Wolfeboro its daily port of call.

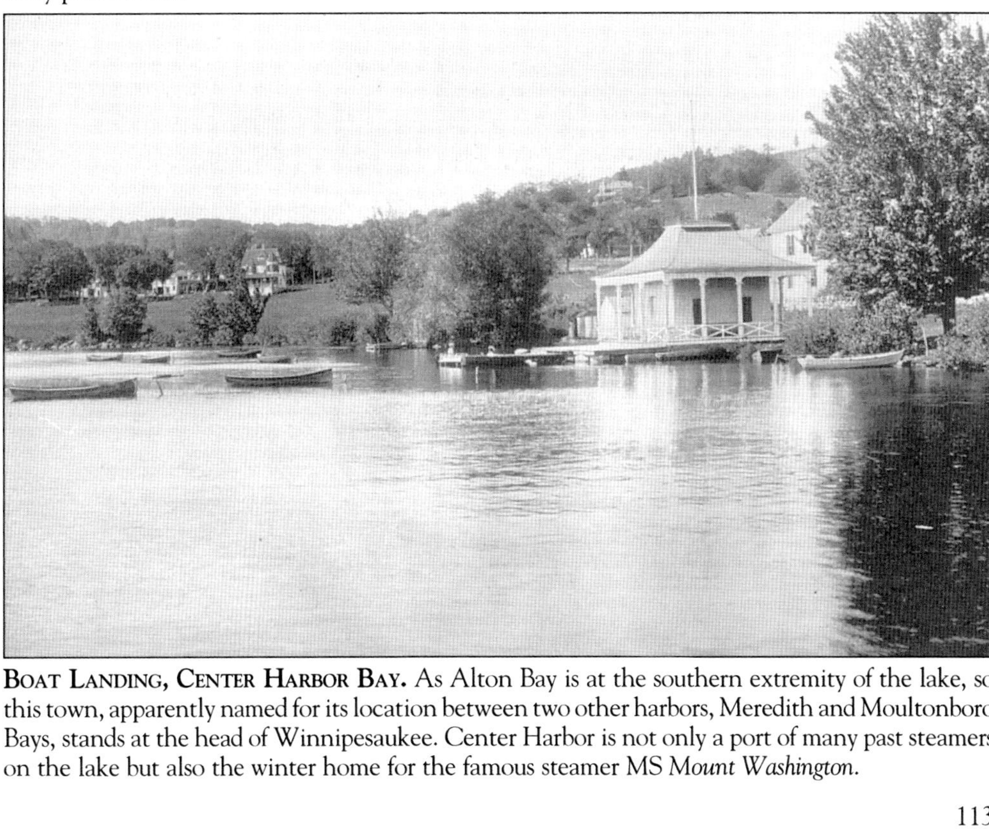

BOAT LANDING, CENTER HARBOR BAY. As Alton Bay is at the southern extremity of the lake, so this town, apparently named for its location between two other harbors, Meredith and Moultonboro Bays, stands at the head of Winnipesaukee. Center Harbor is not only a port of many past steamers on the lake but also the winter home for the famous steamer MS *Mount Washington*.

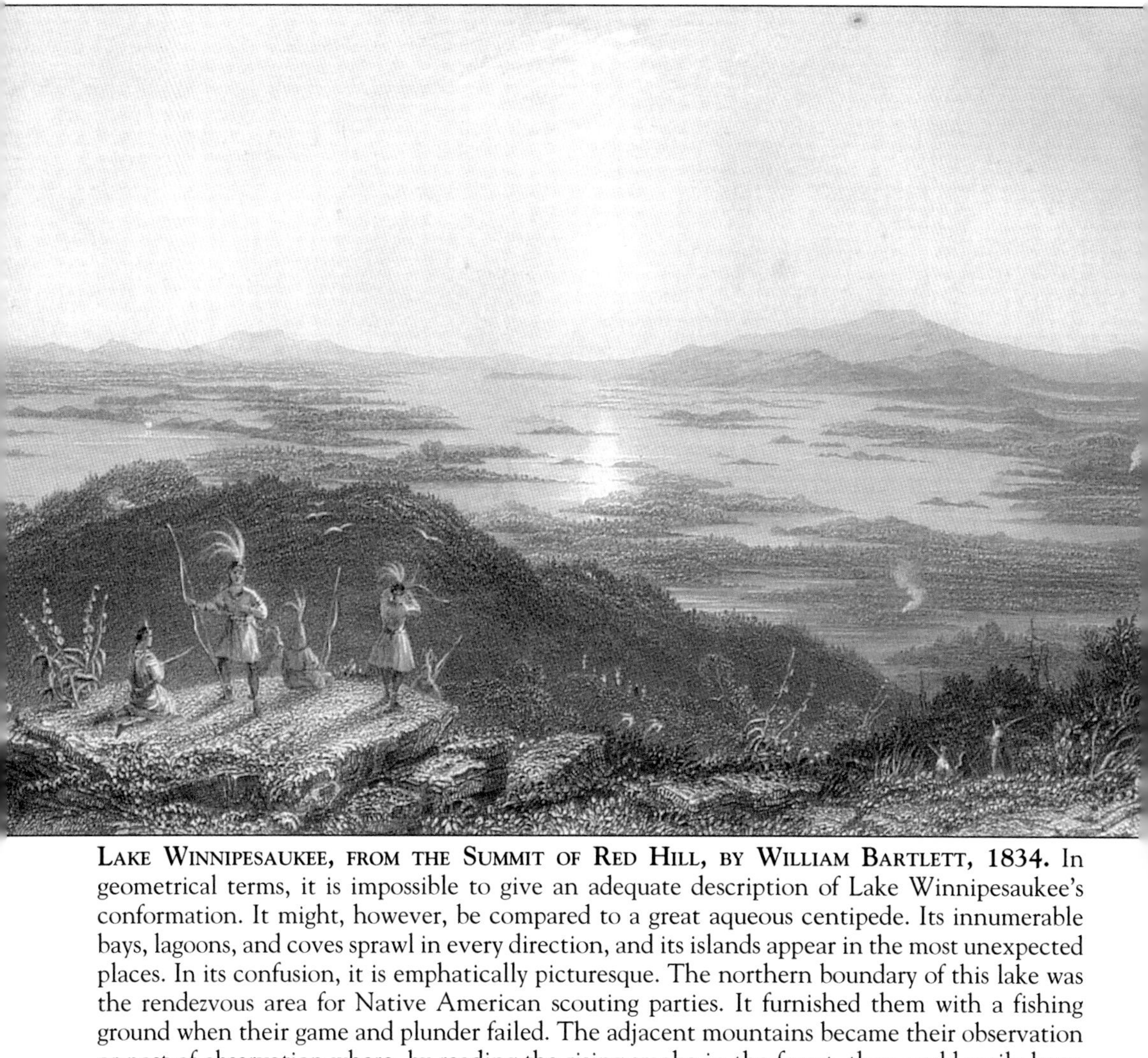

LAKE WINNIPESAUKEE, FROM THE SUMMIT OF RED HILL, BY WILLIAM BARTLETT, 1834. In geometrical terms, it is impossible to give an adequate description of Lake Winnipesaukee's conformation. It might, however, be compared to a great aqueous centipede. Its innumerable bays, lagoons, and coves sprawl in every direction, and its islands appear in the most unexpected places. In its confusion, it is emphatically picturesque. The northern boundary of this lake was the rendezvous area for Native American scouting parties. It furnished them with a fishing ground when their game and plunder failed. The adjacent mountains became their observation or post of observation where, by reading the rising smoke in the forest, they could easily learn the position of every new settler throughout a vast region.

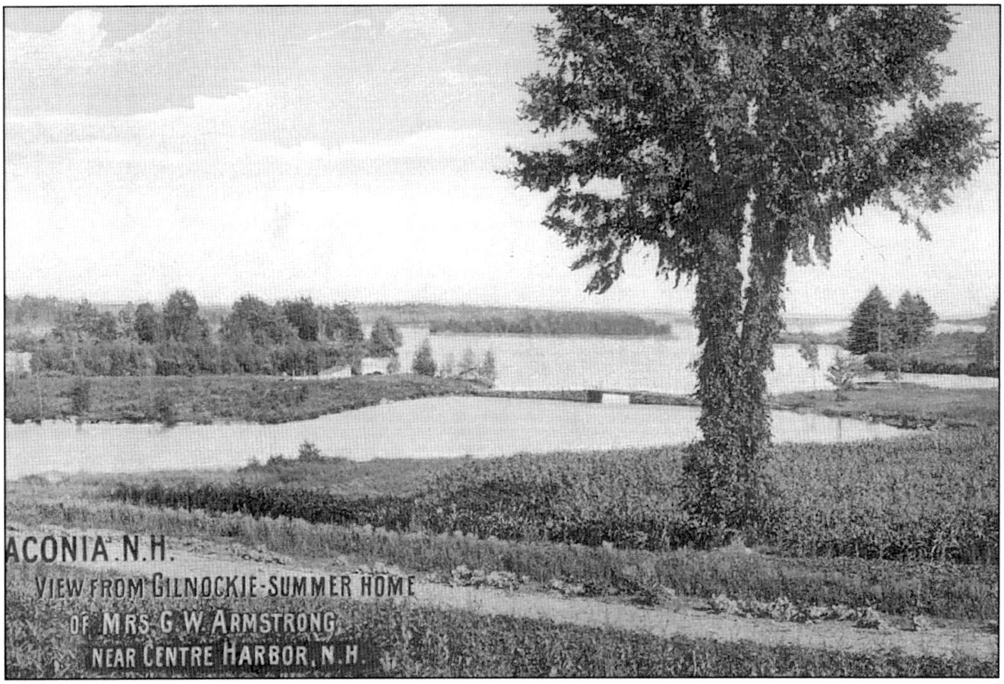

HALF-MILE ISLAND. This island, owned by Mrs. G.W. Armstrong, is located in Center Harbor. The 1916 photograph was taken from the Gilnockie summer home. The connecting bridge to the island no longer exists.

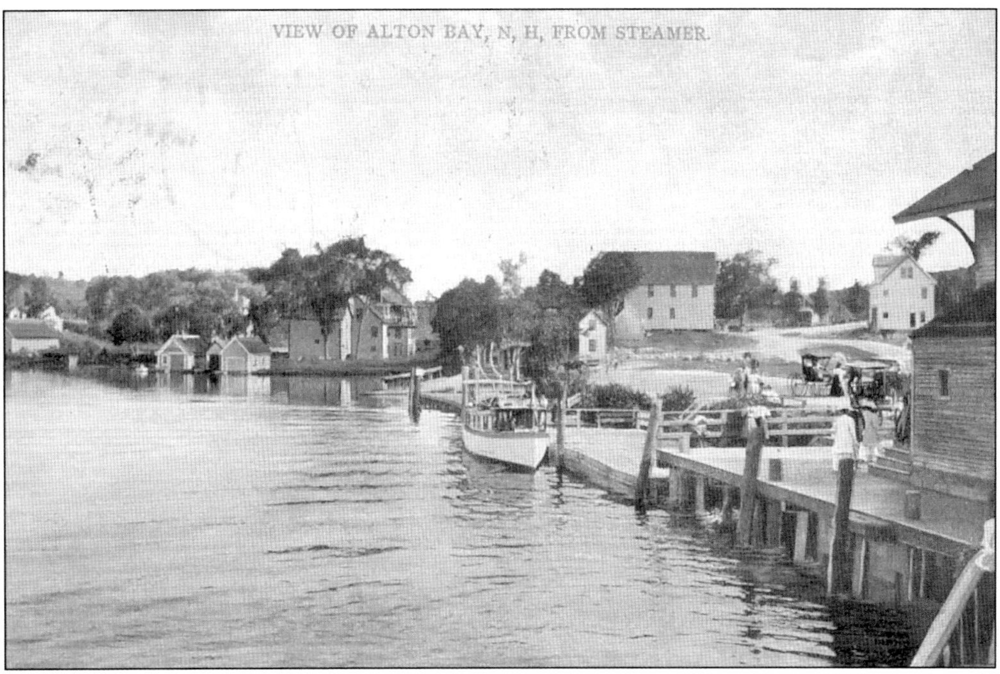

ALTON BAY, FROM THE STEAMER *MOUNT WASHINGTON*, 1911. The village of Alton, situated at the gateway of Lake Winnipesaukee and the foothills of the White Mountains, is one of the most picturesque in all the region.

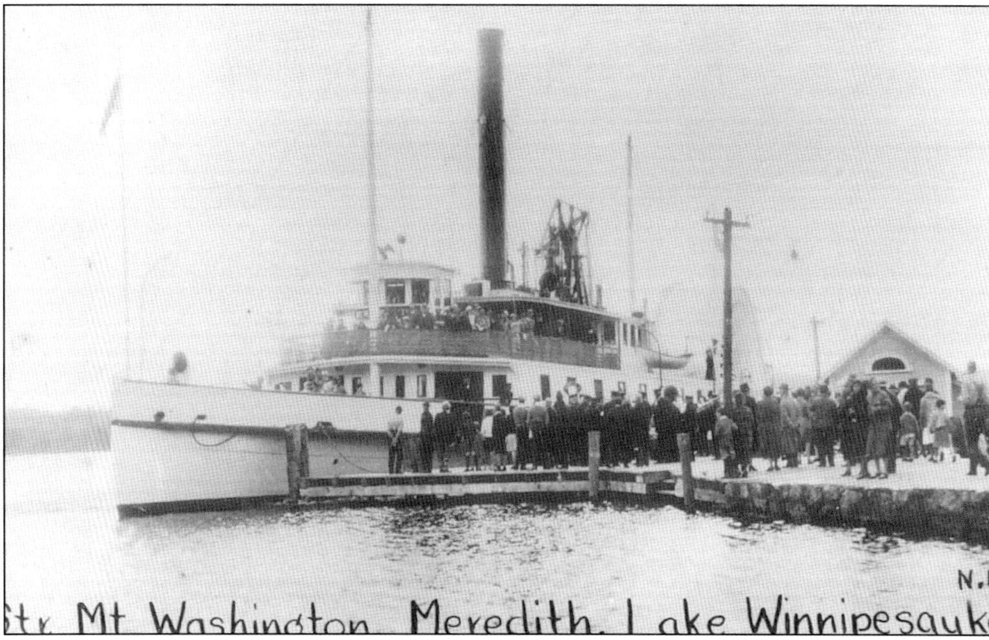

THE SIDE-WHEELER *MOUNT WASHINGTON*, AT THE MEREDITH PUBLIC DOCKS, C. 1930S. In earlier days, it was a rare event to see this vessel at this port. Today, however, the MS *Mount Washington* visits this resort town on a weekly basis.

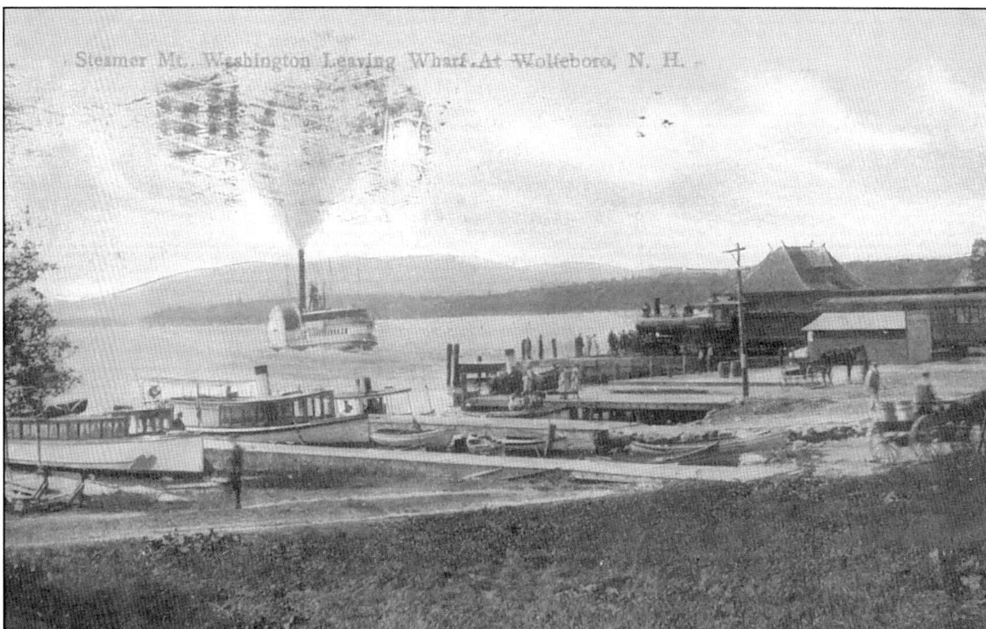

THE STEAMER *MOUNT WASHINGTON*, LEAVING THE WHARF AT WOLFEBORO, 1910. This town has been a regular port of call for the *Mount Washington* since 1872. The town was named after "the late illustrious General Wolfe," and it is the only town in the world to bear this particular name.

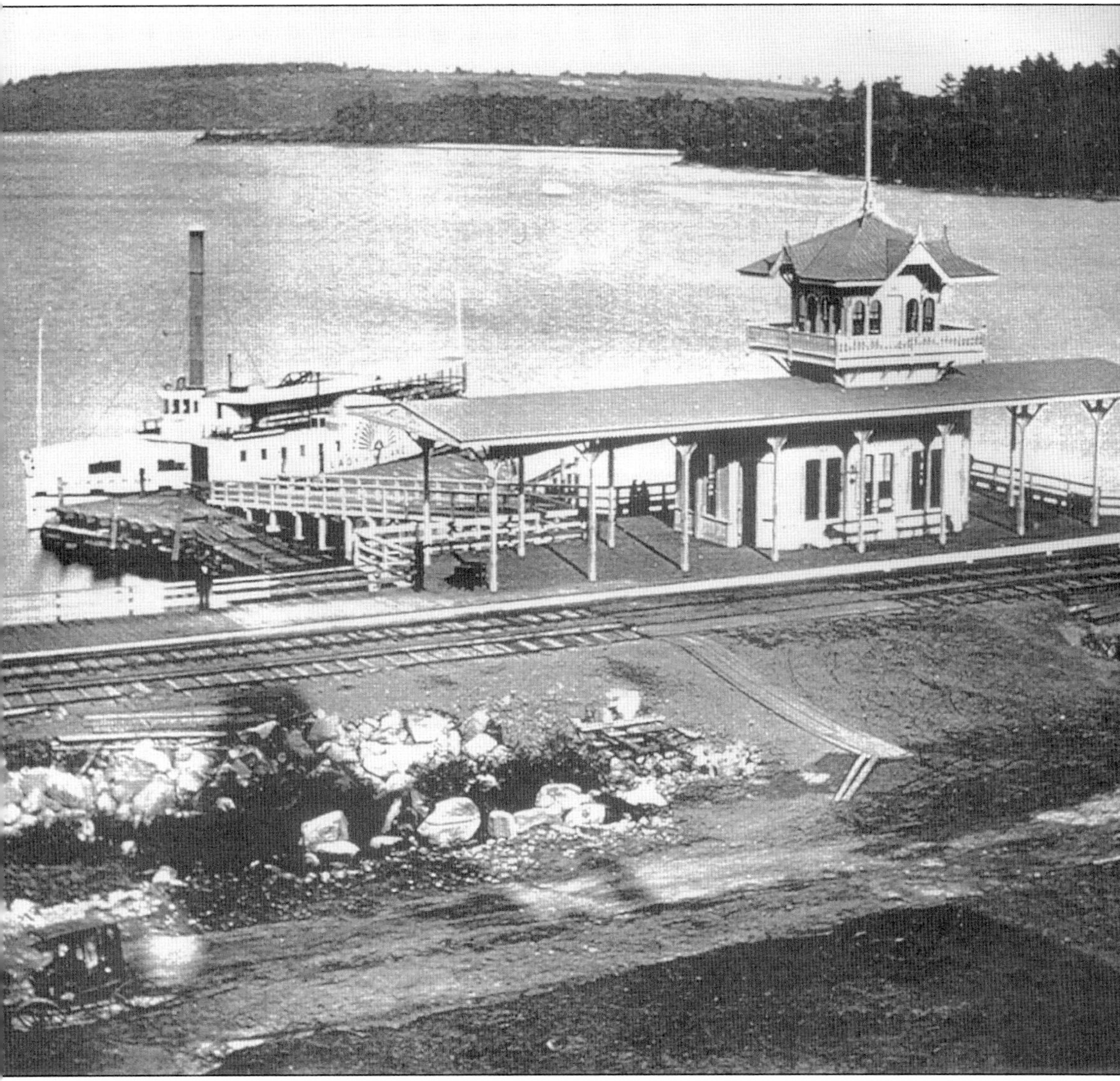

THE SIDE-WHEELER *LADY OF THE LAKE*, AT THE WEIRS DOCK, C. 1880S. From the years 1848 to 1893, this very popular side-wheeler operated as a passenger vessel connecting with Center Harbor, Wolfeboro, and the Weirs. Originally, it was built and operated by the Boston, Concord, & Montreal Railroad Company to provide passenger service for the travelers to the New Hampshire resorts.

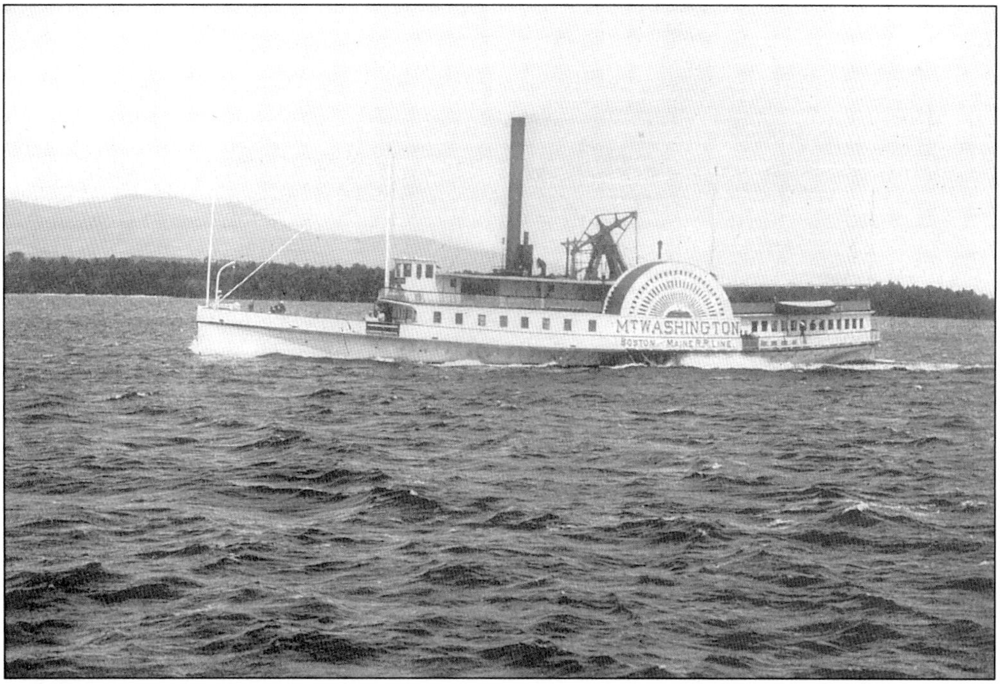

THE STEAMER MOUNT WASHINGTON, SAILING THE WATERS OF WINNIPESAUKEE. From 1872 to 1939, the side-wheeler *Mount Washington* plied these waters. Originally, this vessel was built and operated by the Boston & Maine Railroad Company to provide passenger service for the traveler to the Lakes Region and White Mountains.

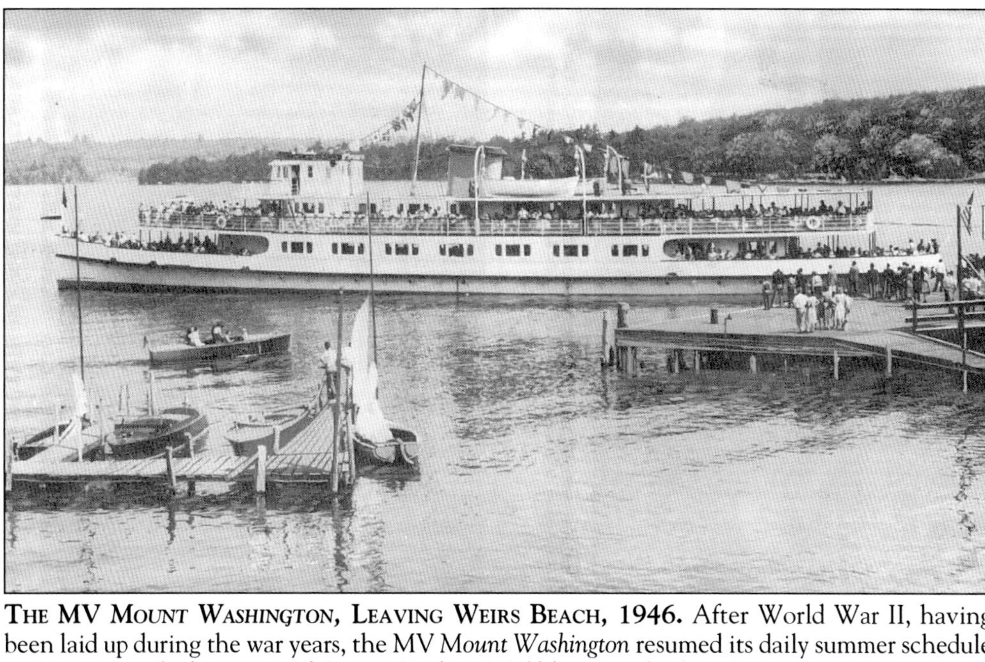

THE MV MOUNT WASHINGTON, LEAVING WEIRS BEACH, 1946. After World War II, having been laid up during the war years, the MV *Mount Washington* resumed its daily summer schedule connecting with the towns of Center Harbor, Wolfeboro, and Alton Bay.

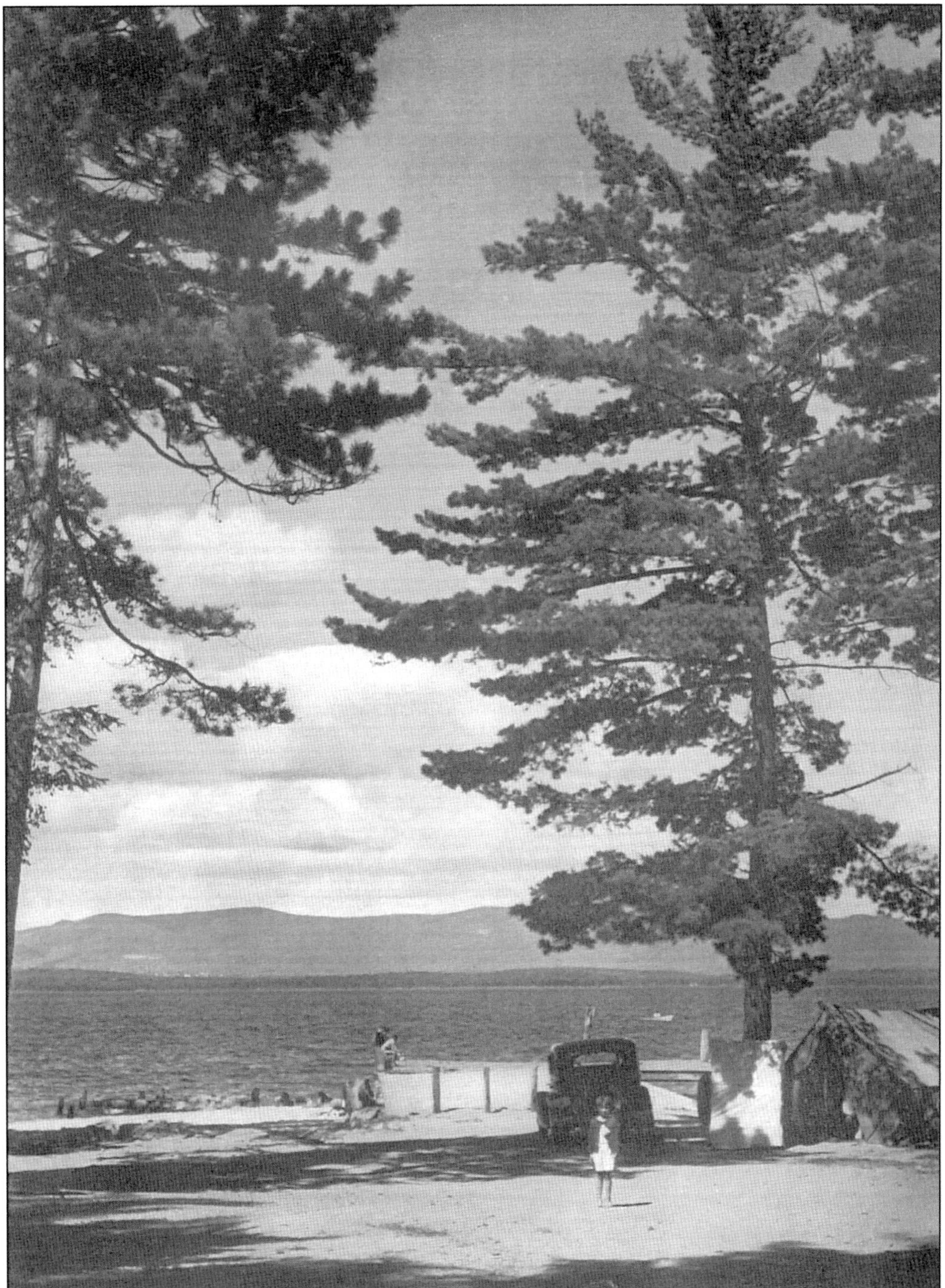

Lake Shore Park and the Ossipee Mountain Range. This view was taken from the pine grove in the mid-1930s. Lake Shore Park has become a very popular summer retreat and has one of the largest bathing beaches on the lake.

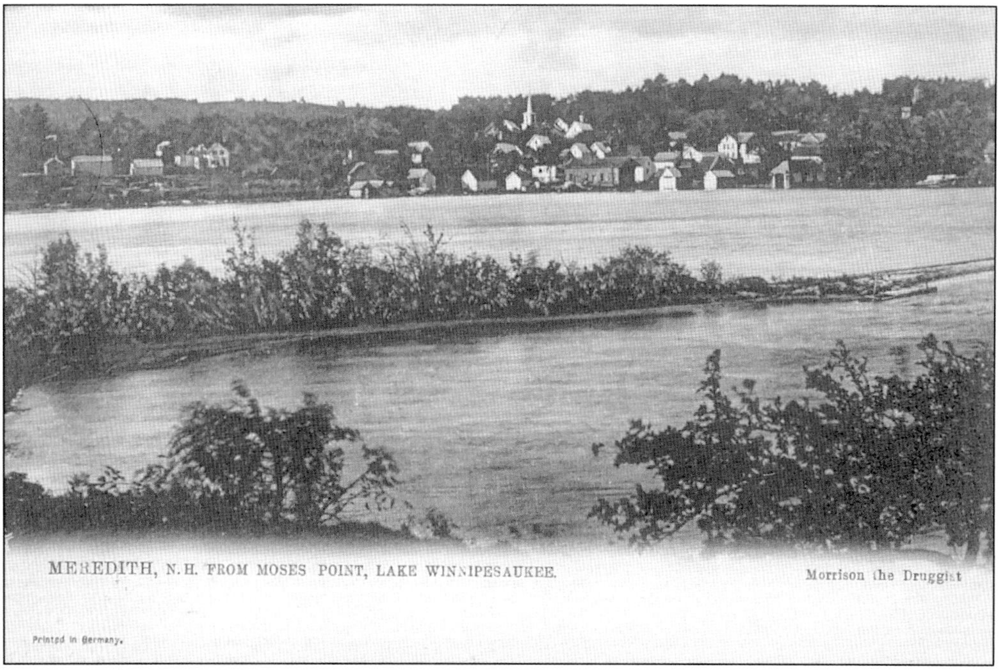

MEREDITH BAY AND VILLAGE ON LAKE WINNIPESAUKEE, FROM MOSES POINT. This town was once called New Salem and is known as such on the famous Holland map of 1784. At that time, its harbor was called Northwest Cove. Within the township, there is another lake, Waukewan, locally called Measley Pond. Lake Wicwas, a small body of water, lies on the outskirts of the village, near the road to Bristol.

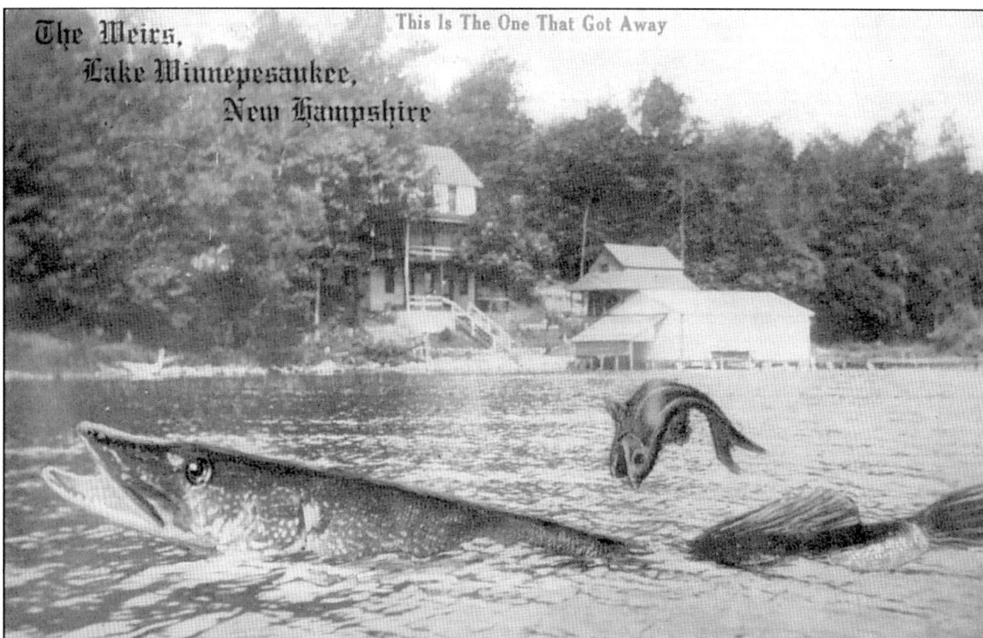

FISHING AT THE WEIRS. "This is the one that got away."

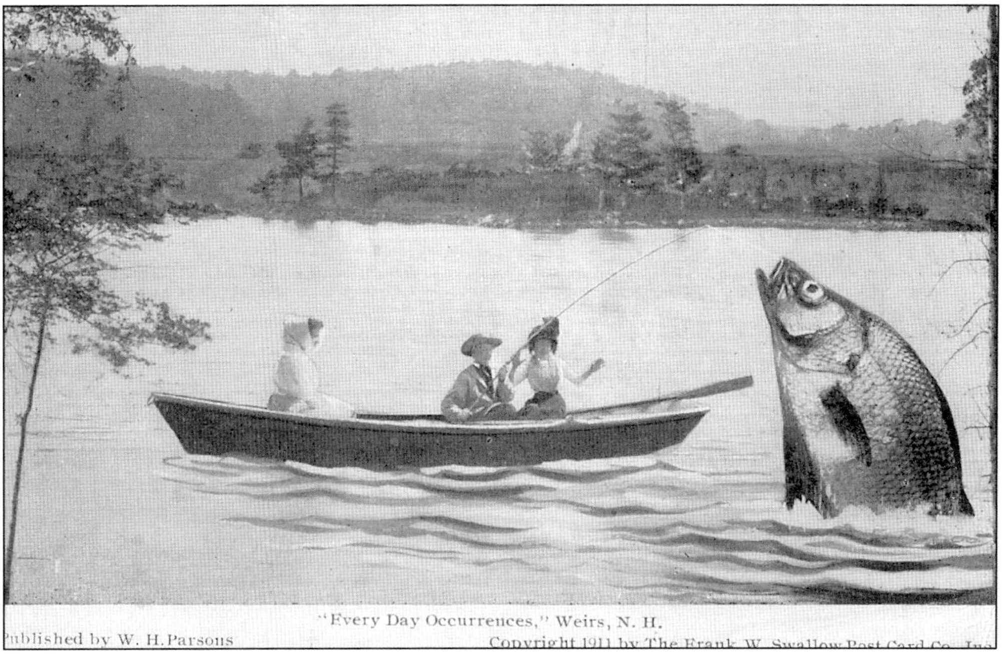

THE WEIRS, LAKE WINNIPESAUKEE, 1911. Catching this trout is an everyday occurrence on the "Big Lake."

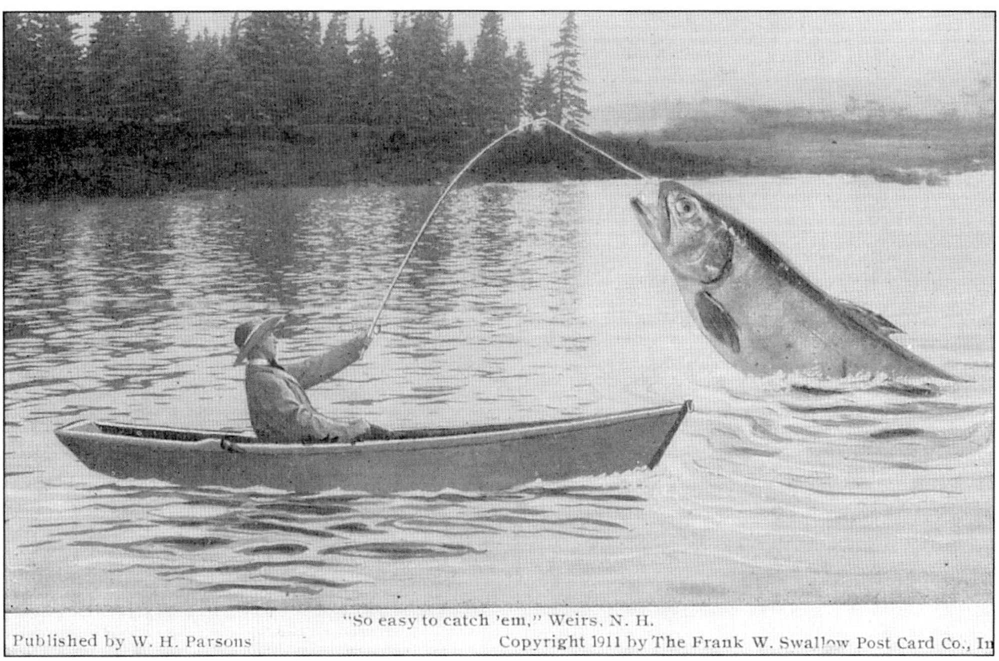

FISHING. "So easy to catch 'em."

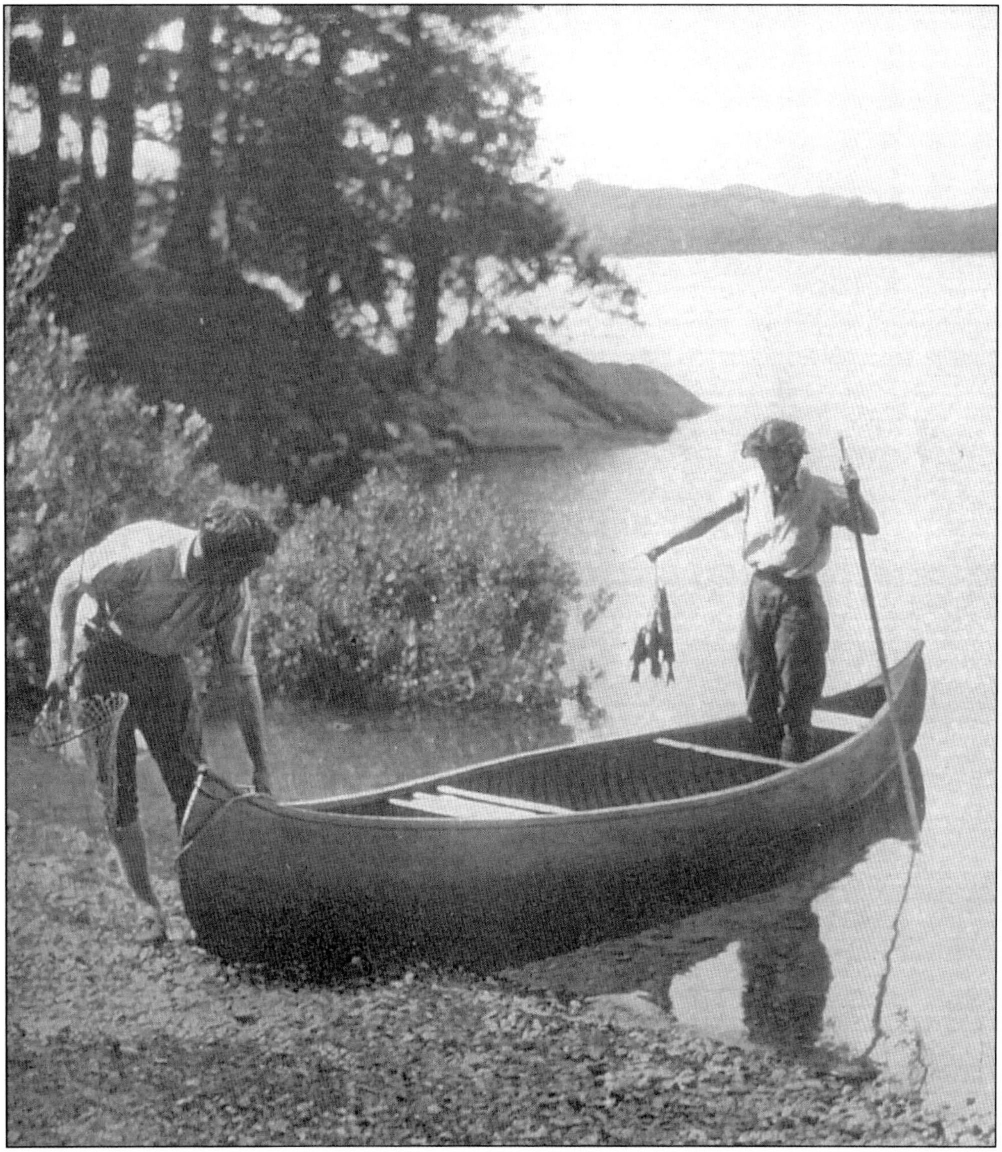

FISHING AT LAKE WINNIPESAUKEE. Fishing is very good in the lakes of New Hampshire, with salmon being stocked and taken from early spring through the summer months. Lake trout are native and are taken from the first of January through the end of September. Bass, pickerel, white fish, shad, and perch are all taken in their proper season.

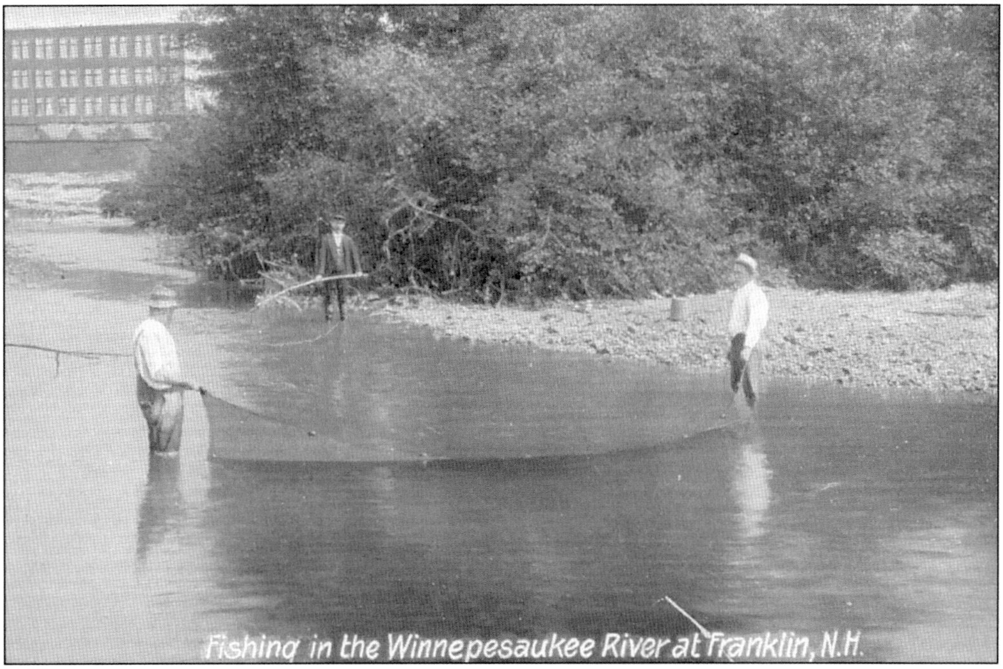

FISHING IN THE WINNIPESAUKEE RIVER, FRANKLIN, 1908. It is at this junction that the waters from Winnipesaukee join the Pemigewasset River to form the Merrimack River, which eventually flows through Manchester, Concord, and finally to the Atlantic Ocean off the shore of Massachusetts.

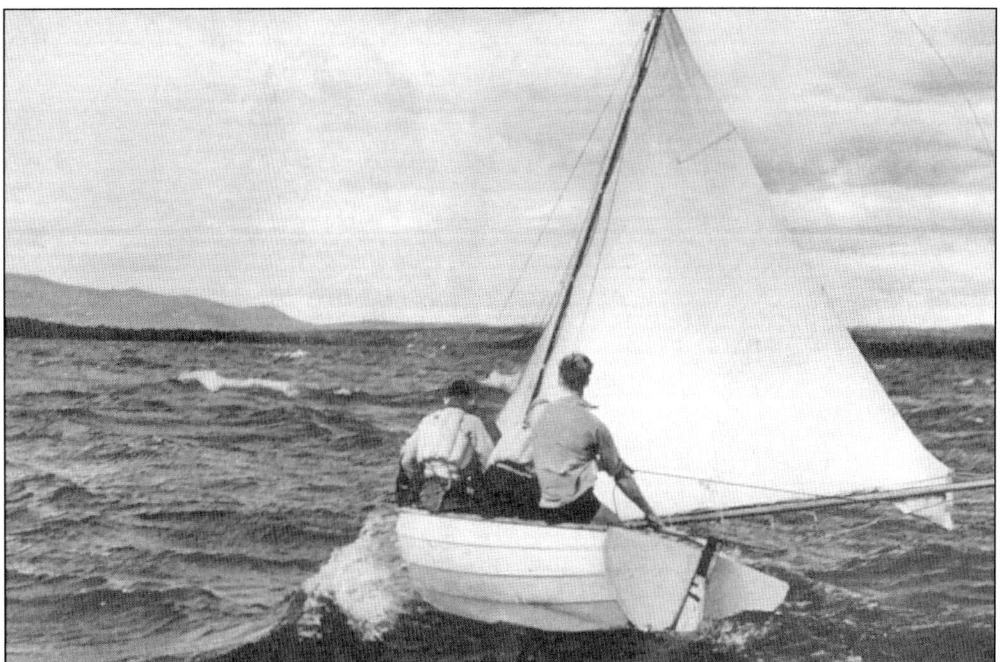

SAILING ON LAKE WINNIPESAUKEE. Sailing is very popular on most New Hampshire lakes, particularly amongst campers.

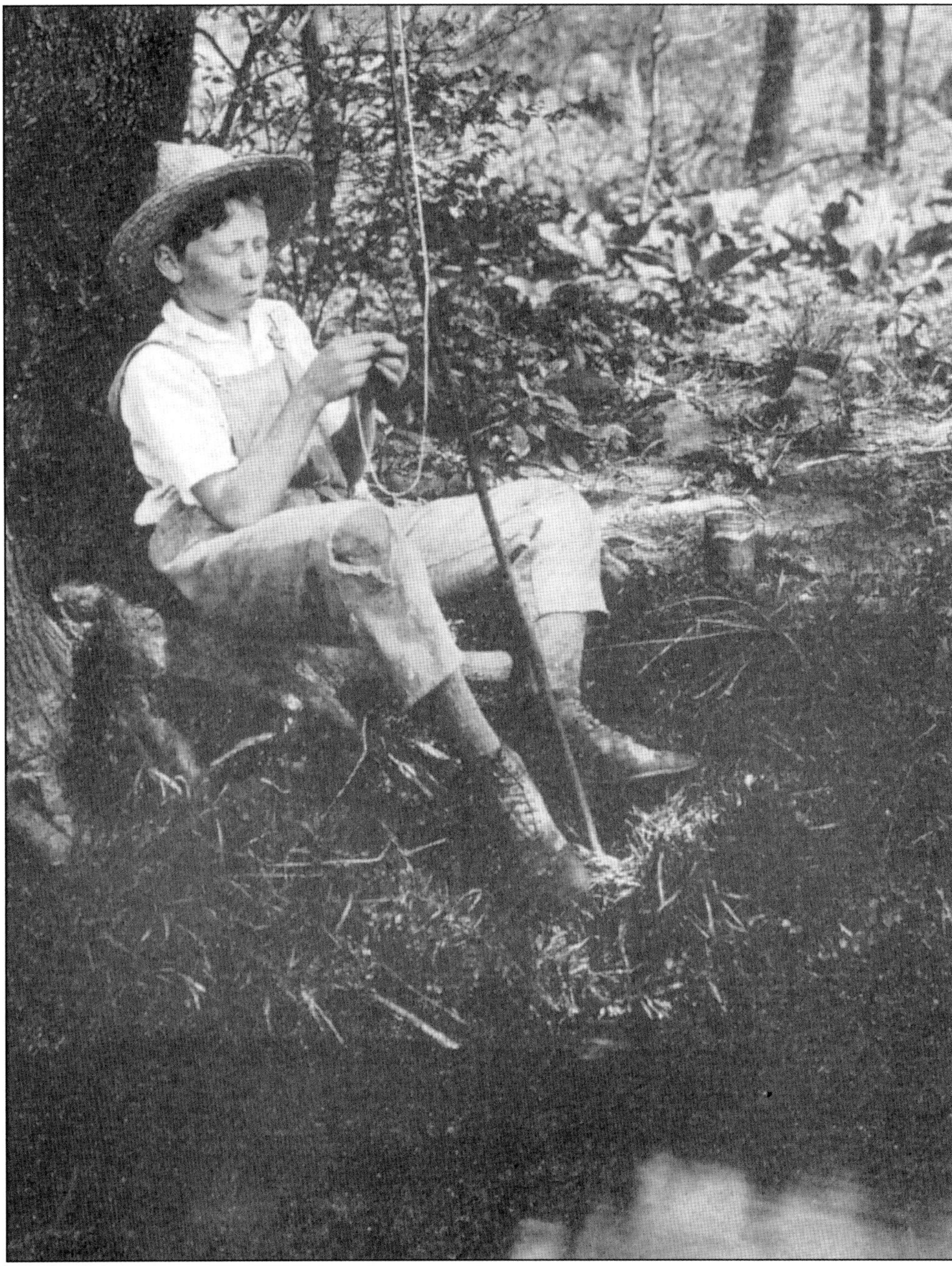

A Boy Fishing on the Banks of Lake Winnipesaukee. This is the life that Mark Twain paints in his *Huckleberry Finn*, and it is the one that is lived on the banks of New Hampshire's lakes and ponds.

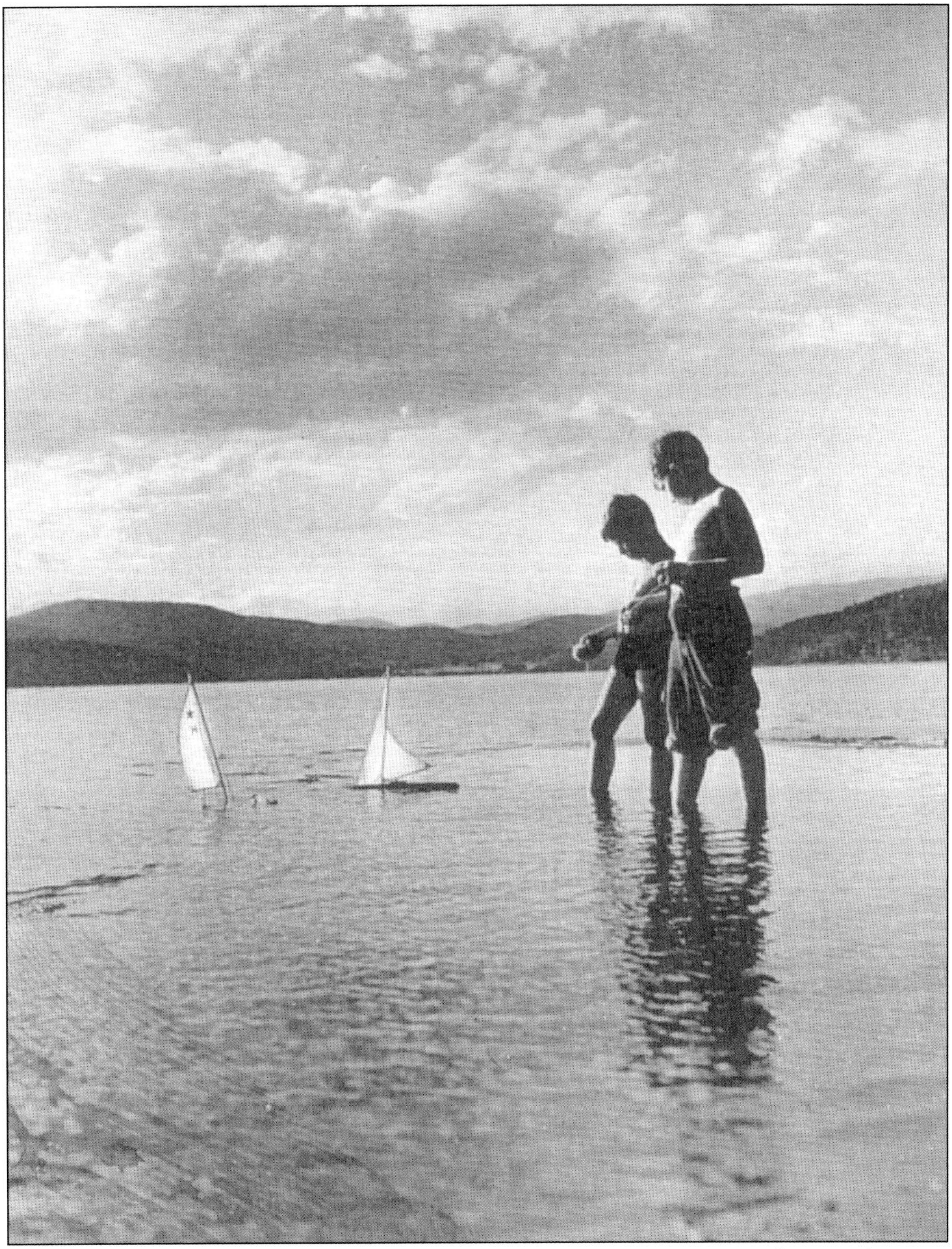

Two Boys with Sailboats. The size of the vessel does not matter at all. It is the sport that counts.

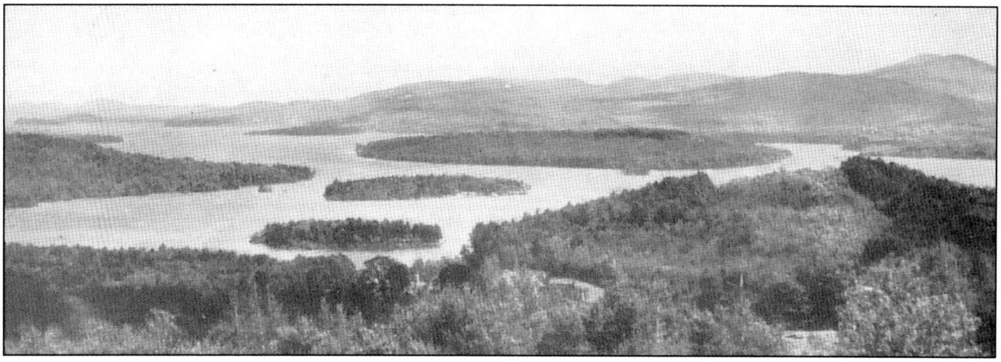

Winnisquam Lake. This lake is bounded by the towns of Sanbornton, Laconia, Tilton, Meredith, and Belmont. The Native American word *Winnisquam* means "pleasant water." With a length of approximately 9 miles and a width varying from a half mile to 2 miles, Winnisquam is considered to be one of the state's most attractive bodies of water. Surrounded by a framework of low rolling hills, it receives the waters of the Winnipesaukee River and, at the southern end, sends them out to form Silver Lake, an expansion of its southern outlet which takes the name of the Winnipesaukee River.

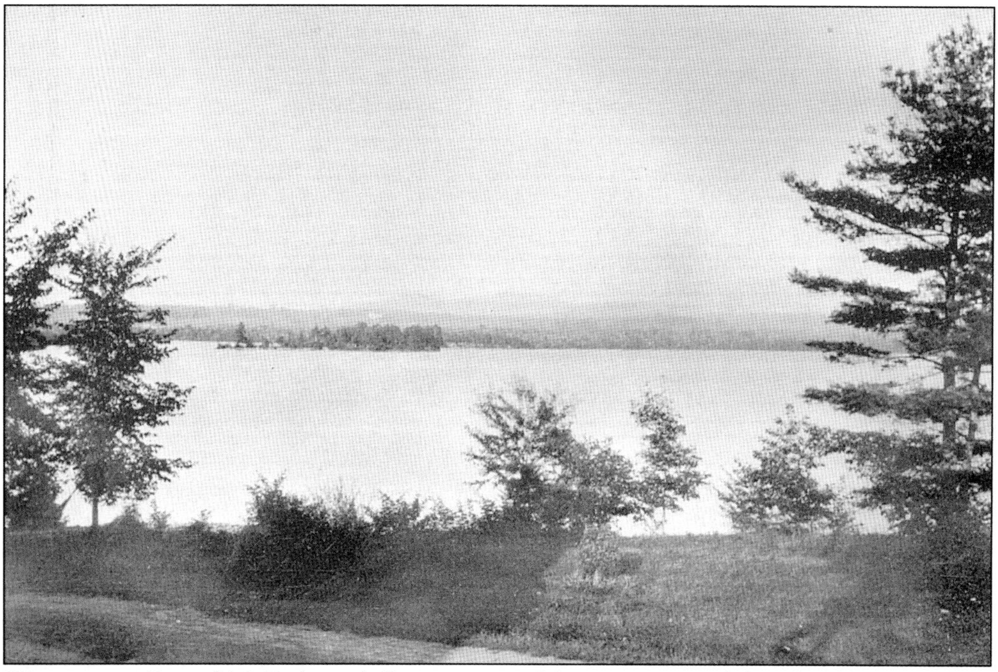

Winnisquam Lake (4,262 Acres), Laconia and Meredith. Meredith rightfully boasts of its scenic attraction, commanding as it does mountain, lake, and island views in nature's wonderful harmony. This is a glimpse of beautiful Lake Winnisquam where it touches the Meredith section, below Winnipesaukee.

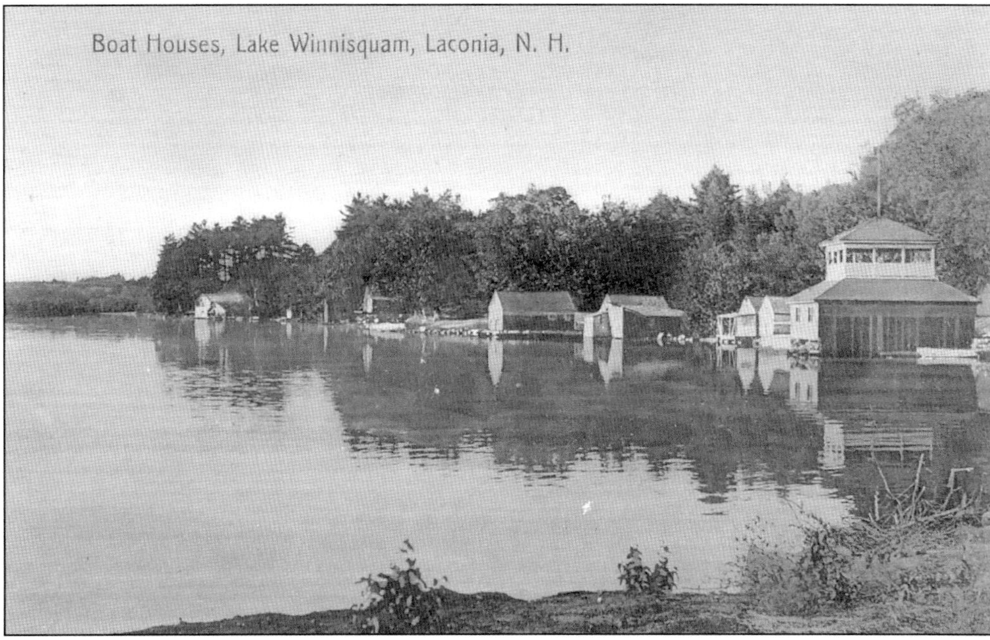

WINNISQUAM LAKE, WITH BOATHOUSES. This naturally spring-fed lake is stocked with lake trout and landlocked salmon. It also contains smelt, whitefish, smallmouth bass, yellow perch, horned pout, suckers, and chain pickerel. In 1984, a pumpkinseed was caught here weighing 12.48 ounces and measuring 9.5 inches.

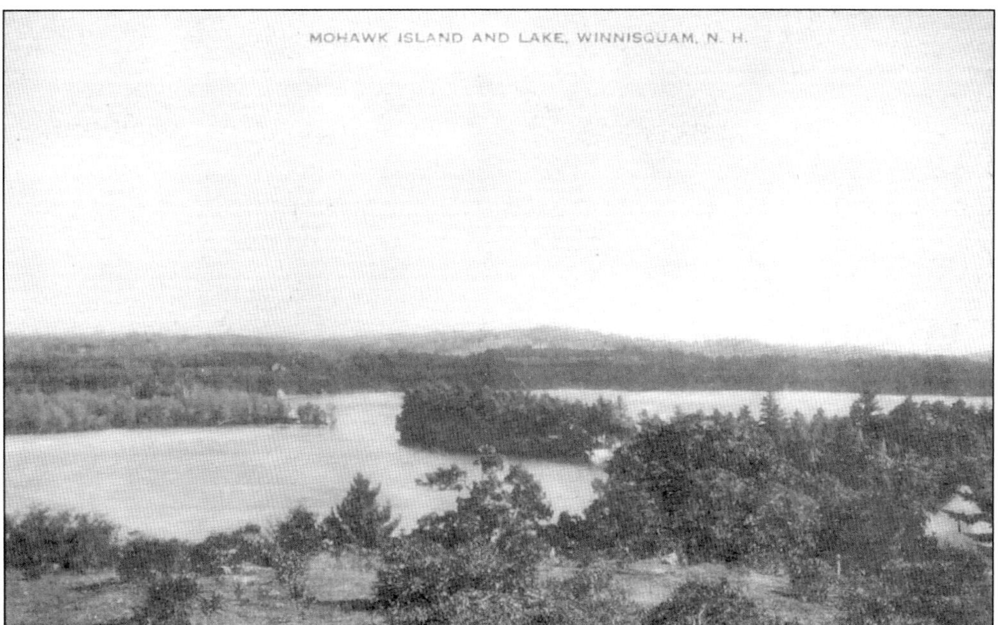

WINNISQUAM LAKE AND MOHAWK ISLAND. Winnisquam is a natural lake, rising 481 feet above sea level. On a clear day from the bridge at the southern section of the lake, the white summits of the Presidential Range are visible.

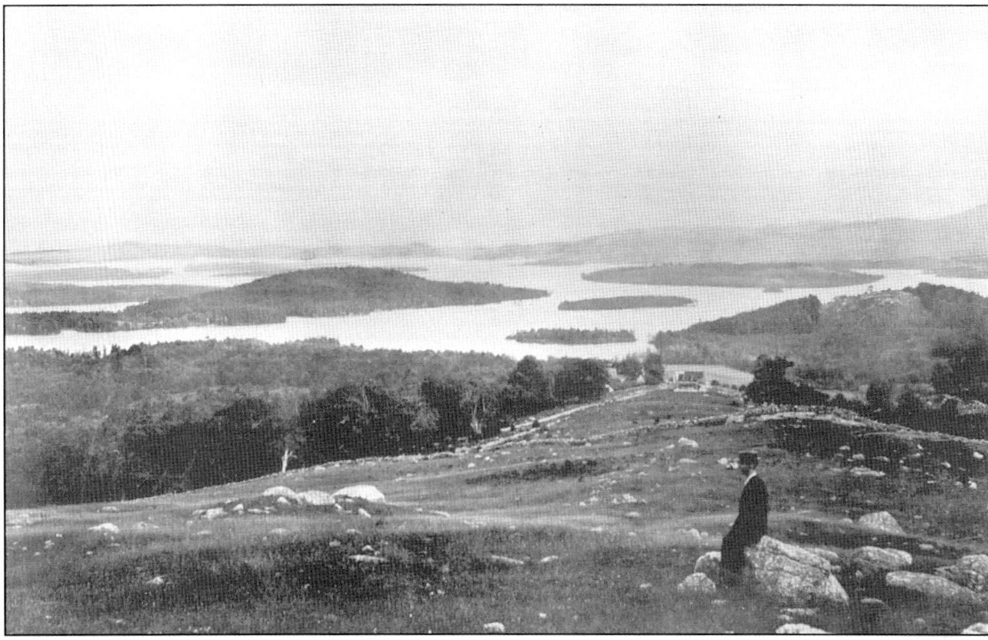

A VIEW OF LAKE WINNIPESAUKEE, LOOKING SOUTH FROM MEREDITH NECK. Visiting New Hampshire in any season is a refreshing way to celebrate life and to regain a breath of fresh air.

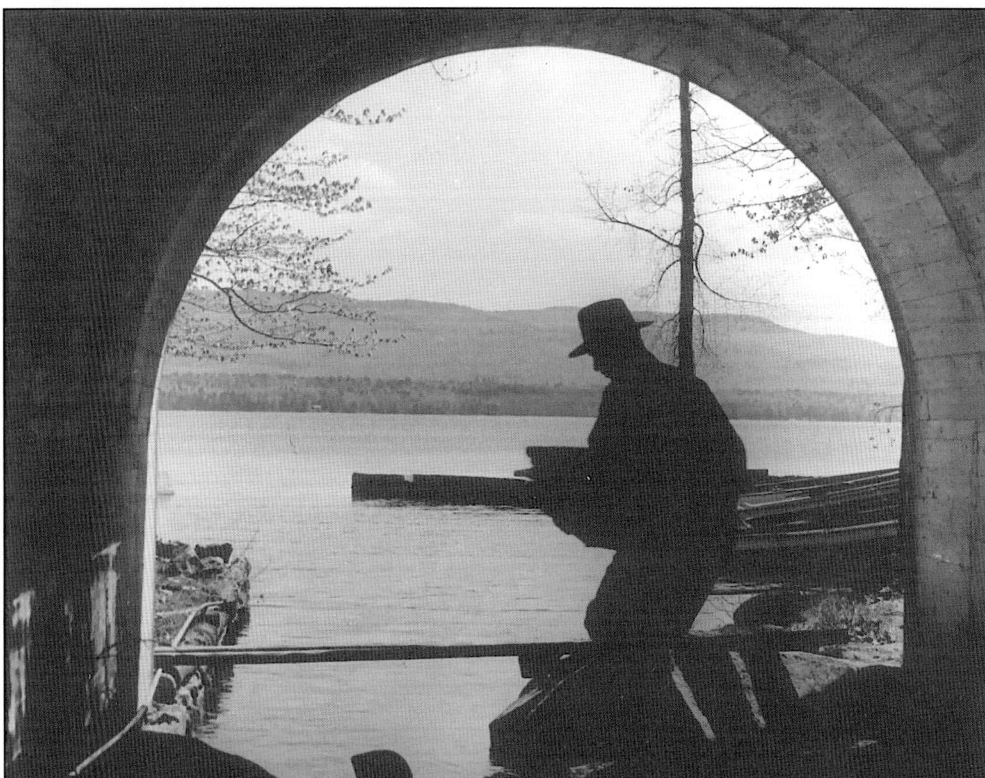

A REFLECTIVE MOMENT AT THE LAKE. This ends today, but there is always tomorrow.